THE ANXIOUS SUBJECT
Nightmares and Daymares in Literature and Film

INTERPLAY 2

Proceedings of Colloquia
in Comparative Literature and the Arts

Editors:
Moshe Lazar
Ron Gottesman

Published under the auspices of
THE COMPARATIVE LITERATURE PROGRAM
and THE CENTER FOR THE HUMANITIES
University of Southern California

THE ANXIOUS SUBJECT
Nightmares and Daymares in Literature and Film

edited and introduced by
Moshe Lazar

UNDENA PUBLICATIONS
Malibu 1983

Library of Congress Card Number: 82-70791
ISBN: 0-89003-117-7 (cloth)
0-89003-116-9 (paper)

© 1983 by Undena Publications

Undena Publications, P. O. Box 97, Malibu, CA 90265

TABLE OF CONTENTS

INTRODUCTION

> I consider heaven-sent a dream which I had some nights past, after falling asleep over Dante's work, which caused me to see a jumble of visions as I slept. . . .
>
> But what frightened me most was to see the bodies of two or three merchants who had put their souls on backwards, and who had all five senses in the nails of their right hands.
>
> Francisco de Quevedo, *Sueños**

> The sleep/dream of reason produces monsters.
>
> Goya, *Capricho No. 43*

This second volume of *Interplay* brings together the papers which were presented at a Symposium in Spring 1981, some of them revised by their authors in light of the animated discussions which followed the lectures. Since Freud had paid relatively modest attention to the nightmare phenomenon, the work of Ernest Jones (*On the Nightmare*) dealing with the mythical creatures of medieval imagination—the Incubus, the Vampire, the Werewolf, the Devil, the Witches—was in the background of several presentations, as were the more recent and important contributions of John Mack (*Nightmares and the Human Conflict*) and Jerome Singer (*The Inner World of Daydreaming*). "Creativity and madness," writes John Mack, "are two alternatives, two possible responses to nightmares or, more accurately, to the critical conflicts that give rise to them. Although madness and creativity

---

*Francisco de Quevedo, *Dreams*, trans. Wallace Woolsey (Woodbury, N.Y.: Barron's Ed. Series, 1976), pp. 6-7, 9.

may coexist, even simultaneously, in the same individual, for a work of art or literature to be successful, the artist's hold on reality, his capacity to relate to the world outside his own mind, must be sufficiently maintained to communicate the quality of shared illusion."

John Mack's observations on the clinical occurrence of nightmares in children and adults were discussed in relation to two clinical case histories presented at the Symposium by psychoanalysts Joseph Natterson and Claude Friedmann, while his comments on the use of nightmares in literature and artistic creativity were discussed in a special session (not presented in this volume) which was co-sponsored by the Center for Medieval and Renaissance Studies of UCLA and whose topic was "The *Sueños* of Quevedo and the Tradition of the Grotesque;" James Iffland (Boston University) spoke about "Quevedo and the Grotesque," and Moshe Lazar (USC) presented a paper on "Children of Saturn in Nightmareland: From Bosch and Quevedo to Goya and Arrabal." The works of Prinzhorn (*Artistry of the Mentally Ill*) and Kris (*Psychoanalytic Explorations in Art*) were discussed in this context as an approach to the artworks of Quevedo, Bosch, Goya, Strindberg, and Kafka; Kris's comments on the "intactness of the ego" (when the ego can not control the regressive process which is at the root of artistic creativity there is no generation of an artwork) were elaborated in the light of Mack's statement: "Creative ability can be a powerful integrating force. The fact that psychosis can exist in a writer or artist despite his creative effectiveness only testifies to the power of the conflicts or the inability of the artist in those instances to deal with them through his work. *One may often discern clearly that a man is wrestling with the same problems in his work as in his madness, only more successfully in the former.*" (*Nightmares and the Human Conflict*, p. 99; emphasis ours).

These writers and artists who successfully work out their inner conflicts and existential anxieties in their artworks are not just projecting actual bad dreams or nightmares; their grotesque distortion of the outer reality is more a mirroring of their "nightmarish" vision of their psychic netherworld. Contrary to writers or artists who tell us about dreams and nightmares, or who use them as a technical device, there are those other creative minds whose works are totally informed by their metamorphosed vision of reality and are shaped as "dreamworks." We distinguish between *dreams* and *nightmares* (as pleasant or uncanny happenings during the sleep, wishfulfilling or defense mechanisms, allowing the individual to peep into his own netherworld and the psychoanalyst to be a *voyeur* for clinical purposes) and *daydreams* and *daymares* which are projections of an ongoing creative process, painful and conscious, by which the "daydreamer" and/or "daymarer" acts out, plays out, works out with artistic skill and success his very personal conflicts. In *The Inner World of Daydreaming*, Jerome Singer has analyzed with great depth and detail the nature and functions of daydreaming in childhood as well as in the adolescent and adult years, its "problem-solving characteristics," and alluded here and there to its use in artistic creativity: had he not limited himself to the clinical context exclusively, Singer might have considered the creative process of the artist as an ongoing daydreaming process. Daydreaming and night dreaming, experimentally analyzed and described as brain wave patterns, eye movements, pressures on the chest, etc., might be very interesting for clinical purposes but bear no common relationship with artworks which are informed by daydreams or daymares. Some artists are daydreamers, others are daymarers. Among the latter, we might consider Bosch, Goya, Strindberg, Kafka, Beckett, Arrabal, and many others; while Ingmar Bergman and Ionesco could be seen as alternating between daydreaming and daymaring though more often dealing with recurring daymares. Kafka has clearly described his situation as a daymarer when he declared: "What is laid upon us is to accomplish the negative; the positive is already given." This thought might be followed up by what John Mack says concerning a major turning point in the works of Goya: "The successful transformation into a creative product of nightmares that emerge in the course of a severe psychological regression may result in works whose originality exceeds that which has gone before." Thus, a daydreamer might become a daymarer. While the dream keeps us asleep and the nightmare arouses us to danger, the daydream and the daymare whether transformed into an artwork or not— should be considered as a conscious creative process. In a *dream*, reality is transformed into fiction but is enjoyed as a pleasurable reality; in a *nightmare*, the fictive reality is experienced as a painful and dreadful reality. On the other hand, in a *daydream*, fiction is created and developed as fiction, and perceived by the daydreamer as fiction; in a *daymare*, the conscious dreamer as an anxious subject projects himself in a fictitious nightmareland which is perceived as a fictive reality, a grotesque metamorphosis of his dread. Artworks in this latter category are characterized by a psychodramatic process in which the artist is both the anxious object and the anxious subject.

A recent work on the paintings of Goya by Fred Licht (*Goya, The Origins of Modern Temper in Art*, p. 188), a truly original contribution to the understanding of this artist, sheds light on the difference between Fuseli representing the traditional perception of the "Nightmare" and Goya as a daymarer: "The theatrical sense is basic to our understanding of Fuseli. And though this theatrical sense is often put at the service of the horrifying, as it is, for instance, in Fuseli's favorite dramatist, Shakespeare, the horror is always resolved in an Aristotelian manner. . . . It is horror attenuated by the presence of a reasoning, sympathetic artist who calculates his effects. . . . We can analyze Fuseli's compositions in the approved, academic manner. But with Goya's fantasies, we enter a different world altogether. Goya himself seems to be helpless in the face of his vision, for he cannot convey them to us intelligibly or by means of conventional compositional schemes." He writes also: "It is a little easier to find literary parallels to Goya's fantasy than it is to find counterparts in painting." Some of these counterparts in literature and in film are the object of the studies presented in this volume.

Nicolas Kiessling, who has published a book on *The Incubus in English Literature: Provenance and Progeny* (1977), elaborates in his study on the concepts of melancholy and nightmare through the centuries and analyzes in detail three schools of interpreters of the nightmare phenomenon: 1) the *rational*, which considers the dream as a product of physiological disorders; 2) *the supernatural*, which describes the incubus and the succubus and phsyical realities; 3) *the imaginative*, which "though not exactly denying the reality of subhuman or superhuman spirits, employed them as symbols or metaphors of man's creative powers." He then describes the merger of both traditions, that of the nightmare and that of melancholy, in the romantic and modern periods.

Focusing their attention on Dostoevsky's *The Double*, Richard Rosenthal and Peter Hodgson approach this work from two different but complementary points of view. In *Dostoevsky's Experiment with Projective Mechanisms and the Theft of Identity*, Rosenthal extrapolates from Freudian and post-Freudian literature his method of analyzing the structure and the meaning of *The Double*. The narcissistic nightmare of *The Double*'s protagonist, Golyadkin, who fails to develop and maintain his own sense of himself, concretizes the mechanism of projection as the central metaphor in the novel. He analyzes in detail this psychological mechanism through which an individual projects on other people undesirable or unacceptable facets of the Self—in order to reject them—or valued aspects of the Self—so as to enhance them. Freud's description of the projection in dream and Melanie Klein's concept of "projective identification" are further elaborated by Rosenthal who, after adding to their considerations the very important observations of Philip Seitz and Peter Giovacchini on "concrete imagery of dreams" and "representational dreams" respectively, is thus able to describe the phenomenon of usurpation "of not just one aspect of another personality, but an entire identity" and to analyze Golyadkin's nightmare ("in which his every step produces yet another Golyadkin ... mocking and displacing him") as a "descriptive-representational dream of ego disruption and fragmentation." A close reading of the text and its narrative devices accompanies the psychoanalytical interpretation of Golyadkin and his doubles. An important section of Rosenthal's study describes, within the framework of an oedipal perspective, the confrontation between the protagonist and his idealized rival, his desire to emulate him and his failure of achieving this wish. Finally, Rosenthal emphasizes the particular relationship Dostoevsky creates between the narrator and the reader, stressing the identification between the protagonist and the narrator, and concludes that Dostoevsky's novella might be seen as a sort of "literary double" of Gogol's *The Nose*.

In *Awakenings to Nightmares*, Peter Hodgson follows up on Rosenthal's analysis of intrusiveness and usurpation of identity, and describes Dostoevsky's challenge to various literary identities in Russian literature, his efforts to dismantle a literary tradition, namely "the philanthropic naturalism of the Russian Natural School." Dostoevsky transforms the reader into an active participant in the construction of the fictional narrative. Hodgson qualifies this participatory role of the reader as that of an "auditor." As a reader/auditor we are forced to play, in *The Double*, three games: 1) the game of nightmares and daymares; 2) the game of the mirrors; 3) the game of the letters. The hopes or illusions of the reader/auditor that an "objective observer" could disentangle the multiple knots between fiction and reality, between sleep and awakening, are finally smashed. (It is in a similar way that the objective observer Laudisi, in Pirandello's *Right You Are–If You Think So*, confronts the illusions of the other characters and disintegrates their hopes of being able to discern between fiction and reality.) Thus, the identity of the reader himself has been called into question: "Is this not the crux of the daymare Dostoevsky has inflicted on us?" Finally, Hodgson brings up the question of the literary relationship between Dostoevsky and Gogol, discards the notion of imitation or parody, and proposes that of *Stylisation* as a strategy common to both of them.

Geoffrey Green, in his study of Jerzy Kosinski's novels, describes the various stations in this writer's use of the picaresque form to represent the nightmarish quest of himself. Establishing a close comparison between the Spanish picaresque novella *Lazarillo de Tormes* (1554) and Kosinski's *The Painted Bird* and *Steps*, Geoffrey Green demonstrates how the writer exploits the picaresque to fictionally dramatize his childhood, suggesting also that "Kosinski's childhood wanderings embody the fictional picaresque genre." Green shows that in his later writings (*Being There, The Devil Tree*, and *Cockpit*) Kosinski departs from the picaresque form when he moves away from the individual—the quest of himself—toward the collective—the anchoring in American life and society. The conflict in his later writings between childhood experiences and the American experiences is therefore given particular attention in this study. The departure from the picaresque structure and form corresponds to an existential separation from childhood of which Kosinski is well aware and which is reflected in the statement quoted by Green: "English helped me sever myself from my childhood, from my adolescence. In English I don't make involuntary associations with my childhood."

In her close textual and structural analysis of Dino Buzzati's novel, *Il*

Deserto dei Tartari, Franca Schettino scrutinizes the reader's response to a narrative text which is "structured like the waking dream experienced by a film spectator." Rather than conveying a "Kafkaesque" (i.e. nightmarish) vision of the world to a reader, Buzzati transforms the latter into a participating spectator who is asked to see cinematically the "text's written reality. . . ready-made, as though in film print." Buzzati, by understanding the anxiety and the fantastic in the protagonist's experience, by shifting the reader's attention from the literal and allegorical story, that of the protagonist, to the represented background (the spatial and temporal spectacle of life), creates a binary mode of narration which produces a dream-like effect on the reader/ spectator. The reader, rather than recalling meanings of the text, is left with a visual experience as having just seen a movie.

The next five studies in this volume deal with nightmares in film. Focusing on both "horror films" and "science fiction films," Noel Carroll uses as point of departure for his considerations Ernest Jones' description of the various types of nightmarish creatures but corrects his over-reductive perspectives (sexuality as a unique frame of reference) on the nightmare phenomenon by adopting the much sounder approach developed by John Mack in *Nightmares and Human Conflict*. Horror film imagery, as the nightmare itself, incorporates "archaic, conflicting impulses." Carroll discerns two major symbolic structures in horror films: *fusion*, "in which the conflicting themes are yoked together in one, spatio-temporally unified figure" (the *Dracula* type); and *fission*, "in which the conflicting themes are distributed—over space and time—among more than one figure" (the *Dr. Jekyll and Mr. Hyde* type). Furthermore, this second type is represented in the horror film by two major modes: 1) *multiplication*, our creation of doubles (*The Portrait of Dorian Gray*, *The Student of Prague*, *Warning Shadows*, for example); 2) *division*, or splitting of one character in time while multiplying him in space (*Dr. Jekyll and Mr. Hyde*). Comparing the plot structures and the fantastic creatures of the horror film with those of the nightmare and stressing their similar use of archaic and mythical imagery, Carroll suggests that the spectator's experience with the "horror" on the screen might relieve him from a possible "nightmare" while asleep at night. Horror films are not nightmares, Carroll states rightfully. He might have called them *daymares*.

In her study on Cocteau's films (*Blood of a Poet, Orpheus, Testament of Orpheus*), Lindley Hanlon presents him as a daydreamer and daymarer for whom the dream is as real as reality and whose artworks are structured as dreamworks. The central figure in these films is Death in her many incarnations, "for it is she who controls the life of the dreamer." Cocteau's artistic creativity reflects the tension between Eros and Thanatos.

In her detailed analysis of Carlos Saura's *The Garden of Delights*, Katherine Kovacs studies his use of dreams and daymares as a recuperative technique and situates him within a specific Spanish literary and artistic tradition pre-occupied with the representation of reality as dream or nightmare (Calderón, Quevedo, Cervantes, Goya, Buñuel). The recuperation of personal and collective memories is presented through a series of reenactments of scenes from the past, through a set of stations in a psychodramatic journey. The movie unfolds on five planes of action, described by Saura himself in his shooting script: 1) recreated past; 2) present; 3) evoked past; 4) oneiric world; 5) future. The narrative and visual shifts from one to another, from the world of daymare to the world of reality, are presented in sound, image, and verb. And as one might infer from the film's title, the daymare world of Hieronymus Bosch is both a cultural background and a visual frame of reference.

Vlada Petric's essay concentrates on the cinematic techniques Ingmar Bergman uses to project dream imagery, nightmares, and states of anxiety on the screen, focusing in particular on *The Hour of the Wolf* and *From the Life of the Marionettes*. Petric analyzes the importance and significance of the variety of shots from different points of view, the use of light and darkness, the pictorial transformations of the characters' faces, and other technical devices, which contribute to the cinematic experience (rather than to the narrative one) of the spectator and which can thus convey the complexities of the protagonists' inner worlds. He also establishes a clear distinction between traditional *mise-en-scène* and the *mise-en-shot* or, even more, the *mise-en-frame* used by Bergman. Petric proposes a very effective method of analyzing Bergman's projection of oneiric visions on the screen.

Analyzing Bergman's films as recurring nightmares, Marsha Kinder proposes to view them as fulfilling four crucial functions: 1) they contribute the primal imagery for a series of specific films, personal dreams informing their main structures (*Naked Night, Cries and Whispers*); 2) they constitute the structure of many important films (such as *Wild Strawberries, Face to Face*); 3) they unify his creative process, his authentic development (*Through a Glass Darkly, The Magician, Silence, Hour of the Wolf, From the Life of the Marionettes*); 4) they are psychodramatic and therapeutic: "acting out of recurring nightmares is therapeutic both for Bergman and his audience." Marsha Kinder focuses then on *The Hour of the Wolf* motif and the three stage pattern of revelation in Bergman's films. In conclusion, Kinder writes, "all of his works feature his marionettes acting out his violent nightmares on theatrical settings, allowing him to project his dual identification with the ravenous wolf and the ravished child."

Scrutinizing Kafka's biographical writings and his literary works, Arnold Heidsieck describes his feelings of isolation and alienation, the perceptions of himself as a stranger in his own world, in his family, and in his social environment. His daymares are transformed in nightmarish stories. Heidsieck examines Kafka's use of animal imagery to project his anxieties and masochistic guilt feelings along with his permanent sense of humiliation and estrangement. The growing perception of himself as a social outcast and as an outsider in his own psyche nurture Kafka's literary daymares.

Concluding the volume are two presentations of clinical case studies by Joseph Natterson and Claude Friedman which allow for interesting comparisons between real nightmares and artistic daymares.

Moshe Lazar

AN ANATOMY OF MELANCHOLY
AND THE NIGHTMARE

Nicolas Kiessling

Melancholy and nightmares, though seemingly disparate, have this in common: both are abnormal conditions that afflict human beings—the first during waking hours, the second while they are asleep. From ancient times to the present learned men have tried to explain and interpret them, poets have embroidered them with legends, and common folk have regarded them with fear and awe. Occasionally they have been merged in literary works, when melancholy could not only be depicted as the outcome, but could also precede the bad dreams or nightmares.

The history of melancholy is marked by an ambivalence that is imaginatively expressed by Milton in "L'Allegro" and "Il Penseroso." "Hence, loathed Melancholy!" says the light-hearted man and "Hail, divinest Melancholy!" responds his thoughtful counterpart. To Galen, the most famous Greek physician of the second century, and those who followed him, melancholy was a "most ignominious and miserable condition of mind." The opposite view, that melancholy was "a most admirable and enviable condition of the mind," owes its origin to a pseudo-Aristotelian source, Problem XXX.1.[1]

Melancholy was considered to be, in traditional and general terms, a physiological imbalance caused when one of the four humors, the dark, thick and heavy fluid melancholia or black bile, became dominant in the body. It could be of a lighter, "natural" variety that was classified as a temperament rather than a disease. The more serious "unnatural" type, caused by a burning of humors within the body, was also called "melancholy

---

[1] These are the views attributed to Galen and Aristotle during the Renaissance. See Lawrence Babb, *The Elizabethan Malady: A Study of Melancholia in English Literature from 1580 to 1642* (East Lansing, MI: Michigan State College Press, 1951), p. 66. The standard source for all students of melancholy is Raymond Klibansky, Erwin Panofsky, and Fritz Saxl, *Saturn and Melancholy: Studies in the History of Natural Philosophy, Religion, and Art* (Great Britain: Thomas Nelson, 1964). For Problem XXX.1, see pp. 15-29.

adust" (burnt melancholy) or atrabiliousness. This severe kind could be brought on by improper diet, bad climate, lack of sleep, uncontrolled passions, or idleness. Its psychological manifestations ranged from despair, insomnia, misanthropy, sedition, and the desire for isolation or darkness, on the one hand, to hallucination and prophecy. Remedies included changes in diet, mental diversions, bloodletting, and purgations—commonly induced by the taking of hellebore or borago.

By the time of the Renaissance melancholy as defined in the Galenic tradition came close to being considered the major cause of dysfunction not only of persons but of countries and institutions. A number of major works on the subject of melancholy were written by medical authorities and religious divines. Most famous of the authors was Robert Burton, whose monstrous compendium, *The Anatomy of Melancholy*, went through six editions between 1621 and 1651. Burton called melancholy a corruption of "one principall faculty of the minde as imagination, or reason." "All the world is melancholy, or mad, dotes, and every member of it," he wrote. The affliction came with Adam's fall and "no man living is free. . . . Melancholy in this sense is the character of Mortality." He searched for and found that kingdoms, provinces, cities, bodies politic, and families were "sensible and subject to this disease."[2]

The pseudo-Aristotelian problem XXX.1, representing the opposite view, begins with the question: "Why is it that all those who have become eminent in philosophy or politics or poetry or the arts are clearly of melancholics?" Those who suffered were distinguished men and included the heroes Heracles, Ajax, Bellerophon (Aulus Gellius called it "a disease of heroes"), and the thinkers Empedocles, Socrates and Plato. Though it was mainly those who were affected by a moderate melancholy who became great, Plato and Democritus asserted that the true poet is touched with madness, which is certainly the extreme kind. John Dryden later expressed this view in his couplet: "Great wits are sure to madness near alli'd; / And thin Partitions do their Bounds divide." Pseudo-Aristotle's problem XXX.1 states that "Many too are subject to fits of exaltation and ecstasy because this heat [from hot bile] is located near the seat of the intellect; and this is how Sibyls and soothsayers arise and all that are divinely inspired, when they become such not by illness but by natural temperament—Maracus, the Syracusan, was actually a better poet when he was out of his mind. Those, however, in whom the excessive heat is relaxed toward a mean, are melancholy, but they are more rational

---

[2]Citations to *The Anatomy of Melancholy* are from the fifth edition, (Oxford: Henry Cripps, 1638). The quotations, in order, are found on 1.1.3.1, p. 31; "Democritus to the Reader," p. 76 (see also p. 17); 1.1.1.5, p. 11; and "Democritus," p. 46 (see also p. 18).

and less eccentric and in many respects superior to others either in culture or in the arts or in statesmanship."[3]

Later, during the Renaissance numerous authorities were persuaded that melancholy fostered intellectual and imaginative powers. Marsilio Ficino, Juan Vives, Philipp Melanchthon, Girolamo Fracastoro, Levinus Lemnius, Andre du Laurens, Cornelius Agrippa, and Thomas Elyot all expressed this opinion. Ficino believed that melancholy produced a "subtle, hot, lucent, agile, and yet stable mind."[4] The actual situation of the melancholy man is described by Jacques Du Bosc. Such persons can "reserve in themselves a privat roome, where to the tempest of Fortune cannot reach. There it is, where the soule retires, to maintaine her self in an eternall serenity; where she gaines an absolute command upon her judgements." "Here finally it is, where wee conserving the image of things delightfull, shall have meanes to have nought but goodly thoughts, . . . and entertaine our Idea on beauty. . . . Who can praise enough this noble musing of the Melancholy, since by it the soule seemes to abandon when she list, the clamorous commerce of the senses."[5] Ficino, even more of a mystic, propounded a theory of spiritual influences on the melancholic, and his contemporary, Cornelius Agrippa of Nettersheim went further, arraying spirits into several classes, "with the lower demons and the melancholy humor responsible for the painter's excellence, . . . the 'middling' demons and melancholy for both the philosopher's excellence and the predictions of the Roman sybil; the highest demons and melancholy, finally, for both the knowledge of the angels' ranks and the foreknowledge of God's decrees."[6] So Robert Burton, who can always be quoted on both sides of the question, summarized: "Melancholy men are of a deep reach, excellent apprehension, judicious, wise and witty."[7]

In the sixteenth and seventeenth centuries in England genial melancholy, the pseudo-Aristotelian version, became almost a fashionable disease. Authors from Shakespeare to Donne and Thomas Browne popularized it.[8] Hamlet could play very well the role of a melancholic, "with a look so piteous in purport / As if he had been loosed out of hell / To speak of horrors" (2.1.78-84);

---

[3] Klibansky, p. 16, for the Gellius quotation; p. 18 for the opening of XXX.1; and pp. 24-5 for the final quotation. For the quotation from Dryden, *Absolom and Achitophel*, lines 163-4.

[4] Klibansky, pp. 258-61; and Babb, p. 61.

[5] Babb, *Eliz. Malady*, pp. 63-64.

[6] Klibansky, pp. 352-59. For the summary of Agrippa's *Occulta Philosophia*, I quote from an unpublished paper by Winfried Schleiner (University of California, Davis), "Melancholy, Genius, and Utopia in the Renaissance," p. 7.

[7] *Anatomy*, 1.3.1.2, p. 186.

[8] Babb, *Eliz. Malady*, pp. 175ff. and Babb, *Sanity in Bedlam: A Study of Robert Burton's* Anatomy of Melancholy (East Lansing, MI: Michigan State University Press, 1959), p. 3.

Jaques, of *As You Like It*, could "suck melancholy out of a song as a weasel sucks eggs" (2.5.10-11); and Duke Orsino, in *Twelfth Night*, tried to induce the melancholy of love by asking for more and more sad music, so that "surfeiting, / The appetite may sicken, and so die" (1.1.2-3).

In the eighteenth century the so-called graveyard school of poets revelled in the decay of classical and Gothic ruins, graveyard visits, and the contemplation of past glories and death. Thomas Warton in 1745 wrote "The Pleasures of Melancholy," in which many of these themes are present. The poet muses, "Beneath yon ruin'd abbey's moss-grown piles / Oft let me sit, at twilight hour of eve." Here in silence he sits "Far in sequester'd iles of the deep dome, / There lonesome listen to the sacred sounds, / Which, as they lengthen through the Gothic vaults, / In hollow murmurs reach my ravish'd ear." To Warton an "elegance of soul refined" was needed to appreciate those pleasures.[9]

In the late eighteenth century this aspect of melancholy was intensified into what the Germans call "Weltschmerz," as in Goethe's famous novel, *The Sorrows of Young Werther*, or in Thomas Gray's "Elegy." In that poem the epitaph of the author—or his alter ego—stated that "Melancholy had mark'd him for her own." A melancholy gloom that inspired an exploration of the twilight regions of the mind became a feature of Gothic novels around 1800 and of the Romantic movement itself. Typical among American writers would be Charles Brockden Brown, with the baleful ventriloquist in his novel *Wieland* and the two victims of melancholy and sleepwalking, Edgar Huntly and Clithero Edny, in the novel *Edgar Huntley*; Edgar Allan Poe, reiterating the gloomy "nevermore" in "The Raven"; and Nathaniel Hawthorne, whose own life for a time was an exemplar of melancholy. In his mother's home, meals were served to him privately in his room, and he never went out for a walk until after dark. Thus the classical view that melancholy affected "eminent persons," and creative artists, was valid through the nineteenth century.

This so-called genial melancholy was not accepted by all theologians or physicians from the sixteenth through the eighteenth century. A number of writers declared that the prophetic powers of melancholics were non-existent. Henry Howard wrote that "sooner shall a man finde out a pure virgin in Sodome, then a true Prophete in the cave of melancholy." The physician John Harvey lists false prophets, including "our common melancholique and *Saturnine* prophets, wherwith the world hath long space beene perilously seduced."[10] In the latter part of the Renaissance clerics especially emphasized

---

[9] Lines 28-9 and 202-5. See also Eleanor M. Sickels, *The Gloomy Egoist: Moods and Themes of Melancholy from Gray to Keats* (New York: Columbia University Press, 1932), pp. 35-7.

[10] Babb, *Eliz. Malady*, p. 50.

a corresponding devil theory. Melancholy, write Campanella, "is the black dregs of burnt blood, [and] does not cause sagacity and foreknowledge, as many labor to prove (and Ficino in particular.)" "The dark humor mixed with blood generates only horrible spirits, . . . and causes lycanthropy, fear, and vile thoughts. . . . They take pleasure in dirty and fetid places, sepulchures and dead bodies, because the infected spiritus seeks out his likeness."[11] Robert Burton investigated the so-called visions of melancholic persons and he lists several authors who argued that the visions were the work of the devil. Demons found that melancholy men were easily misled. One of Burton's favorite authors, Andre Du Laurens, asserted that the melancholic person is more apt to be troubled "by the intercourse or medling of evill angels . . . [who] oftentimes . . . foretell & forge very strange things in their imaginations."[12] The generating of "only horrible spirits," and "medling of evill angels," as we shall see, comes close to what supposedly happened in nightmares. This negative view culminates after 1660 in England, during the neoclassical period, when genial melancholy was associated with dreadful things like lycanthropy, necrophilia, and madness. John Locke perceived even a worse association: it was "melancholy . . . mixed with devotion" that produced the new religion, Enthusiasm.[13]

Contemporary psychiatrists or psychologists accept, at least to a layman's eye, the rather broad and negative definition of melancholy. Sigmund Freud, for example, gave the following definition: "The distinguishing mental features of melancholia are a profoundly painful dejection, abrogation of interest in the outside world, loss of the capacity to love, inhibition of all activity, and a lowering of the self-regarding feelings to a degree that finds utterance in self-reproaches and self-revilings, and culminates in a delusional expectation of punishment. This picture becomes a little more intelligible when we consider that, with one exception, the same traits are met with in grief."[14] Subtypes that one can find in a psychiatric dictionary include melancholia abdominal, activa, passiva, cataleptic, climacteric, complacens, excited, gravis, hypochondriacal, involutional, and a half-dozen more. Robert Burton described most of these in great detail and a number of others which are currently described under different illnesses, for example, melancholia anglica (suicidal insanity), canina (lycanthropy), flatuosa, panphobic, and religious. Melancholy, then, has always been identified as a morbid mental

---

[11] Schleiner, p. 15.

[12] *Anatomy*, 1.3.3., p. 212. For the Du Laurens quotation, see Babb, *Eliz. Malady*, p. 49.

[13] Schleiner, p. 48.

[14] Sigmund Freud, *Collected Papers*, trans. J. Riviere (London: The Hogarth Press, 1925), 4:153.

state in which depression is a paramount feature. In certain periods, melancholy became closely associated with dreams and nightmares. Long before Sigmund Freud defined them as "disguised fulfillments of suppressed desires,"[15] dreams and especially nightmares had inspired theories and legends that merged with those that had grown up around melancholia.

In folklore and literature the nightmare is an oppressive dream or vision which profoundly disturbs the dreamer. It is usually of a sexual nature. Within the limits of this definition, the variations are numerous. In the most traditional form, an attacker, the nightmare itself, oppresses by weighing down, sitting or lying, on the dreamer. The attacker could be male, hence it would lie on and be called an incubus, or it could be female, and lie under, and be called a sub or succubus. The vividness of the attack often obscured, to the dreamer at least, the distinction between dream and reality. In a Fuseli painting, "The Nightmare," the nightmare sits on the breast of a sleeping woman. The pose of the woman is erotic, but the look on her face seems to be more of terror than of ecstasy.[16] What will she be thinking of when she awakens? Will she want to recreate the experience? Has she learned anything from the dream? These questions fascinated romantic poets and thinkers, and they provided answers.

There have been three schools of interpreters of the nightmare: the rational, who debunked the dream as nothing more than a product of physiological disorders; the supernatural, who took the incubus and succubus to be physical realities; and the imaginative, who utilized the legends about dreams and nightmares in a creative way "to point a moral or adorn a tale."

The rational school of interpreters argued that the nightmare dreams were produced mainly by physical causes or conditions, such as overindulgence in eating and drinking, eating the wrong foods, fevers, epilepsy, and other illnesses. Aristotle, Hippocrates, Galen, and Soranus subscribed to this theory, yet each harbored quaint, even supernatural, ideas on the subject. They still believed that tiny demons inhabited certain foods and that when these foods were ingested, the demons entered the body with them and produced flatulence, alimentary upsets, and nightmares. Next to wine and hemp, the worst sinners in this respect were common beans. Pythagoras as early as the sixth century B.C. had forbidden them to his

---

[15] John E. Mack, *Nightmares and Human Conflict* (Boston: Little, Brown and Company, 1970), in a chapter on "Nightmares and Creativity" (p. 93), develops the thesis that "a nightmare or other dream has furnished the source of inspiration for the creative product, if it has not actually provided the literal content of the work itself."

[16] For the nightmare paintings of Fuseli, see Nicolas Powell, *Fuseli: The Nightmare* (London: Allan Lane, The Penguin Press, 1973), passim, esp. pp. 19 and 67-77.

followers.[17] The rationalist school had its adherents from classical times to the Renaissance, but it was not, before the eighteenth century, the predominant school. The founding of the Royal Society in 1660 provides a watershed date after which the rationalist school becomes influential in England. Night monsters were generally regarded with skepticism. Dryden even questioned Shakespeare's wisdom in creating Caliban in *The Tempest*. Such a creature was not to be found "in Nature," yet Shakespeare "makes him a species of himself, begotten by an Incubus on a witch."[18]

Interpreters of the supernatural school even in ancient times perceived the nightmare as something more than a mere dream. The vividness of the experience prompted them to invent a miscellany of names, each indicating a different trait of the nightly visitor: ephialtes, mora, incubus, silvester, pilosus, faun, satyr, and pan. An encounter with such a figure was always traumatic and could result in death. It could also result in conception for a woman. Closely related to this tradition was the mythological fact that gods often ravished women. Zeus, for example, performed this act in various forms, as a swan, bull, a golden shower, and in the case of Amphytrion, in the shape of the woman's husband. The tradition is not limited to Indo-European peoples. In Jewish lore Lilith is the predominant seducer who roamed at night looking for partners in her orgies. Adam's offspring by her were a race of demons, spirits, and ghosts. The Old Testament does not mention Lilith, but it does include a passage in Genesis (6.1-6) which alludes to the unfortunate union between sons of god and daughters of men—giants were the result. In the apocryphal Book of Enoch, so-called Watchers, or fallen angels, united with humans, and the offspring were evil spirits and giants.[19]

Early Christian writers continued this tradition. In medieval literature the stories of the sexual tormenter are rife. Monks and nuns who tended to suppress the sexual impulses more than average persons were especially prone to attacks by the nightmare. Clerics discussed the theoretical problems in good scholastic fashion by asking such questions as: Can the devil appear in the form of a man and unite sexually with wretched women? Can a woman conceive by an incubus? Does the devil actually perform sexual intercourse or does he only maintain the illusion of the act? If there are offspring of

[17]Wilhelm H. Roscher, *Ephialtes, Abhandlungen der philologisch-historischen Class der königlich sächsischen Gesellschaft der Wissenschaften* (Leipzig, 1900-3), 20, No. 2, pp. 18-23.

[18]John Dryden, *Troilus and Cressida* (London: Abel Swall, 1679), "The Preface," p. b^r.

[19]For the Book of Enoch, esp. 5.1-5, 7.21-25, and 10:1-6, see *The Apocrypha and Pseudepigrapha of the Old Testament*, ed. R. H. Charles (Oxford, 1913), 2. 191-3 and 198.

these acts, are the offspring human or spiritual? How did spirits, if they were
only composed of air, obtain the material seed? Thomas Aquinas had a ready
answer to the last question. The incubus demon could "steal the semen
of an innocent youth in nocturnal emissions and pour it into the womb of a
woman.... Therefore it seems that a man is able without a miracle to be at
one and the same time both a virgin and a father."[20] St. Anthony was one of
the most famous resisters of spiritual tempters, and attacks upon his virtue
by the night monsters are the subject of numerous medieval and renaissance
paintings. Merlin, the magician in the Arthurian stories, was, according to one
tradition, the most famous offspring of a cleric. His mother, a nun, was
tempted and succumbed to a demon of the night and the result was conception. Children thus conceived tended to be more illustrious than the
average, and Aquinas presents one of the current theories about why this
was the case. Demons, he argued, could perform the acts during auspicious
astronomical seasons as well as with exceptional male and female partners.[21]

As usual, Robert Burton supplies further evidence. He cites a cloud of
witnesses, from Augustine, the church father, to Paracelsus, the sixteenth-
century father of modern chemistry, and Justus Lipsius of Louvain (1547-
1606), also a university scholar, to prove the reality of the incubi. Paracelsus
allowed that some of these creatures, "nymphs and pygmies," were benefi-
cent, but others, "sylphs, gnomes, and salamanders," were malign. Lipsius
believed that there never was a time or a city that had so "many lecherous
devils, Satyres, and Genii" as his own century or his hometown of Louvain.[22]

The imaginative school of interpreters, though not exactly denying the
reality of subhuman or superhuman spirits, employed them as symbols or
metaphors of man's creative powers. Divine inspiration was often linked with
man's creative energy. Thus Socrates had a spirit or demon who guided him
in matters of conscience. Epic writers in the classical tradition would never
begin work without the invocation of the Muses. Inspiration also came by
way of dreams and oracles. Christians understandably classified all Greek
stories of gods, spirits and oracles as manifestations of the devil and his angels.
Yet the Judeo-Christian tradition was plentifully supplied with accounts of
divine communications by way of dreams (Abraham, Jacob, Daniel), visions
(Ezekiel, Jeremiah, Paul), and angelic visitations (Sts. Antony, Theresa, and

---

[20] For the types of questions asked, see, for example, Ulrich Molitor, *De Laniis et
Phitonicis* (Leipzig: Arnoldus de Colonia, 1495), chapter 6. For the quotation from
Aquinas, see *Summa Theologiae*, 1a. 51, 3, 6; and Russell Hope Robbins, *The Encyclo-
pedia of Witchcraft and Demonology* (New York, 1959), p. 28.

[21] For Merlin, see Nicolas Kiessling, *The Incubus in English Literature: Provenance
and Progeny* (Pullman, Wa.: Washington State Univ. Press, 1977), pp. 48-50; for a discussion of theological views regarding the incubi, pp. 21-8.

[22] *Anatomy*, 3.2.1.1, pp. 435-6.

John of the Cross). During the English Renaissance authors frequently used figures from the world of spirits to illustrate man's quest for knowledge. In Marlowe's *Dr. Faustus* the demonic Mephistopheles inspires Faustus and endows him with creative powers; in *Macbeth* witches conjure up sinister prophecies concerning future events; and in *The Tempest* Ariel and other benevolent spirits enable Prospero to peer into the nature of things and to manipulate events.

It remains now to show a most dramatic merger of the two traditions, melancholy and the nightmare, in the romantic and modern periods. In the pre-romantic period the lonely, isolated, and meditative melancholic could be regarded as potentially more creative and perceptive than an ordinary person. At the same time spirits of the night and the nether world often served as symbols to explain man's creativity and insights. Romantic authors like Keats, Hawthorne, and Yeats were attracted to both themes and presented melancholia as the result of a devastating revelation transmitted by a nightmarish spirit, or as a condition which made the artist receptive to a demon of the nightmare genre.

The motif of the demon lover, the spirit which causes melancholia, appears nowhere more poignantly than in Keats' ballad, "La Belle Dame Sans Merci." It tells of a knight who has met a beautiful "lady in the meads," "a faery's child" with long hair, light foot, and wild eyes. In her strange language she tells him, "I love thee true." The knight is bewitched and the union between the two is complete: "there ... [he] shut her wild, wild eyes / With kisses four." She then lulls the knight to sleep. When he awakens, the vision has dissipated, as happens frequently in fairy tales. But the memories of the inimitable vision remain forever to haunt the narrator. He will wait on the cold hill's side, "alone and palely loitering" until the La Belle Dame returns. The ballad is best interpreted as a metaphor of an artist who sees into the depth of things and then, his vision ended by a return to reality, hovers between two worlds, an outcast of both. He becomes a melancholic recluse until the end of time.

Hawthorne's *Young Goodman Brown* is one of several Hawthorne stories of persons who become isolated because of what they learn from a fearful dream. The hero of the short story falls asleep in a forest and dreams that he is called away for an evening initiation into the devil's communion. He leaves his wife Faith and enters a dark forest accompanied by a devil. His reluctance at taking part in the ceremony is swept away when he sees that every so-called upright citizen of his New England community, including his good wife, Faith, is there to participate in the devil's communion. When he awakens and returns home, he cannot respond to the loving welcome of Faith or to any of the seemingly decent villagers whom he had seen at the devil's communion in his dream. The narrator concludes: "Alas! it was a dream of evil omen for

Young Goodman Brown. A stern, a sad, a darkly meditative, a distrustful, if
not a desperate man did he become from the night of that fearful dream."
Upon his death, the narrator continues, "they carved no hopeful verse upon
his tombstone, for his dying hour was gloom." Like Keats' forlorn knight
Young Goodman Brown had been turned into an incurable melancholic by
a devastating vision.

William Butler Yeats, in his fifteen-line poem, "Leda and the Swan,"
retells the rape of Leda by Zeus, in swan form: "A sudden blow: the great
wings beating still / Above the staggering girl." The results of the rape were
visible to all: "a broken wall, a burning tower, and Agamemnon dead." The
line refers to the abduction of Helen, the destruction of Troy, and Agamemnon's murder by Clytemnestra. The immediate results do not seem to be
fortunate for mankind. But Yeats sees more important issues at stake when
he asks a vital question in the last lines of the poem. "Being so caught up, so
mastered by the brute blood of the air, / Did she put on his knowledge with
his power / Before the indifferent beak could let her drop?" For Yeats that
question was all-important, for he believed that man would not survive unless
somewhere, somehow, he could transcend his limitations and have at least a
vision of the divine. The myths of Leda, of Semele and Zeus, and of the Virgin conception of Christ, in Yeats' view, reveal allegorically how man's vision
can be extended beyond normal limits. It is the role of the poet to ask "the
overwhelming question," to perceive the truth and beauty, and to interpret
them for men. Even as a boy Yeats brooded over these matters "As I climbed
along the narrow ledge I was now Manfred on his glacier, and now Prince
Athanase with his solitary lamp, but I soon chose Alastor for my chief of men
and longed to share his melancholy."[23] Yeats was referring to Shelley's poem
Alastor. Alastor, an idealist like his creator, Shelley, is plunged into melancholy when he seeks in real life the counterpart of his high thoughts and
visions of beauty. Yeats realized at an early age that the "mystic sympathy /
With nature's ebb and flow," can be attained momentarily, but never retained
and that solitude and despair follow, once the transitory goal is achieved and
lost.

No poet ever maintains communion with the mystic otherworld or with
the divine. Or to state it on another level, no poet can ever retain forever
his creative powers. The result of lost vision is melancholy. But melancholy
is actually the starting point as well as the end point for creative artists.
Thus the classical view that poets and writers are naturally predisposed to
melancholy is still valid. Melancholy played a prominent role in the works
cited above, and in each case—Keats' knight and a beautiful but merciless

---

[23] *The Autobiography of William Butler Yeats* (New York: MacMillan Company,
1916, rpt. 1969), "Reveries," xiv, p. 39.

lady, Hawthorne's Young Goodman Brown and a disillusioning dream, and Yeats' Leda and the "brute blood" and the "indifferent beak" of the swan— the nightmare dream serves as the focal point for the action. To Keats, Hawthorne, and Yeats, the mood of melancholy both allowed the perception of truth and followed the moment of perception.[24] Hence we can see that the traditions of the nightmare and melancholy are components of the central theme in some of the most moving works of literature written in the nineteenth century.

Washington State University

---

[24] Mack, p. 108, cites the research of Greenacre in pointing out that "creative activity ... may relieve, but not solve conflicts." The cycle of melancholy, creation, and melancholy continues throughout the creative period of an artist's life.

DOSTOEVSKY'S EXPERIMENT WITH PROJECTIVE MECHANISMS AND THE THEFT OF IDENTITY IN *THE DOUBLE* *

Richard J. Rosenthal, M.D.

"TWIN GAVE HIM 'BAD NAME'– BROTHER HELD IN SLAYING"

DIEPPE, FRANCE (UPI)–Philippe Levasseur, 25, strangled his twin brother, saying the twin was stealing his identity and giving him a bad name, police said Monday.

Levasseur's twin, Gilbert, was considered a trouble-maker and had begun identifying himself as Philippe, police said. No one could tell them apart.

According to police, Gilbert refused to pay his check at a restaurant Saturday and told the owner to take his complaints to Philippe Levasseur.

Police said Philippe sought out Gilbert and the two began arguing. Words turned to blows and Philippe strangled Gilbert. Philippe surrendered to police later. (Los Angeles Times, August 10, 1976.)

This story, which appeared in newspapers around the world one hundred thirty years after *The Double* was published, would have probably pleased Dostoevsky, who avidly read the papers of his day for things to write about, and who on a number of occasions found real life duplications of stories he had already written. The newspaper account shares several features with Dostoevsky's novella, such as its ambiguous tone and the specific scene in the restaurant. A good twin murders his bad twin, an apparent contradiction. How do we know for sure, since we are told that no one could tell them

*An earlier version of this paper was presented at the Symposium of the International Dostoevsky Society, Rungstedgard, Denmark, August 18, 1977.

apart? At least we can be certain there were two brothers, and they looked alike; Dostoevsky's novella is more complicated.

Written at a time when the twenty-four year old author was struggling to find his own personal and literary identity, *The Double* is about an individual's failure to develop and maintain his own sense of himself.[1] Since the senior Golyadkin's identity is dependent upon the validation of others, his double's intrusion into every aspect of his external or social world results in his ceasing to exist. In essence, a narcissistic nightmare has been created.

The story was deeply disturbing to Dostoevsky's contemporaries, and both public and critics rejected it. It was not the *idea* of the double itself which upset them, not even the theme of a usurped identity, since contemporary readers, like Dostoevsky himself, were familiar with the long literary tradition of the doppelgänger, and in particular the work of E. T. A. Hoffmann.[2] Hoffmann's recognition of a latent or unconscious second self, antagonistic to the conscious personality and projected into the external world as a real or imagined double, was well-known and frequently imitated. Critics could not, it seems, accurately say what it was that disturbed them most about Dostoevsky's story.[3] Nor could the young author say just what he believed he had accomplished in it, though he made it clear he felt *The Double* to contain one of his greatest literary discoveries.[4] Thirty years

---

[1] "The most natural need of man," wrote Dostoevsky, "is to become conscious of, to realize, to give shape to, his *I* in real life." "Peterburgskaja letopis'," *Stat'i*, 13, 29. Quoted by Robert Jackson, *Dostoevsky's Quest for Form* (New Haven and London: Yale Univ. Press, 1966), p. 28.

[2] Letters to his brother, Mikhail, August 9, 1838 and January 1, 1840 in *Letters of Fyodor Michailovitch Dostoevsky to his Family and Friends*, trans. E. C. Mayne (New York: Horizon Press, 1961), pp. 3-5, 11. See also Ralph Tymms, *Doubles in Literary Psychology* (Cambridge: Bowes and Bowes, 1949); Charles Passage, *Dostoevski the Adapter* (Chapel Hill: North Carolina Press, 1954); and Passage, *The Russian Hoffmannists* (The Hague: Mouton, 1963).

[3] Well known is the response of V. G. Belinsky, the leading critic of the day and the man who had only just previously hailed Dostoevsky's genius for *Poor Folk*. Belinsky condemned *The Double* as being "fantastic." What he objected to was its author's abandonment of realism, a charge Dostoevsky seemed to be still defending himself against years later when he wrote that "true events, depicted with all the exclusiveness of their occurrence, nearly always assume a fantastic, almost incredible, character," *The Diary of a Writer* (1873-1881), trans. B. Brasol (New York: Braziller, 1954), p. 90. Similar statements appear throughout the *Diary*: for example p. 468, where he relates in some detail how reality will always exceed anything the writer can imagine, or again, on p. 491, where, in describing *The Meek One*, he writes, "I called it 'fantastic,' although I consider it real in the highest degree."

[4] Letter to Mikhail, October 1, 1859. *Pis'ma* 1, 257. Quoted by Victor Terras, *The Young Dostoevsky 1846-1849* (The Hague: Mouton, 1969), p. 20.

after publishing it he wrote "I have never pursued a more serious idea in my entire career as a writer."[5]

What he was attempting to do, I believe, was most clearly described in a letter written to his brother: "The *outward* must be balanced by the *inward*. Otherwise, with the absence of outward events, the inward will take too dangerous a sweep upwards. Nerves and fantasy will take up too much room. From want of habit every outward event will appear to be of colossal and, somehow, of frightening importance. One begins to be afraid of life."[6] The effects of this imbalance, between the outward and the inward, its relationship to problems of identity, was explored by Dostoevsky in this and in his subsequent work, enabling him to put psychological mechanisms and states of mind into literary form. *The Double* is an extended experiment in this use of spatial imagery and movement. It is here that we first encounter Dostoevsky's most important character type, his underground man, that we come to appreciate the *dynamic* interaction of his doubles, and that we experience some of the stylistic devices which have such a powerful, albeit disturbing, impact on the reader.

There is an interplay, generally, between what is internal, or intrapsychic, and what occurs "out there" in the so-called real world where other people have separate and independent existences from our own. Golyadkin is overly dependent on the opinions of others. However, in a sense there really are no others in his world. With the exception of his double, the most important characters either never appear or remain undescribed. When Golyadkin does exchange words with other people—his doctor, his servant, various employees from his office—he, but often they, have so many expectations as to what the other wants to hear, so many preconceptions of what society deems appropriate, that what occurs is a series of brilliantly written non-conversations, in which neither side makes contact with the other. The effect is rather like the experience of trying to play tennis with oneself by hitting the ball and then running over to the other side of the net. What Golyadkin hears in these interchanges are his own thoughts, sentiments and suspicions echoed back to him.

The failure to see or hear what's really out there, because we are too busy attributing what is *us* to *them*, is, of course, the mechanism of projection. A psychological mechanism is given concrete representation in *The Double*, and becomes a central metaphor in the story. Since I will be utilizing this concept throughout my discussion, let me briefly review the subject of projection,

---

[5] *Diary of a Writer*, p. 883.

[6] *Letters to Family and Friends*, p. 43. The statement is frequently taken as a confession of the author's own psychic imbalance; he offers it as advice to Mikhail, who was himself undergoing personal difficulties at the time. It was not written with reference to *The Double*, nor in the context of one of their discussions of literature.

including some of its more primitive forms, before seeing how they appear in the text of Dostoevsky's story.

I. THE INS AND OUTS OF PROJECTION

In its most well-known application, unacceptable aspects of the self are disavowed and attributed to some person or group or some other part of the external world. (It's not *I* who is ambitious, angry, unfaithful, etc. it is *he*.) However, highly valued aspects of the self may also be projected, for example to protect them, or to bolster one's regard for the person into whom they are projected. We also project aspects of our selves into others in order to transiently identify with them in order to better understand them, the process known as empathy. Projection, and the related mechanism of introjection, are basic to the building up of identifications, and of an identity.

In one of his earliest writings dealing with identification, Freud described projection utilized in a dream in order to vicariously gratify an unconscious wish. By attributing what is unacceptable to the self to another, it is not only disowned, it is gratified by a "community" with the other person.[7] Freud's paper on the Schreber case, his most extended discussion of paranoia, also emphasized the significance of projection in maintaining an object relationship.[8] Melanie Klein introduced the term *projective identification* in order to emphasize that the process does not stop with the simple projection, but also consists of the fantasies the individual has about what he has done.[9] There is a continued relationship, she maintained, both with the projected aspects of the self and with the person or object into which they are projected. The individual may feel persecuted by these others or in identification with them. He may feel a need to control them in order to control those aspects of himself which have been projected into them, or conversely, he may feel controlled by them. Specific fantasies may lead to feeling trapped or suffocated, depending upon what it is he feels he has done and where he identifies.

One group of fantasies deserving special mention are those in which the organs of perception are used to omnipotently penetrate or invade the other. Seeing, hearing, or smelling may be used, not to receive stimuli from the

[7] *The Interpretation of Dreams* (1900), *The Standard Edition of the Complete Psychological Works of Sigmund Freud*, ed. James Strachey et al. (hereafter abbreviated *S.E.*), 24 vols. (London: Hogarth, 1953-74), IV, 320.

[8] "Psycho-analytic Notes on an Autobiographical Account of a Case of Paranoia (Dementia Paranoides)" (1911), *S.E.*, XII, 9-82.

[9] "Notes on Some Schizoid Mechanisms," (1946), in *Developments in Psychoanalysis*, ed. Joan Riviere (London: Hogarth Press, 1952).

object, but to put parts of the self, in fantasy, into them, usually for purposes of control.[10] To see someone from a great distance, for example, or to follow their every movement with one's eyes, supports this primitive belief of having power over them. To see means to invade or possess, and to know. (This would include "knowing" in the biblical sense, thus those fantasies of preco-cious sexuality in which projective identification is confused with sexual intercourse.) Since the first object of these fantasies is the young infant's mother, one can appreciate their role in dealing with helplessness and depend-ency.

Excessive use of such primitive projective mechanisms may leave an indi-vidual feeling internally depleted, and this inner sense of impoverishment will then render him less able to protect himself from the experienced in-trusiveness of others. It will also leave him uncertain as to his own psychic boundaries, resulting in a confusion between inner and outer reality (fantasy or dream versus life).

Golyadkin is in the tradition of petty clerks troubled by their ambition. He wants to move ahead in a number of ways, including the most concrete one achieved by putting one foot in front of the other. (To project, accord-ing to the dictionary, means to throw or hurl something forward.) Essentially Golyadkin wants to be out front, where he will be appreciated and admired. Due to his excessive reliance on projective mechanisms, however, his subse-quent confusion as to where he leaves off and the other person begins, all his efforts at self-assertion are experienced as being at someone else's expense, hence a kind of theft.

Not knowing where the boundary is between oneself and an other, leads to a preoccupation with greed. The question one would repeatedly be asking oneself would be "Am I being too demanding, or am I merely asking for what I am entitled to, while it is the other who is exploiting me? Which of us is asking for too much?" Often this is then dealt with by a kind of overcompen-sation: "If I ask for even more, then I'll know I'm not being taken advantage of," or conversely, "If I'm self-effacing then I can't be accused of being greedy or of coming on too strong." More than likely there's a vacillation between being overly-aggressive one moment and self-effacing the next. It is important to remember, however, that while there may be this oscillation, the external situation may remain constant, and what shifts back and forth is merely the subjective interpretation of it.

What one perceives depends upon where one identifies, and what it is one believes one has done. Spatial concepts are basic to the mechanism of projec-tion, as is the rather remarkable but universal notion that various aspects of

[10] See Wilfred Bion, "On Hallucination," *International Journal of Psycho-Analysis*, 39 (1958), 341-49, rpt. in *Second Thoughts* (London: Heinemann, 1967).

one's personality, perhaps especially one's feelings, are concrete "things" which can be removed from inside oneself and given to another person. (A corollary is that once expelled from within, these "objects" take on a life of their own.) There is an additional kind of concrete thinking which is characteristically associated with more massive forms of projective identification. When the boundary between subject and object has, in effect, been eliminated so that the two are fused, other distinctions are erased as well. It no longer becomes possible to think *about* something, or talk *about* something; the thought or word becomes the thing itself.[11] A patient winces when I speak to him, and tries to duck the words which are experienced as being hurled at him like boulders. Since thoughts and words now take up room, they squeeze out the mind or self which produced them. Someone in such a state of mind may typically complain of feeling "stuffed," or have a headache, or produce dreams and fantasies in which two objects are competing for the same space.

Needless to say, what I have been describing are a spectrum of fantasies which occur intrapsychically; nothing, so far as we know, has actually been put into the other person. Projective identification, however, is a bridging concept between the intrapsychic and the interpersonal. Simultaneous with the fantasy are often subtle, usually unconscious, affective or cognitive communications and behaviors which induce complementary or identical states of mind in the recipient. The latter may feel intruded upon, controlled, or driven to act inappropriately. In other words, the recipient of the projections is manipulated to respond in such a way as to verify the projective fantasy.

What import, if any, does this have for the relationship between Dostoevsky and the reader of his novella? The empathic reader brings with him a particular involvement and sensitivity to projective mechanisms. When we read we not only take in with our eyes, but we also put something of ourselves out and into the characters and situations about which we are reading. We impose our fantasies and expectations on the literary work to make it resemble ourselves. Norman Holland, among others, has emphasized how in the act of reading there is a loosening of boundaries between self and nonself, inner and outer, and a temporary fusion or confusion with the literary work.[12] In anticipation of pleasure the reader relaxes his defensive autonomy

---

[11] See Hanna Segal, "Notes on Symbol Formation," *International Journal of Psycho-Analysis*, 38 (1957), 391-97 and Herbert Rosenfeld, "Contribution to the Psychopathology of Psychotic States: The Importance of Projective Identification in the Ego Structure and the Object Relations of the Psychotic Patient," in *Problems of Psychosis*, ed. P. Doucet and C. Laurin (Amsterdam: Excepta Medica, 1969), p. 118.

[12] Norman Holland, *The Dynamics of Literary Response* (New York: W. W. Norton,

and lets the novel effect him. It is this vulnerability which Dostoevsky manipulates.

In *The Interpretation of Dreams* Freud had concluded that the mind was able to observe itself, and to give pictorial representation not only to its inner thought contents but also to its own mental states and processes.[13] He did not follow up on this idea, being more interested in the interpretation of thought content as it related to conflict. But he did refer to the work of Silberer, and accepted the latter's observations as to how his own fantasies, produced in the transitional period between sleep and wakefulness, sometimes pictured the state and functions of his mind, rather than the content of his thoughts. Freud was sufficiently impressed with Silberer's work as to label it "one of the few indisputably valuable additions to the theory of dreams."[14]

In the 1960's Philip Seitz pursued this further in a series of articles dealing with the representation of mental processes and structures in the concrete imagery of dreams.[15] His observations suggest that dreams of this type occur most frequently in the transitional states of mind associated with entering or recovering from a narcissistic regression—and also in those individuals with borderline pathology who hover between unstable object interest and narcissism. Seitz referred to Eissler's report that during such transitional narcissistic states, symptoms as well as dreams often contain magnified but distorted representations of the patient's own mental processes, states and structures.[16]

As psychoanalysis has become more involved with the treatment of character disorders, and particularly the narcisisstic and borderline personalities, there has been greater recognition of those dreams which Peter Giovacchini has labelled "representational": dreams which describe mental structures, their defects and states of collapse.[17] Typically the imagery is of a house in which the floor has been pulled out from under foot, walls crumble, rooms

1968) Ch. 3. The question of such fusion-confusions occurring in the process of *writing* is relevant, but beyond the scope of the present article.

[13]*S.E.*, V, 344-45, 503-6.

[14] "On Narcissism: An Introduction" (1914), *S.E.*, XIV, 97.

[15] "Representations of Structures in the Concrete Imagery of Dreams: A Clinical Method for Investigating the Structural Theory," presented to the Chicago Psychoanalytic Society, Jan. 22, 1963. Abstr.: *Bulletin of the Philadelphia Association for Psychoanalysis*, 13 (1963), 89-94. See also "Representations of Adaptive and Defense Mechanisms in the Concrete Imagery of Dreams," presented to the Chicago Psychoanalytic Society, Jan. 24, 1967.

[16]Kurt Eissler, "Notes Upon the Emotionality of a Schizophrenic Patient and its Relation to Problems of Technique," in *The Psychoanalytic Study of the Child*, 8 (1953), 235-50.

[17]See "Dreams and the Creative Process," in *British Journal of Medical Psychology*,

are empty, or threatening figures are trying to break in from without, or else the dreamer is unable to return home, or to regain some lost or stolen possession. The subject of the dream is the identity struggle of the dreamer, frequently the disruption or fragmentation of his or her self image. A distinguishing feature of neurotic dreams, the wide gap between manifest and latent content, is absent. Little appears to be disguised or transformed, and thus we are not surprised by the dreamer's paucity or absence of associations. Frequently the dreaming process itself appears to be concretized, or the dream is "acted in," so that what takes place in the analyst's office, or elsewhere in the patient's present life, is its dramatization or enactment.

Thus we might think of dreams as either falling into two distinct classes, or as being characterized according to their position on a developmental continuum, with these descriptive or representational dreams at one end and the more familiar disguised conflict dreams at the other. The descriptive-representational dreams are much closer to primitive fantasies than those dreams which were of interest to Freud. Nightmares and night terrors often appear to be either "failed dreams" or dreams of this more primitive type. Much of the anxiety associated with such nightmares is not related to their conflictual content, but is due to the regression to a primitive level of mental functioning, reminiscent of an early period of development when inside could not easily be differentiated from outside, or self from non-self. This is what accounts for the uncanny feeling which often accompanies such dreams, the experience of reencountering one's own concretized mental processes, mechanisms and structures.

Golyadkin's dream, in which his every step produces yet another Golyadkin until there is a multitude of doubles mocking and displacing him, might well be regarded as such a descriptive-representational dream of ego disruption and fragmentation. But so too might the entire story! There is a dream-like, or nightmarish, quality throughout *The Double*. The disturbing sense of ambiguity and vagueness was noted by Dostoevsky's contemporary readers, but there is also the strong sense of uncanny dread, and the feeling shared with the protagonist of increasing loss of control.

In the four day period encompassed by the narrative, Golyadkin is frequently in the transitional state between sleep and wakefulness, and there are suggestions that he may have dreamed part or even all of his story. In

39 (1966), 105-15. Giovacchini uses the term "representational" in the manner of Joseph Sandler and Bernard Rosenblatt, "The Concept of the Representational World," *The Psychoanalytic Study of the Child*, 17 (1962), 128-45. Heinz Kohut's "self-state dreams" are similar, or perhaps a sub-group of such dreams. *The Analysis of the Self* (New York: International Universities Press, 1971) and *The Restoration of the Self* (New York: International Universities Press, 1977).

the language of such dreams, as well as the woken-state language of primitive fantasy, the mechanism of denial may be represented as an act of murder, while the fantasied possession of aspects of another, or the invasion of the other's space, is presented as robbery. These twin crimes of robbery and murder recur throughout Dostoevsky's work; psychic mechanisms are thereby put into a moral and social context, as well as a literary one. It is in such concrete fantasies of intrusiveness and usurpation that the notion of stealing, not just aspects of another personality, but an entire identity, first begins.

II. GOLYADKIN'S SEARCH FOR A PLACE TO HIDE

When we are introduced to Golyadkin in the opening paragraph of the story, he is getting up from his night's sleep and is not quite sure whether he is awake or dreaming. His first action is to run to the mirror: a look at his external reflection will tell him how he is feeling. The narrator then describes the various objects in the immediate environment as Golyadkin might see them. The walls of Golyadkin's room, his furniture, his clothes look familiarly back at him. The autumn day peers into the room with a sour and bad-tempered grimace. When he picks up his wallet and looks at his money, it seems to look back at him in friendly and approving fashion. His samovar rages and hisses angrily, while lisping and babbling at him. The reader accepts these uses of projection; they are animistic or anthropomorphic in a way that is befitting the telling of stories. There is no question of confused identities or of qualities being attributed where they don't belong. When Golyadkin's servant, Petrushka, appears wearing a man-servant's livery that doesn't fit because it was made for somebody else, it is treated as a good-natured joke.

A moment later, however, when Golyadkin in his rented carriage is seen, first by two fellow employees and then by the head of his department, we realize by his embarrassment that he, Golyadkin, is where he doesn't belong. His response is to deny the uncomfortable reality by first pretending that he wasn't seen and then, failing that, to pretend that it isn't he, but somebody else who looks like him. He responds to a potential confrontation by denying his own existence. "It's quite all right; this is not me at all, Andrey Philippovich, it's not me at all, not me, and that's all about it." [18]

It is at this moment that the reader might first suspect that the previous series of pretenses are not just literary convention, but have been introducing a pathological way of relating to the world. Golyadkin's negation of himself

[18] *Notes from the Underground/The Double*, trans. Jessie Coulson (London: Penguin Classics, 1972), p. 132. All references to the novella are to this edition; subsequent pagination will be given in the text.

in this scene is a consequence of his apparent overconcern with how other people regard him. His need to favorably impress these others, and to avoid their disapproval, is a reflection of his need to receive something from them. Something which should come from within, which should be a part of the self, is missing and felt to come from the outside world. (This kind of dependency is particularly humiliating to admit to, and so Golyadkin loudly proclaims his independence, and emphasizes how he never does things to court favor or influence others.)

It is not enough to say, as some critics have suggested, that Dostoevsky is depicting his hero's self-consciousness. While it is true that Golyadkin takes himself as his object, his failure is in not also taking himself as subject. Projective mechanisms are utilized in his repeated efforts at viewing himself from other people's perspective, and in getting them to think and act for him. We learn that "he would have paid anybody handsomely to tell him exactly what action to decide on," (p. 209), and that he seeks out authority figures in order to throw himself at their feet. "I put my fate in your hands" he yearns to tell His Excellency, or anyone with any authority who will listen. "Give a man your protection and favor. . . . I myself stand aside from the whole business" (p. 266, also pp. 243, 269). While some of Golyadkin's subservience may be understood as natural to the bureaucratic society in which he lives, his responses clearly go way beyond such expectations, and what is truly horrifying is the enthusiasm with which Golyadkin gives up aspects of his personality. His willingness to abdicate any sense of responsibility makes him a non-participant observer of his own life. He repeatedly states this intention to "stand aside." "I'll be just an . . . onlooker, an outsider and no more, and then whatever happens I'm not to blame" (p. 279).

What appears to be Golyadkin's dependency on others is fraudulent, actually a kind of pseudo-dependency, since he not only utilizes these others for functions which he could better provide for himself, but they serve mainly as recipients for his projections. Golyadkin will find mirrors everywhere, even on his boss's shoes. The various authority figures therefore remain anonymous and interchangeable. *No one* is allowed to exist in their own right, including, of course, Golyadkin himself.[19]

Golyadkin's statements about how he is looking for "his own place" in the world, in order to "be himself," are belied by all his efforts. He appears determined to be anyone but, and we observe him pushing himself, or various

---

[19]Victor Terras describes him thusly: "Being more 'like everybody else,' seeking none but formal social relationships, pursuing no ethical values but only external symbols of social status, possessing no emotional ties or spiritual aspirations—this ultimately reduces Golyadkin to a state of virtual non-existence as a human being." *The Young Dostoevsky*, p. 62.

aspects of himself, where he and they don't belong. This intrusiveness, through physical as well as psychic boundaries, gives concrete representation to the mechanism of projection. Literally, there is one gate-crashing scene after another.[20] Within a relatively short space of time, Golyadkin first visits his doctor at an inappropriate hour; then goes to a dinner party to which he hasn't been invited and, after being refused entrance, crashes the party; then hides outside his place of work when he oversleeps, and after not daring to go in, enters just before closing when he is sure to be most conspicuous; then makes an uninvited visit to his department head's home; and then goes to see his boss at home and barges into the middle of an important meeting; and finally hides outside a fancy ball to which he was also not invited and then comes inside, again in the most conspicuous manner possible. Golyadkin, the outsider, intrudes into someone else's space, with projection concretely represented as movement between inside and outside, or across the barrier between self and non-self.

As is true of people with this kind of boundary problem, Golyadkin is quick to give up his own space. He disclaims responsibility for his actions, speaks of himself in the third person, moves as if mechanically propelled by someone else, blames enemies and, when feeling particularly uncomfortable, looks for a mouse hole to crawl into and wishes for his disappearance or annihilation. It is here that one of Dostoevsky's most important metaphors begins, with his hero's withdrawal into his corner, or behind a screen, or underground, ostensibly in order to avoid insult by others. It is Golyadkin's self-abnegation, initially in order to protect himself from painful feelings, which then causes him to feel overwhelmed by his "enemies." This leads to even further withdrawal, essentially more of the same thing, although now being done in the name of protecting himself from these others. It is just such self-abnegation, his "standing aside," which brings forth the birth of a double.

Golyadkin's doubles seem to multiply in response to the increasing fragmentation and emptying out of his personality. First the narrator presents himself as a doppelgänger, then Golyadkin Jr., then in Golyadkin's nightmare within a nightmare, each step taken in his effort to run away from himself only causes another Golyadkin to spring up, "*as if from under the ground . . . so that finally there had sprung up a terrible multitude of perfect replicas*" (pp. 230-231, italics mine).

Dostoevsky represents his character's state of mind through a repeated contrasting of internal emptiness with external clutter or confusion, essen-

---

[20] Ronald Hingley has observed the series of "gate-crashing scenes" that play such an important role throughout Dostoevsky's work. See *The Undiscovered Dostoyevsky* (London: H. Hamilton, 1962).

tially the same way in which this psychological state is typically represented in dreams. For example, when Golyadkin responds to his shame and mortification at his benefactor's by wanting "not only to run away from himself but even to annihilate himself, to cease to be, to return to the dust," he is at that moment overwhelmed by external persecutors in the form of "the snow, rain, and all the conditions for which there is not even a name," and we are told that "all this together had crushed down on Mr. Golyadkin, as though purposely joining in league and concert with all his enemies" (p. 166).

This stylistic device is repeated throughout the story. One more example: near the end of the novel, Golyadkin tries to render himself invisible by hiding behind a woodpile. While in hiding he vows to disengage himself from any responsibility for what will happen, and he ignores all his feelings, including his feeling that he shouldn't be there. When he is discovered and led into his former benefactor's drawing room, he is at his most helpless. Again we get a description of external bombardment, this time by "masses of people, a flower show of ladies" (p. 281) all surrounding and pressing in upon him.[21] The crowd engulfs him, and "all those eyes fixed on him seemed to be oppressing and crushing him" (p. 283). And, as if that were not bad enough, the crowd turns into an army of doubles. "He imagined that an endless string of Golyadkins all exactly alike were bursting noisily in through all the doors of the room" (p. 284).

What is being represented are the fantasied consequences of projective mechanisms, specifically the imbalance between "inside" and "outside" and the projective evacuation into fragments which then take on a life of their own and return as persecutors. Having contrasted Golyadkin's social isolation (the "absence of outward events") with his narcissistic ruminations, a kind of "internal clutter" if you like, I then gave several examples of how his excessive reliance on denial and projection leads to a perceived inner emptiness (variously described in the story as numbness or deadness, or as being asleep, false, spurious, shrunken, helpless, weak, paralyzed, blind, etc.) contrasted with external clutter. Sensing that he is doing something wrong, Golyadkin either attempts to arbitrarily reverse the process, or focuses on the boundary itself, and tries to turn it into a screen to hide behind.

The previous success of Golyadkin's efforts at self-effacement is clear. He is regarded as so insignificant that no one, not even his servant, bothers to look at him; therefore no one notices the striking resemblance of the double

---

[21] This scene prefigures Svidrigailov's suicide, with the myriad of flowers adding to the final persecutory fragmentation of his world. See my article "Raskolnikov's Transgression and the Confusion Between Destructiveness and Creativity," in *Do I Dare Disturb the Universe? A Memorial to Wilfred R. Bion*, ed. James Grotstein (Beverly Hills, Calif.: Caesura Press, 1981).

until it is pointed out to them. When Golyadkin finally appeals to His Excellency, the man for whom he has been working asks, "Who are you?" Even his own double doesn't recognize him, and this after they had spent an entire evening together.

That Golyadkin looks insignificant is particularly important since an unusual degree of power is attributed to visual forms of representation within the story. How things appear is equated with how they are, as when Golyadkin looks in the mirror to see how he is feeling. He changes his large notes into smaller ones, and even though he has lost money on the transaction, the fatter wallet makes him feel as if he has more. When he goes on a shopping spree, he makes an extraordinary number of expensive purchases but no money is exchanged and nothing actually received; all is pretense, done for appearance sake. Most significant of Golyadkin's early reactions to his double is shame that somebody would look like him, and he is ashamed to be seen with him.

Conflicts about how one appears are usually paired with a disturbed attitude toward the activity of looking. Golyadkin is made helpless under the gaze of others. His own glance, in equal measure, projects venom, in fantasy powerful and space-annihilating. It is his fantasy of visual omnipotence which allows him to imagine he can cause the ballroom chandelier to fall merely by looking at it, thereby turning a helpless situation into a heroic one. The activity of looking not only erases distance but gives one power and control over people. When Golyadkin wants to diminish the influence of his former landlady he refers to her as "one-eyed" (p. 236). A glare brings together guilt and shame, and in so doing seems to banish one to a state of non-existence. When Golyadkin's German physician takes on the full role of judge and jailor in the final paragraph of the story, his eyes glow like red coals in the darkness.[22]

In addition to appearance, Golyadkin's oscillation between intrusiveness and self-effacement is physically represented in his speech patterns and in his movement. The author's intention for Golyadkin was first described in a letter Dostoevsky wrote his brother, in which he attempted to convey the style, and voice of his character: "By no means does he want to go forward, pretending that, why, he is just not ready yet, and that for the present he is who he is, that he is nothing, not on your life, and that, I dare say, if it's already come to that, then so can he, and why not, for what reason."[23]

[22] See Andrew Peto, "Terrifying Eyes: A Visual Superego Forerunner," *The Psychoanalytic Study of the Child*, 24 (1969), 197-212.

[23] Konstantin Mochulsky, in quoting this letter, notes that "Dostoevsky's heroes are born out of speech; this is a general law in his creative processes." *Dostoevsky His Life and Work*, trans. Michael Minihan (Princeton: Princeton Univ. Press, 1967), p. 40.

Golyadkin has difficulty making a statement or even asking a direct question; to *get to the point* is regarded as terribly aggressive. Golyadkin's blocked speech somehow then leaves his thoughts to meander on their own, as if still hoping to arrive at their goal. Words tumble on after one another, pleonastically stuffing themselves into some space, fighting for centrality, or perhaps fighting to avoid it, since Golyadkin never does say what he means. On one occasion he asks himself why it is that he always keeps talking about the wrong thing. Rather than being used for communication, his words function as masks, shields, or weapons.

The function of speech as a screen to hide behind is suggested by the lack of originality in all his utterances. Everything is borrowed, a stringing together of proverbs, platitudes and commonplaces. This shield doesn't work and Golyadkin continues to fear exposure. Just as he believes other people can see through him, he believes they know what he is going to say before he says it. Consequently he refers to events as if the listener already knows what is on his mind, or he refers to everything as indirectly as possible, a language of allusion, while wondering whether he hasn't, in fact, said too much. He is always defensive, always apologizing.

Golyadkin's movements have already been well described by Vinogradov and by Terras.[24] The latter writer reminds us that Golyadkin is middle-aged, very short and quite stout, so that his sudden rapid moves don't fit; they seem to belong to someone else. In fact, these movements have a life of their own, as if someone else is moving him. Golyadkin is referred to as a puppet or jack-in-the-box, "as if somebody had touched a spring inside him" (p. 158). These sudden moves are both manic and intrusive—he is always jumping in where he doesn't belong. Andrey Philippovich sees him as if he "looked ready to jump straight down his throat" (p. 150) and reacts by anxiously jumping backwards and slamming the door just as Golyadkin bounds swiftly up the stairs right at him.

Golyadkin deals with his uncomfortableness about how other people might view him by the most primitive form of denial, he shuts his eyes and believes himself invisible. "And he would get through, he would certainly get through, looking neither to right nor left, he would slip through, that was all, and nobody would notice" (p. 157). At other times he worries about his intrusive behavior. "That's just like you," he chastizes himself, "You go plunging straight in" (p. 183). Later on he again admonishes himself: "'Won't that be too much,' he thought; 'aren't I going too far? It's

---

[24]V. V. Vinogradov, "Towards a Morphology of the 'Naturalist' Style" (1922), rpt. in *Dostoevsky & Gogol: Texts and Criticism*, trans. and ed. Priscilla Meyer and Stephen Rudy (Ann Arbor: Ardis, 1979), pp. 217-28. Terras, pp. 130-33.

always the same: I always overdo things'." This inhibits any purposive movement on his part and prevents him from ever asserting himself effectively.

Golyadkin's movement is contrasted with that of his double. Golyadkin Jr. also tries to be someone else, but is successful at it. Perhaps because he's not hampered by shame or guilt, he scampers and skips, turns and twists, minces and darts and prances and wriggles his way through the second half of the story. He proceeds to play one role after another. Golyadkin Jr. has no inner life of his own. Or to put it another way, since he can be anybody, he is nobody, or at least not himself. Golyadkin Sr. is envious of and feels "mocked" by his double's ability to do just that which he himself is unable to do, to move rapidly and freely over all boundaries, to change identities. On a more rational and reasonable level, Golyadkin Sr. believes that his double has unlimited confidence and self-respect, that he charms everybody gracefully and easily and that he not only accomplishes the things that Golyadkin would like to do, but he does them without any effort. He is admired and admitted to those places from which Golyadkin Sr. is kept out.

Golyadkin Sr.'s comparison of himself with his double, and his envy of his double's ability to "overstep all the boundaries," anticipates Raskolnikov's relationship with Svidrigailov. Unlike his double, Golyadkin Sr. does have something to lose by crossing these psychic barriers: his sanity. His anxiety about going too far is related to his progressive inability to distinguish the boundary between himself and others. What better way of representing Golyadkin's confusion than by having him think he's looking into a mirror when he's looking at another person. Or is he looking at another person? Golyadkin can't defend himself because he can't tell when the other has gone too far. Did he or Golyadkin Jr. eat the eleven cakes? He puzzles over what Andrey Philippovich's words meant at a time when his superior hadn't said anything, he himself had done all the talking. He sees used dishes on a restaurant table and, wondering whether it was he who had dinner, offers to pay. As he, himself, states, "Anything is possible" (p. 258).

Golyadkin's name is derived from the word for "naked" and in the manner which I have been suggesting he is without clothes, indeed, without skin.[25] There is an emphasis throughout *The Double* on clothes as a defensive structure, a kind of psychic skin separating self from non-self. Golyadkin's disintegration is represented by his losing his clothes. He loses first one galosh, then the other, then the rest of his clothes begin to tear and come apart. His double is described initially as "a man who for want of his own clothes is wearing somebody else's" (p. 186). Golyadkin lacks an adequate boundary

---

[25] Belinsky described Dostoevsky's talent as "an ability, one might say, to slip into the skin of another person, even if that person be a complete stranger." Quoted by Terras, p. 109.

between himself and others, and without it he can't hold his identity together. Not only is he vulnerable to being intruded upon, but without this
covering to protect him he is also exposed, and that which he might most
wish to conceal can be seen by all.

III. An Oedipal Story

This story of intrusiveness and usurpation can also be taken up from an
oedipal point of view. After all, the oedipal myth is of the child's precocious
intrusion into parental territory, usurping the role of one parent with the
other. There are a number of retaliatory fantasies, one of which is of a
younger sibling coming along and usurping the child's place with the beloved
parent. Golyadkin, we notice, has several rivals. Vladimir Semyonovich, who
is the boss's nephew, has not only just received a promotion at the office but
he is soon to be the son-in-law of Golyadkin's former benefactor. Thus he is
the favored son of several of Golyadkin's symbolic fathers. Throughout the
story Golyadkin frequently refers to these men as fathers, thus making this
view of his relationship with them explicit.

It is in the interview with the German physician, Dr. Rutenspitz, that
Golyadkin first expresses how upset he is at being disregarded.[26] He snidely
hints that Vladimir Semyonovich's interest in marrying Clara Olsufyevna is
not out of love for her so much as it is a way of achieving position. It is this
position which seems to be the object of Golyadkin's jealousy and it is just
such favor which he had lost prior to the beginning of the story. Golyadkin
describes his rival as a baby, "with the milk not yet dry on his lips" (p. 141).
A moment later he spitefully envisions him as biting into a lemon. Clearly,
Golyadkin felt he had seniority and saw his place usurped by the newcomer.

Golyadkin's downfall begins on the anniversary of Clara's birth. As his
benefactor's only child, she is a rival also and his attitude toward her makes
much more sense if she is viewed as a sibling rather than as a primary object
for his love. When he receives the letter from her in which she supposedly
tells of her love for him and asks him to elope with her, his response is
striking. He doesn't utter a single comment about ever having loved her or
wanting to marry her, but instead expresses his outrage at how her father

---

[26] Robert Rodgers stresses the physician's role as the ultimate father surrogate, noting
that he shows up both at the apartments of His Excellency, and at the home of Golyadkin's benefactor, Berendeyev. At one point Golyadkin suspects the doctor of trying
to poison him, and at the novella's conclusion it is Dr. Rutenspitz who condemns him to
hell or the insane asylum. *The Double in Literature* (Detroit: Wayne State Univ. Press,
1970), pp. 35-37.

spoiled and fussed over her. He can't stand all the attention she received: "They stuffed her with sweets and chocolates, and the silly old man slobbered over her; you're my sweetheart, you're my darling, he says, you're my pretty one" (p. 264). Again, as with his jealousy of Vladimir Semyonovich, Golyadkin portrays his rival as orally indulged and greedy. Nowhere in the story is Clara's mother mentioned, but a maternal figure is brought in at this point and blamed for being behind all his difficulties. This woman is Golyadkin's former landlady.[27]

Throughout the story everyone accuses Golyadkin of mistreating her, and there is the suggestion that it is because of this that he is no longer entitled to anything. What Golyadkin is guilty of is misrepresenting himself in order to get food and lodging, apparently by pretending he will marry her. If we think of this woman as representing the mother who originally provided nourishment and shelter, the significance of Golyadkin's "crime" is clear. It is his sense of having received something fraudulently, in effect through stealing, which leads to his viewing of subsequent events as inevitable retribution. Golyadkin, however, then denies any wrongdoing by shifting the blame to the landlady herself, referring to her as "the old witch," and insisting that it was *she* who had betrayed *him*.

But then he shifts his reproach again, now blaming Clara, "The old witch is a good woman, the witch isn't to blame, it's you, madam, who are to blame for everything" (p. 265). Clara is the intruder who usurps his place! It's no wonder that he fantasized the chandelier falling down to crush her! A younger sibling, sometimes the feared unborn child, may represent the ideal or perfect person. Golyadkin's reasoning, like that of many an older brother, would be: If I were good enough, my parents wouldn't need to have more children. Thus the arrival of a younger sibling is experienced as a failure; the shame and humiliation of not having lived up to parental ideals.

When Golyadkin experiences the humiliating rejection at the hands of his benefactor, the man who had been like a father to him, he initially tries to annihilate not only his memory of the experience, but the self that had experienced it, and he then tries to reconstruct the lost relationship with his benefactor by establishing just such a relationship with Golyadkin Jr. The senior Golyadkin takes on the role of patron and protector and treats the newcomer as he himself would like to be treated. This kind of relationship, in which the love object represents the self, and one identifies with the beloved parent,

---

[27]Notably, we find an absence of couples anywhere in the story; none of the father figures appear to have wives. What better way to prevent the birth of a younger sibling! The exception is a solitary reference to the wife of Dr. Rutenspitz, who, we are told, had brought him his coffee (p. 133).

treating the other as one was or would have liked to have been treated, was described by Freud.[28]

Children frequently create imaginary companions or fantasied twins in response to narcissistic humiliations such as the birth of a younger sibling.[29] The imaginary companion serves both for the projection of unacceptable impulses and feelings and as an idealized self representation, a way of preserving the child's shattered narcissistic omnipotence. The relationship with such a fantasied twin or companion is frequently satisfying. After a period of months or years the imaginary companion becomes unnecessary, and is given up or forgotten. There are instances, however, where the imaginary companion turns upon his little master and attacks him, or becomes a persecutor who lives on as an object of terror.[30]

In Golyadkin's case we see how all the roles his double plays originate in the wishes or intentions of Golyadkin Sr., however they are caricatured and played out with a vengeance. I have already demonstrated, for example, how one of Golyadkin's desires, to be able to move forward in word and deed, to be both straightforward and assertive, is mocked by the blinding speed and supernatural dexterity, the increasingly unreal movement, of Golyadkin Jr. Not only does the self attempt to spoil the idealization, to devalue it through caricature and ridicule, but the idealized or ideal self is seen as attempting to rob from the *limited self*.[31] The double's role as a usurper of Golyadkin's position becomes more overt, so that it is he who becomes the ultimate rival.

Golyadkin's "namesake" of course is felt to be a younger brother or son

[28] The idea first appears in "Leonardo da Vinci and a Memory of His Childhood" (1910), *S.E.*, XI, 100-02 and is then repeated four years later in the classic essay on narcissism (*S.E.*, XIV, 88). See also Dorothy Burlingham, "The Fantasy of Having a Twin," *The Psychoanalytic Study of the Child*, 1 (1945), 207.

[29] Various authors estimate that between 13% and 33% of all children have imaginary companions. See studies cited by Humberto Nahera, "The Imaginary Companion," *The Psychoanalytic Study of the Child*, 24 (1969), 169. The "arrival" of the imaginary companion soon after the birth of a sibling is noted by Nahera and others. See Sheldon Bach, "Notes on Some Imaginary Companions," *The Psychoanalytic Study of the Child*, 26 (1971), 159-71, and Wayne Myers, "Imaginary Companions, Fantasy Twins, Mirror Dreams and Depersonalization," *Psychoanalytic Quarterly*, 45 (1976), 503-24.

[30] Anna Freud, *The Ego and the Mechanisms of Defense* (New York: International Universities Press, 1946). Alan Eisnitz refers to the case cited by Miss Freud, and presents one of his own, in "Mirror Dreams," *Journal of the American Psychoanalytic Association*, 9 (1961), 461-79. See also Ronald Benson and David Pryor, "'When Friends Fall Out': Developmental Interference with the Function of Some Imaginary Companions," *Journal of the American Psychoanalytic Association*, 21 (1973), 457-73.

[31] Remember how Golyadkin Jr. tricked the senior Golyadkin into thinking his work was blemished, so that he could whisk it away and then take credit for it as his own. Thus what had been accomplished through hard work is credited to an omnipotent aspect of the personality, which then becomes viewed as indispensable.

from the beginning. Upon his first appearance, Golyadkin admits his suspicion that something like that was being prepared, "that there was *somebody else* in reserve" (p. 173). Although they look as alike as two peas in a pod, the reader nevertheless experiences the double as quite a bit younger. He is called junior, shows spryness and quickness of movement, as well as playfulness and, characteristically, he kicks his legs like a baby. Like the other rivals he is orally indulged, and at Golyadkin Sr.'s expense. Golyadkin is made to feel more and more excluded, while observing that "the scoundrel looks like the court favorite" (p. 248). At the end of the story, just before going off to the lunatic asylum, it is with bitter irony that Golyadkin observes how nice it is that they are all gathered at the home of his benefactor, "just like a family before somebody leaves on a long journey" (p. 284).

IV. THE OMNIPOTENT RIVAL

The most outstanding characteristic of Golyadkin's double is his capacity to imitate, to fit in anywhere by adapting to other people's expectations and values. This is one goal of the narcissistic personality—to anticipate what other people want and ingratiate oneself, thereby gaining approval, love, or validation. (Wishes to "stand out," to be an individual or rebel, of course, counteract it.) It had been Golyadkin's effort in this first direction, not the work of any external rival, which robbed him of any identity of his own. It is also responsible for his feeling of fraudulence; both he and his double are open to the accusation of being imposters or counterfeits.

When we look at Golyadkin Jr. we see how clearly he embodies not only those characteristics and personality traits which Golyadkin is trying to disavow, but those which the senior Golyadkin most greatly admires.[32] His double is his idealized self! That the gap between such an idealized self and one's limited, everyday self could cause untold suffering was well known to Dostoevsky, who wrote that the tragedy of the underground man lay

[32] Although he does not refer to *The Double*, Freud in "The 'Uncanny'" (1919), *S.E.*, XVII, 234-36, analyzes Hoffmann's *The Sandman* and discusses the theme of the double. He relates it to a conflict within the ego between a split-off critical faculty or conscience and those aspects of the self which it finds reprehensible. The latter, he observes, are frequently repressed. Significantly Freud notes that it is not only offensive material which may be incorporated into the idea of a double, but "all the unfulfilled but possible futures to which we still like to cling in phantasy, all the strivings of the ego which adverse external circumstances have crushed." This, of course, is the *ego ideal* which Freud had already described in his essay on narcissism (*S.E.*, XIV, 94, 95), where he had recounted how the view of one's own lost perfection is projected before oneself and taken as an object.

precisely in this "consciousness of his own deformity . . . *the consciousness of what is best and the impossibility of attaining it*." [33] This unbridgeable gap is a constant source of humiliation.

Golyadkin is ready to forgive his rival anything, for just one word of approval. He repeatedly falls for his double's tricks because he wants so desperately to be liked by him. What he wants is to be reconciled with those aspects of his own personality which are embodied in Golyadkin Jr., but this is impossible. Since the gap between them is too wide, the hopelessness of bridging it has led to attacks on both the ideal self and on the *limited self*. The pyrotechnics of Golyadkin Jr., itself the subject for caricature, in its turn serves to ridicule the pathetic Golyadkin who is stumbling over chairs, stepping on women's feet and on their dresses, and bumping into servants carrying trays, while all the while trying to look inconspicuous and at ease. [34]

Basically the envied rival is a self who doesn't suffer such limitations, but who can be all things to all people, shifting gears effortlessly and never experiencing hurt or humiliation in social situations, in fact never having to be vulnerable. This kind of rival appears over and over again in Dostoevsky's fiction, as a double who represents idealized aspects of the hero and with whom the hero continues to unfavorably compare himself. The hero's efforts to have a relationship with him are an effort to regain the perfection and power associated with his own lost infantile omnipotence. The more impossible this becomes, the more he attacks both his limited self and his rival.

These omnipotent rivals have a number of features in common: (1) There is an emphasis on appearances and on "looking good." They are invariably physically attractive and well-dressed. (2) They possess the right social graces and know how to behave in society. (3) They are favored in the eyes of the love object, whether it be a woman or a surrogate parent. (4) They easily move across (psychic) barriers. (5) They are untouchable emotionally, i.e. "above it all." This is felt to give them power. (6) They are not dependent on others. As a consequence, they don't get hurt, although they often hurt others. (7) Their freedom consists, in the final analysis, of a freedom from guilt. (8) However, they are, or are often accused of being, spiritually empty.

---

[33] Quoted by Coulson in her Introduction, *Notes from Underground/The Double*, p. 10. From *The Notebooks for a Raw Youth*, ed. Edward Wasiolek (Chicago and London: Univ. of Chicago Press, 1969 [1965]), p. 425.

[34] Significantly Golyadkin Jr. represents the kind of *perfect twin* which many people take to be their standard of normality, the way things should be. Viewing oneself from such a perspective, the normal, limited personality has to be seen as hopelessly inadequate. See Bion's description of the splitting of the self and the reciprocal interaction or dialogue which takes place between the various personality organizations in "The Imaginary Twin" and "The Differentiation Between the Psychotic and Nonpsychotic Parts of the Personality," both in *Second Thoughts*.

Examples might include Svidrigailov, de Grieux in *The Gambler*, Zverkov and the six-foot lieutenant in *Notes From The Underground*, Stavrogin in *The Possessed*, and Velchaninov in *The Eternal Husband*. Readers familiar with Dostoevsky's work will have no difficulty thinking of others. (It is my impression that in Dostoevsky's own life Turgenev played such a role.) Significantly, Dostoevsky doesn't allow these characters, or their relationship with the hero, to remain static; in several instances, the perspective is such that the story is told from the point of view of the omnipotent rival.

One feature of these personalities requires particular comment: their relative absence of feelings. One's feelings, of course, are what makes one most vulnerable, and most human. But they are precisely what Golyadkin regards as his greatest limitation, and what he attempts to annihilate in himself. His most specific tirade against such feelings occurs in the final chapter when he is telling Clara (in her absence, of course) what marriage to him would be like. Don't expect any "billing and cooing and talking about our feelings" (p. 277). A wife should just provide the food and drink, he tells her, and forget about such things as tenderness or emotional intimacy. You'll be lucky if you get an indifferent kiss every week or so.

To the extent that Dostoevsky's protagonist disavows his needs and desires, his awareness of them in others is experienced as demanding, even draining; if he should recognize that he cares about a woman, he would feel enslaved by such feelings, including any feelings about having hurt or disappointed her. The relationship itself becomes viewed as a trap, with marriage felt to be the most suffocating, and claustrophobic of all.[35] The omnipotent rival is believed immune from such feelings, and from such involvements. Most typically, he substitutes *sensations* for feelings, and there is an emphasis on physical movement to provide the excitement which replaces passion.

V. WHERE THIS PUTS THE RIVAL

It might be tempting, not only to see Golyadkin's problem within the psychopathological confines of the narcissistic and borderline disorders, but

---

[35] In *Crime and Punishment* there are five male characters defined in terms of their respective attitudes toward women. Surprisingly, it is the healthiest of them, Razumihin, who describes matrimony as a kind of death-in-life (Part III, Chapter I). Raskolnikov's efforts to escape from a suffocating relationship with his mother make up the central theme of the novel. The two characters who understand him best tell him that what he is most in need of is "fresh air." See "Raskolnikov's Transgression and the Confusion Between Destructiveness and Creativity."

to leave it there.[36] Dostoevsky, however, is not presenting us with a case history; what is important is experiential. The intrusive projection into others, the subsequent confusion between what is real and what is not, and the precarious dependency on someone else for what one feels one should provide for oneself, become not just aspects of Golyadkin's difficulty, but problems for the empathic reader. The over-all effect is the realization of what it feels like to be a Golyadkin.

I began by pointing out how the action of the story consists of a series of gate-crashing scenes. The reader, to the extent that he or she identifies with Golyadkin, experiences anxiety about going where one doesn't belong, and an anticipation of being caught, exposed and humiliated. I then went on to illustrate how the theme of intrusiveness and usurpation works on a number of different levels of the story. This theme has its most direct impact on the reader through the interaction with the narrator.

Early in the story the narrator encourages the reader's trust by being benign and reasonable, but to the extent that the reader accepts the opinions of someone called a narrator, the reader is dependent on someone else for perceptions and evaluations which one usually provides for oneself. The precariousness of this kind of dependency is brought to the reader's attention each time there is a sudden shift in the story and what is presented differs from what lies within the reader's normal expectations.

When the narrator makes extended use of projection to describe how the walls of Golyadkin's room, his furniture and clothes all look back and greet him, we accept this as a device appropriate to its literary context, and only a moment later sense how it also represents Golyadkin's disturbed way of viewing the world. By then, however, we've already been identifying ourselves with a Golyadkin who looks to the external world, even to such inanimate objects as samovars and paper money, for signs of approval or disapproval. That these shifts cause the reader to question the uneasy co-existence of literary and psychological realities becomes clearer, but also more disturbing each time there is such an occurrence.

For example, midway through the story there is a chapter in which the narrator describes the ball at the home of Golyadkin's benefactor. The things

---

[36] I am aware of the variety of previous diagnoses which have been entertained: Otto Rank thought Golyadkin was a classic portrayal of a paranoid state, *The Double: A Psychoanalytic Study*, trans. Harry Tucker (Chapel Hill: Univ. of North Carolina Press, (1971); Lawrence Kohlberg found classic symptoms of an obsessive compulsive character, "Psychological Analysis and Literary Form: A Study of the Doubles in Dostoevsky," *Daedalus*, Vol. 92, Spring 1963; John Todd and Kenneth Dewhurst were most impressed by the autoscopic phenomena, "The Double: Its Psychopathology and Psychophysiology," *Journal of Nervous and Mental Disease*, Vol. 122, 1955. Others have regarded Golyadkin as a case of multiple personality or a paranoid schizophrenic.

I could tell you, he says, if I were only someone else, a Homer or Pushkin, and then he proceeds to tell us in the most elevated and hyperbolic language, pausing his long winded description only long enough to remind us that out of feelings of inadequacy to the task, he will remain silent. The reader will recognize in this a familiar literary convention, a topos of the epic. To the extent that the reader passively accepts this convention, on another level he begins to feel more and more uncomfortable, for the narrator's pomposity appears in marked contrast with the protagonist's deflated state at that moment, Golyadkin wishing to sink into the ground or hide in a mouse hole.

Not only is the narrator introducing himself as a character for the first time, with practically every one of his sentences beginning with the first person pronoun, but he has turned mocking and cruel with regard to Golyadkin. The narrator seems to be showing off, his verbal dexterity the equivalent of Golyadkin Jr.'s dance. The reader finds himself in the uncomfortable position of colluding with the betrayal, but then remembers that this is "only" a literary convention, and that the narrator is doing what narrators do. Besides, the narrator is not a real person, and neither for that matter is Golyadkin. The literary and psychological realities play off each other; both seemingly present within the same space, each causing us to question what we are accepting in the other.[37]

For the reader to deny the narrator *his* "identity" is to perhaps miss an important alternative point of view with regard to this chapter, namely that the narrator has been thrust as a character into the action of the story only as a result of Golyadkin having usurped his position. After all, just prior to this Golyadkin had tried to view the ball as a "detached observer," a role more appropriate to narrators. Vinogradov presents this argument, and further notes how "When Golyadkin again returns to his role as 'main actor,' the narration resumes its former objectivity."[38]

While such reasoning "makes sense," it is based on the kind of concrete thinking associated with primitive projective mechanisms. It is also illustrative of my thesis that Golyadkin's self-negation is not the passive withdrawal it may have initially appeared to be, but is invariably at someone else's expense. Utilizing the battle imagery of the text, Vinogradov points out how Golyadkin's penetration into "enemy territory" (assaulting Andrey Filippovich,

---

[37] "The literature of the fantastic leaves us with two notions: that of reality and that of literature, each as unsatisfactory as the other." Tzvetan Todorov, *The Fantastic: A Structural Approach to a Literary Genre*, trans. Richard Howard (Cleveland and London: Case Western Reserve Univ., 1973), p. 168.

[38] "Towards a Morphology of the 'Naturalist' Style," esp. Section II, "The Compositional Principles of *The Double*," rpt. in *Dostoevsky & Gogol: Texts and Criticism*, pp. 223-28.

accosting Anton Antonovich, attempting to abduct Clara and invade her father's home) is accompanied, not only by a dissolution of reality, but by an apparent merging of narrator and hero.

Vinogradov documents the stylistic devices by which this latter effect is brought about. Golyadkin's thoughts and speech pop up in the narration, first in quotes, then increasingly without demarcation. Golyadkin also increasingly patterns his behavior on literary models. The narrator, meanwhile, is observing events as Golyadkin would observe them, as if from inside his consciousness, and parodying his protagonist, in effect becoming his double. We progressively cannot tell who is speaking, Golyadkin or his narrator.

As the reader progresses further into the story, both he and Golyadkin miss the luxury of the detached outside observer, the so called narrator-from-above. As Bakhtin has noted, it is as if the narrator cannot back far enough away from Golyadkin to give a summarizing, integrated view of him.[39] This lack of perspective seriously interferes with the reader's efforts to distance himself, to achieve objectivity and detachment, and is one of the factors contributing to the disturbing claustrophobic feeling which many people experience when reading Dostoevsky. The narrator's seeming inability to summarize, to give an overview, results in prolixity, generally regarded as one of the novella's artistic flaws. It is my impression that this wordiness functions for the reader in a manner similar to the multiplicity of doubles, or the flowering profusion of party-goers who crush Golyadkin at the story's climax. Both protagonist and reader are overwhelmed by external clutter, the imbalance between outward and inward. It is not just Golyadkin Jr. but the very words with which the story is told which dance or run away, adding to the sense of going too fast, and of things being out of control.

The words seem to keep the reader moving forward, yet they convey very little of the specific information needed to orient oneself. This goes beyond the question of whether Golyadkin is awake or asleep, hallucinating or conversing with another, reading a real letter or not. There's a hunger on the reader's part for missing information about the externals of Golyadkin's life. Other than Golyadkin, the character with the most "palpable" reality in the story is his double, and he of course is playing a different role practically each time we encounter him. His slippery elusiveness is a characteristic of the story itself. For example, crucial events which occurred before the story began, and to which the various characters are reacting, are only hinted at—so we keep reading, in the hope of finding out what we think we somehow are supposed to already know.

---

[39]Mikhail Bakhtin, *Problems of Dostoevsky's Poetics*, trans. R. W. Rotsel (Ann Arbor, Mich.: Ardis, 1973 [1929]), p. 188.

As we go further and further into the story, the "facts" become less and less certain. Why does Golyadkin's doctor now have a heavy accent when he didn't before? Is he, as Golyadkin suggests, a double for the other Dr. Rutenspitz, hence an evil imposter? Has Golyadkin succeeded in projecting his own split-self personality on to the entire world, so that it is all fraudulent?

One of the difficulties with an excessive reliance on projective mechanisms is that one cannot take anything for granted. Projections are returned or taken back—no, it is not *he* who is ambitious, angry, unfaithful, etc.—it is, after all, only *me*. What one has built up, as one's view of the world or one's view of oneself, seems to suddenly collapse. There is not only an all-or-nothing quality to this, but I have heard it frequently described as a feeling of having to go back to the beginning, returning to "square one."

Readers have this experience with *The Double*, the feeling of the whole or part of the story collapsing on us. Each morning when Golyadkin wakes up we wonder whether what preceded his awakening might not have all been a dream. But Golyadkin also has mental lapses in which he "wakes up" to find himself somewhere without knowing how he got there. There is a cyclical pattern to the story, with later events "mirroring" earlier occurrences, thereby casting doubt as to the "reality" of what happened. By the time of Golyadkin's final nightmare, the boundary between dreams and reality no longer exists: Golyadkin can no longer dream, nor can he awaken.

In order to appreciate the ultimate collapse of the story, however, one would have to be reading it under the conditions present for Dostoevsky's contemporaries. The primary Russian literary model in the 1840's was Nicholai Gogol, and when Dostoevsky burst on the scene with his *Poor Folk*, he had been hailed as "the new Gogol."[40] But when, just a few months later, the young author took Gogol's "The Nose" for his model, he was accused of going too far, and of exceeding the bounds of respectable influence or imitation. Thus the theme of intrusiveness and usurpation carried itself right up to an accusation against Dostoevsky himself, and *The Double* was itself viewed as a double. The charge of stealing another's identity, when made in the literary domain, is plagiarism!

"The Nose" was also about someone with a deficient sense of self, but in the case of Gogol's protagonist his deficiency received concrete representation in the form of a missing body part which appeared in the outside world and threatened to supplant him. This was a common enough theme in the

---

[40] According to Yury Tynyanov, "Nekrasov speaks to Belinsky about a 'new Gogol,' Belinsky calls Gogol 'the father of Dostoevsky,' and even Ivan Aksakov, sitting in Kaluga, hears news about the 'new Gogol.'" See Tynyanov's "Dostoevsky and Gogol: Towards a Theory of Parody, Part One: Stylization and Parody," rpt. in *Dostoevsky & Gogol: Texts and Criticism*, p. 101.

tradition of the doppelgänger, but Dostoevsky utilized not only Gogol's theme, but his "literary father's" style and language and rather specific elements of the story. A quote from a contemporary critic, K. S. Aksakov, conveys the outrage that was felt: "Dostoevsky constantly mimics Gogol, frequently imitating him to such an extent that what results is no longer imitation, but appropriation. *We do not even understand how this tale could have appeared. All Russia knows Gogol, knows him almost by heart; and here, in front of everyone, Mr. Dostoevsky rearranges and repeats outright whole sentences from Gogol. . . .* From the rags of the once-beautiful clothing of a true artist Mr. Dostoevsky has sewn himself a garment and brazenly shows himself to the reading public."[41]

Notably this effect was deliberate, with Dostoevsky seeming to take every opportunity to remind his readers of his predecessor. A number of sentences, including the opening paragraph, are almost identical, and in the original version of *The Double* Dostoevsky kept referring to noses, in a sense rubbing the reader's nose in what he was doing. On the more sophisticated level of interpretation Dostoevsky was raising questions as to the difference between influence and imitation, in the development of a literary style, or a personality. How much should come from outside of oneself, and how is one to use it? On another level, Dostoevsky's contemporary readers, with an allegiance to Gogol, must have felt in the same uncomfortable position as they did with respect to the intrusive narrator, of either having to reject what they were receiving, or of colluding in the usurpation, and hence sharing the guilt.

The novella, then, is a kind of literary double, playing off the work of Dostoevsky's predecessor in a way similar to Golyadkin Jr.'s interaction with Golyadkin Sr., or the narrator's interaction with his protagonist. Like these previous pairs of doubles, the interaction is two-way. Thus, in his comparison of "The Nose" with *The Double*, Bem notes how the allusions to Gogol "suddenly and unjustifiably intrude" into Dostoevsky's story.[42] We are

---

[41] The quote originally appeared in the *Moscow Literary and Scientific Symposium* for 1847, pp. 33-34. It is cited by A. L. Bem, "'The Nose' and *The Double*," rpt. in *Dostoevsky & Gogol: Texts and Criticism*, p. 229. See also p. 281 n. If Dostoevsky did, in fact, utter the words attributed to him ("We are all descended from Gogol's Overcoat") Aksakov's remark gives them an ironic twist. Joseph Frank believes the statement is probably apocryphal, and notes that it had also been attributed to Turgenev. *Dostoevsky the Seeds of Revolt, 1821-1849* (Princeton: Princeton Univ. Press, 1976), p. 332 and p. 377 n.   Aksakov's image of the stolen garment not only echoes the plot of Gogol's *Overcoat*, but resonates within *The Double* itself, where both Petrushka and Golyadkin Jr. appear dressed in "borrowed" clothes. As Dostoevsky's biographers are fond of observing, life seems to inspire art, and then to imitate it.

[42] Bem, p. 233. Bem's phrase highlights the importance of quickness and surprise in creating the *confusion*. A patient tried to describe this by recalling how he had once

reminded of how Golyadkin's speech patterns intruded into the narrator's territory as if usurping the latter's identity, although our initial reading had it the other way around, with the narrator puffing himself up at Golyadkin's expense. Clearly it is in the tension between both possibilities that Golyadkin's implied question "Which of us went too far?" attains greatest significance.

There is a well-known drawing used to demonstrate visual ambiguity in which a design, looked at one way resembles a duck, looked at another way, a rabbit. With a blink of the eye figure and ground have reversed themselves. This might be the experience of the reader with the reversals of the fantastic and commonplace in Gogol's story. All is external; the reader remains at a healthy distance and is never personally threatened. What Dostoevsky has done is to place the reader inside Gogol's character, just as M. C. Escher does to those ducks and rabbits, by seeming to "lose the boundary." Not only are the conventions and characteristics of both media (in Escher's case, that of two dimensional space) used to create the illusion, but the spectator is drawn into the work by the need to validate his perceptions. In the process of active participation he gets more disoriented, seeing things simultaneously from different points of view, and even appearing to confirm what he knows to be impossible.

In summary, I have been utilizing a psychoanalytic perspective—specifically, my experience with the existential problems of borderline and narcissistic patients, and the concepts of primitive projective mechanisms and fantasies—to look at some of the difficulties inherent in reading an early Dostoevsky novella, *The Double*, a work which was regarded as a failure but which is pivotal for all of Dostoevsky's subsequent development. Dostoevsky's stylistic innovations are intimately related to his "psychology." I have attempted to show how the story is an extended experiment with spatial imagery and movement, used to give literary representation to shifting mental processes and states of mind, and how this occurs on various levels of the narrative structure.

I have not meant to suggest that the complex subject of identity can be understood only in terms of these projective mechanisms, or that such states of mind as those described are peculiarly abnormal. To some extent we all struggle against deep urges to yield up our identities, to erase separations

---

driven his car at an excessive speed, lost control and driven into a tree. Just before impact he remembers seeing the tree headed straight at him. His point is well-taken. At such speed it becomes problematic which of the two is the aggressor (although in terms of the consequences it may not matter). Golyadkin comments: "They say that the bird flies of its own accord to the fowler. Quite true, I am prepared to agree: but which is the fowler here and which is the bird?" (p. 148).

and differences, and to get others to think and feel and act for us; sometimes, like Golyadkin, we try to clothe ourselves in an omnipotent other self, a self we could have been or secretly believe we someday still will be, a self who is free of the painful awareness of just those limitations which define our boundaries and make us who we are.

UCLA School of Medicine

AWAKENINGS TO NIGHTMARES

Peter Hodgson

Dr. Rosenthal has captured your imagination with the idea that *The Double* is a disturbing work because it raises the question of personal identity. His description of projective identification provided us with a primer of terms and a scenario for the identity crisis he was analyzing. In the interests of symmetry, let me adhere to the same format. Starting with the idea that *The Double* challenged several literary identities when it first appeared, I'd like to suggest a couple of terms of my own and the scenario for an analysis of another kind. Mine is an analysis of historical and theoretical matters. It is designed to demonstrate that Dr. Rosenthal's insights into the workings of the human psyche can be applied to the workings of a literary sensibility.

Dostoevsky called *The Double* a poem; and it certainly is not a novel or a short story. I think he called it a poem to draw attention to the fact that it was a special kind of storytelling exercise instead of an ordinary fictional narrative. Now the story does not seem to have impressed the general public in 1846 as anything out of the ordinary; to most it appeared to be yet another imitation of Gogol. But it made a marked impression on certain readers. It was a peculiar disappointment, even a threat, to the progressive critic, Vissarion Belinsky, and the circle of liberal Westernizers which had grouped around him by the middle of the 1840's. They were the ones who had seen to publishing Dostoevsky's first work, *Poor Folk* just a month earlier in one of their almanacs. *Poor Folk* had been the talk of the Petersburg literary world for nearly a year by that time. And had *The Double* delighted Belinsky the way *Poor Folk* did, it would have secured Dostoevsky's place as the foremost progressive writer of his day. But because it so disturbed the Europhiles, it sufficed to cast Dostoevsky into a kind of purgatory from which he was not to emerge before his arrest and exile at the end of the decade. This rejection, coming immediately on the heels of such an enthusiastic reception, was a defensive response to *The Double*, defensive because Dostoevsky's story was felt to have challenged the identity of a new progressive school of fictional writing, the Russian Natural School, which had taken shape only a few years before.

The Double did not in fact call into question the stylistics or subject matter of the new school, the way a literary parody would. On the contrary, it was an assault which seemed to have come from within the new school itself. Before the appearance of *The Double*, Dostoevsky was for Belinsky the very hope and future of progressive Russian fiction writing, Gogol's heir apparent. First, he was obviously a man of extraordinary originality and creative power. But, more important, he appeared to be addressing, in a compassionate manner, just the kind of social problems which were supposed to be motivating the Natural School. Dostoevsky's *Double*, on the other hand, however Gogolian it seemed, did nothing to promote Belinsky's idea of humanitarian, or "philanthropic" naturalism. On the contrary, it attacked its basic premise.

This premise is an aesthetic imperative as old as Aristotle, namely mimesis, the idea that art should represent or imitate reality. Belinsky had vulgarized the idea by reducing it to a simple expedient. He declared that literature should be a mirror of reality so that he could arrogate to the critic the right to determine just what kind of reality constituted the appropriate content for fiction. It was his intention to send young Russian writers out into the city, like cub reporters, to "cover" the urban scene. But for some reason Dostoevsky's Golyadkin who, like Gogol's Poprishchin, is driven mad by his dehumanizing environment, was not what Belinsky had in mind. He called the story "fantasy," and said that sort of thing belonged in a madhouse, not in literature. So it appears that Dostoevsky had put some kind of spin on the ball. *His* clerk and *his* urban scenes had called into question Belinsky's identity, his status as the arbiter of content in Russian fiction. But was this challenge to Belinsky's authority enough to challenge the legitimacy of the Natural School? On the face of it, no!

The truth is, the scope of Dostoevsky's challenge was broader and deeper than it appeared. The first thing to consider is that both Belinsky and the Russian naturalists were taking their cue from a new realistic current in West European writing. Its prototype was the French *physiologie* or physiological sketch. These short tableaux were spawned by the newspapers and journals which had recently come to dominate the world of letters. They were pseudo-scientific slices of urban life which pretended to dispense with literary technique—plot, character, development, stylistic ornament, in order to perform a taxonomical operation on the urban landscape. They sorted out its fauna into genera and species and arranged these according to station and privilege along the vertical index of the five-story Parisian apartment house. The fancy folk were on the *bel étage*, tradespeople below, and the rest of the citizenry in descending order of importance from third floor on up to the garret. It was the natural scientist Geoffrey St. Hilaire who inspired Balzac's efforts in this new form.

Now when we consider how faithfully the Russian natural school imitated the French physiology, often producing urban landscapes which looked a good deal more like Paris than St. Petersburg, we stumble on a curious terminological double which forms the basis of my theoretical analysis. Under Belinsky's direction, Russian naturalists had set out to *imitate* contemporary Russian reality, but what they were doing was *imitating* literary models from another language and from a vastly more sophisticated urban context. Imitation, then, both in the form of an aesthetic imperative generally called mimesis, and as a technical strategy sometimes called plagiarism, was the procedural basis of the natural school. The disturbing threat implicit in *The Double* derives from the fact that what the bold young Dostoevsky was doing was not imitation in either sense of the word. Instead, Dostoevsky was practicing an irreverent form of literary enactment or burlesque. He was furthering a tradition established by Gogol in the early 1830's and developed by an unacknowledged current of reluctant naturalism in the forties. This disruptive literary strategy of Dostoevsky's was first discovered by Russian Formalist critics in the 1920's. They called it Stylization. Stylization is, like parody, an agent of change in literary history. It challenges traditional systems which have gone stale, or for some other reason have proven inadequate to the cultural circumstances in which they are operating. On the one hand, Stylization calls attention to the various component parts of the system by exposing them, or laying bare their conventionality. It shows the reader that they are just the stuff of make-believe, and not *real*. At the same time, a Stylization forces the reader to recombine the parts of the dismantled system into another more viable form.

"Imitation" and "Stylization," then, are your terminological points of reference. The scenario of usurped identities I propose to you consists in Dostoevsky dismantling a literary tradition, namely the philanthropic naturalism of the Russian Natural School. He found this tradition both stale, because it was not really any different from Romanticism in its basic assumptions about life and art, and inadequate to the Russian experience, because it was foreign in origin and only partly digested by its Russian imitators. At the same time, however, Dostoevsky is engaging his reader in the task of rearranging the exposed parts of this system: the city, the clerk, the boss, the servant, ambition, insanity. By the ritual enactment of deconstruction and reconstruction, reader and author are establishing the aesthetic principle for a new literary system. Dostoevsky and all the reluctant naturalists used a metaphor to herald their new anti-mimetic principle. It was the pun. Consider that the pun reveals words to have two meanings (literal and figurative) and therefore not to be stable, dependable labels or reflections of things in the real world.

And, by the same token, the pun suggests that readers, like clerks, are doubles. They have a literal or mirror identity which is inappropriate to interaction with a work of art, and a figurative identity which is the proper vehicle for transposing them into the world of a story.

Here we can make a connection between Dr. Rosenthal's world of human anxiety, and the detached world of literary theory by considering how, to put it in Golyadkin's terms, the pun challenges the boundaries between "inward" and "outward." Childish puns, and the ones which make you groan, play on the similarity in sound or even spelling between two different words.

> As a rule, I hate opera, but Boris is good enough for me.

But the literary pun, called syllepsis or zeugma, is a little bit more complicated. It juxtaposes the literal and figurative meanings of one and the same word.

> Who was that lady I saw you with last night?
> That was no lady, that was my wife.

The example usually adduced in literary encyclopedias is from Pope: "She stained her honor and her new brocade." The pun draws attention to the relationship between life and art by insisting that there is a boundary between them. Applied as a structural principle in a story like *The Double*, the pun shows that fiction cannot be a mirror of reality, because the real world cannot be transposed directly into a narrative text. A wretched matchgirl, shivering on the street, cannot be willed onto the page by a critic, or a writer, however compassionate he is. She must be mediated through a body of stylistic techniques. These techniques are deployed in order to realize or execute a particular strategy. The fact that matchgirls or petty clerks are pitiable, even deplorable social phenomena may or may not be an important consideration for the literary strategy operating in a given narrative. Dostoevsky invites his reader to respect the boundary between non-fictive life and fiction, to come to terms with the literary matchgirl, within the confines of her literary existence, and according to the rules of this existence.

If we understand the narrative text to be an arrangement of words, each subject to a literal and a figurative interpretation, then we can imagine the text as a whole to have the same potential. The reader is inclined to ignore this when he is confronted with a cookbook, instruction sheet, or scientific treatise. He is expected to interpret these literally, projecting their meaning back onto the real world where the physics of 3-D space, gravity, and time hold more or less fast. But a story is different. If we project the characters, settings, and incidents of a work of fiction back onto the real world we violate their figurative identity. Figurative interpretation does not dislodge the fictional entities from the text. Instead it invites the reader to project himself into the world of the text.

That seems to be what a child listening to a fairy tale does. And the native Russian narrative tradition in which Gogol and Dostoevsky worked, in many ways a naivist tradition, wanted to restore the ambience of live oral narration to literary fiction. This is why Dostoevsky saw Belinsky and his imported physiology as a perversion of the relationship which should obtain between reader and narrator. Belinsky was breaking down the boundary between life and literature, forcing the reader to project the fiction onto reality. This was the converse of his premise that the world projected itself directly onto the mirror of the page. You see how he ignored the problem of narration altogether, to say nothing of the verbal medium, the stylistics of the narration. Dostoevsky wants to show us that the real world is removed from fiction by a complex transformation process and of only secondary importance when we are heeding the telling of a story. He draws our attention to this narrational process itself, where the reader and the author interact to recreate the fiction. Dostoevsky, like other creative prose writers before him and since, one thinks of Rabelais, Cervantes, Sterne, Lewis Carroll, insisted on the integrity of his story-telling medium. He did this by forcing the reader to come to terms with that medium by assuming a role which was complementary to his own. This active, participatory role of the reader, his figurative identity in the figurative construct of the narration, can be called auditor. And Dostoevsky's first job in *The Double* is to get the auditor to meet and join with the narrator (which is, of course, Dostoevsky's figurative identity).

It is the narrator who invites us into the story of *The Double* by telling us, in a conventional literary way, that Golyadkin, a conventional clerk, woke up one morning in a room with certain appurtenances, also conventional, and so forth. . . . The narrator is mediating between us and Golyadkin. However, Dostoevsky has contrived a narrator who will abandon us as soon as we abandon our role as auditor. And, furthermore, Dostoevsky has contrived a narrative which will force us to do just this, because it involves us with a character whose identity is as unstable as that of a pun. Dostoevsky knows that we will not just accept the fact that there is more than one Golyadkin. He knows that unlike children, we will try to hold the story accountable to the rules of the real world. We look of course to the narrator for help in this endeavor, putting a literal interpretation on him. But when we do, we find that he is not there. In fact, he has been preempted by his own character, much the same way Golyadkin, Sr. was preempted by Golyadkin, Jr. (his double). The narrator is, after all, literally just a construct of words, and what has happened is that he has been assimilated into the stylistic identity of his character (who is also literally just a construct of words, although on a different level of the narration).

The way this works is that Dostoevsky violates the boundaries between these two levels of the text. At the beginning of the story, the narrator talked a certain way, and "our hero," as he called Golyadkin, was quoted as having talked another way. Then, little by little, Dostoevsky allowed Golyadkin's diction and speech mannerisms to penetrate the narrative in the form of momentary insights into Golyadkin's state of mind or point of view. This is, in itself, a perfectly conventional literary device, an extension of the technique whereby indirect discourse replaces direct discourse or quotation. This is the device the French call *style indirect libre* (indirect free discourse). But Dostoevsky exposed this device by realizing it. He let Golyadkin gradually take over the level of discourse occupied by the narrator, and usurp his identity. Finally, the narrator could not talk in his own voice, even when it was clear that he should be doing so. What this means for the poor reader is that when we need the narrator to establish the identity of Golyadkin, he *is* Golyadkin.

Here we are, rational adults, trying to come to terms with a story where neither the character nor the narrator has a stable identity. They both seem to have disappeared into the same vortex. Remember, Dostoevsky has designed this complicated subterfuge in order to confront the literal reader with his own figurative role as auditor in the enactment of the story. He is showing us that we have obstructed our active participation as auditors by interfering in our capacity as literal-minded readers. What has the interfering reader been doing? Well, Dostoevsky has seen to it that we have had a very busy time indeed. It turns out that we have been playing a number of games, rather like hide and seek games. The point of these games is to make sense out of the facts of the story, to answer the question, "Is Golyadkin, Jr. an out and out hallucination, or is there some basis in the reality around him for Golyadkin's paranoia and curious doubling?" The procedure of the games is to impose literal interpretations on various components of the narrative, which means trying to move literal and figurative worlds into congruence. The result of the games is that we find these worlds to be incommensurate.

Let's look at three of the games we are forced to play. We will notice that the games themselves, like the pun, are metaphors for lessons which Dostoevsky wants us to acknowledge as we act them out. The first is the game of Nightmares and Daymares. If Golyadkin is asleep and dreaming then we are off the hook, we tell ourselves, because of course anything can happen in a dream. We accept dreams the way we should be accepting stories. But we cannot determine whether or not Golyadkin is really asleep. He wakes up two or three times as the story gets under way, and we don't know which of these are false starts. Any one of the subsequent awakenings far into the plot could be the only real awakening. Or, if none were, and Golyadkin never did wake up, then how did we get into his dream? Who dreamed the narrator? Could we have done so? Even in the unlikely event we could work all this out, the solution would not be able to restore, retroactively, all the figurative identities we have literalized in the course of the game.

The next game is the game of the mirrors. Funny, Belinsky didn't catch this one. Golyadkin wakes up and looks in a mirror in order to ascertain that he is really there. Subsequently, however, he looks into mirrors at several points in the story where he is having trouble with his double, most prominently in the pastry shop where there is a large mirror behind the counter on which are displayed the infamous cakes. This is a game which tempts us to explain the double as a hallucination set into motion by Golyadkin's seeing himself in the mirror. But when we try to get the whole story to conform to this literal interpretation, our supposition breaks down. Could the reflection have eaten the cakes? What about all the times when there is a doubling, but no mirror? If art cannot mirror reality, how can it mirror art?

The third game is a game of letters (the kind you mail). Here, we are trying to find out if there is some sort of conspiracy afoot. Letters are texts, reality encoded onto the page, and surely we can interpret them literally. But what if the encoded reality is, like the mirror image, a figurative entity in the first place? And besides, these letters are clearly not to be taken at face value. Like the narrator, they are being assimilated into the stylistic No-Man's-Land of Golyadkin, so that by the end of the story they all sound as if he wrote them. We cannot be any more sure of even their real existence than we can of Golyadkin's. It's like the girl on the old Morton Salt Box.

Observe that the harder we try to make literal sense out of the facts which bear on Golyadkin's identity, the more forcefully the futility of what we are doing is brought home to us . The more remote we get from Golyadkin's figurative identity and our own, the more we find ourselves trying to hold accountable to reality other figurative components of the narrative which sooner or later our rational mind (prompted by Dostoevsky) is going to insist are just part of a story. The games Dostoevsky has set up for us are no-win games, and our losing them is the point of the exercise.

Just when everything seems hopeless, Dostoevsky plays the cruelest trick of all on his beleaguered reader. He offers us recourse to an objective observer. It brings to mind Lucy holding that football for Charlie Brown every fall. But who could be more reliable than kindly old Anton Antonovich, the fellow who supervises the clerks in Golyadkin's office? Unlike Petrushka, the servant, to whom we first turned for some sort of verification, Anton Antonovich has no stake in the intrigues, real or imagined, which whirl around Golyadkin. Nor is he like the powerful bureaucrats whose eminence renders them inaccessible to Golyadkin, and therefore to us. We hold our breath as Golyadkin tries to bring himself to ask Anton Antonovich the all important question: Is he or isn't he? And by some miracle the inarticulate booby does manage to get the point across. And Anton Antonovich is going to respond. But what kind of response do we get?

> "Ah, yes! Striking resemblance; same last name. . . . I meant to ask you, perhaps from your home town. . . . Did I tell you about my aunt on my mother's side. . . . "

So there you have it: the final humiliation. We were maneuvered into staking everything on the hope that Anton Antonovich would act like an entity in the real world. Our last hope is dashed, and we are thrown back onto the figurative world of the story.

Had we been monitoring our desperate struggle we could realize that there is nothing left but us and the fact of the text. But as the story draws to a close, Dostoevsky—clearly a man with no human feelings—deprives us of the very narration itself. Remember the part of the story where Golyadkin hides behind the stove, down in the vestibule of his office building, and sends the doorman up to reconnoitre for him? The narrative informs us that Golyadkin himself suddenly runs up the stairs and gets embroiled in a whole set of adventures. Then, just as suddenly, he finds himself back downstairs behind the stove. Neither he nor we know how he got back there. The only reasonable conclusion one can come to is that he never really left his hiding place. But doesn't this eradicate the portion of the narrative we have just been following? And what about the scene later when Golyadkin "comes to" and finds himself staring at an unfinished plate of food in a cafe. Is it not the same meal he began near the beginning of the story? This is like the successive awakenings, but if we acknowledge the possibility that we have been returned to the beginning of the story because Golyadkin never did really split in two, we are in an even stranger position than we were when we found ourselves locked outside his dream. For if there is no doubling, there is no game, and what's more, there is no story, either. But then what have we been doing? No matter what we grasp at, character, narrator, setting, incident, plot—they have all dematerialized. The fabric of conventional responses whereby we, as auditors, incorporate ourselves into a fiction has been rent, exposed, vitiated by the inappropriate demands of our literal interpretations. We have forfeited our access to the text. We are all that is left.

Or are we? Hasn't our own identity been somehow called into question here? Is this not the crux of the daymare Dostoevsky has inflicted on us? Does *The Double* perhaps transcend the function of literary stylization?

☆   ☆   ☆

Let us consider the notion of Stylization in a slightly broader historical context. The term was invented, by Yuri Tynianov, to explain the relationship between Gogol and Dostoevsky. Not imitation or parody, the term was originally meant to convey the spirit of a quasi-adversarial relationship between a writer of an older, and one of a younger generation, like the one described by Harold Bloom in his *Anxiety of Influence.* I would like to suggest that Stylization was actually a strategy common to both Dostoevsky and Gogol. Gogol practiced it in his early Ukrainian tales and his Petersburg Tales, in *Dead Souls*, and most clearly in his late work, *The Overcoat.* An example of Dostoevsky applying Gogol's standard manner of Stylization was *Poor Folk*, and just as nobody in the 1840s discerned the Stylization in Gogol, whom they dubbed the father of the Natural School, so everybody was happy to accept *Poor Folk* as a naturalistic work. Had Dostoevsky left well enough alone, he would have been on safe ground. What Dostoevsky did instead was notice that in one of Gogol's stories, *The Nose*, the Stylization had been executed at such a white heat of creative intensity that the result was a fundamentally different kind of narrative, a sustained grotesque. This was not a supernatural "fantasy" which denied physical reality, nor merely an assault on a literary tradition, but an assault on the reader himself. It was not just a reexamination of the boundaries between life and art, but a breaking down of the boundaries between the reader and the text. Dostoevsky decided to try this himself. In his second work, *The Double*, he succeeded.

Now let's compare a Stylization and a grotesque. In *Poor Folk* as in *The Overcoat* a reader finds that now and then he is inclined to make a sentimentalized, literal interpretation of this or that component in the story, and he gets caught in the act. Some other component in the system will suddenly disorient him, exposing his false step and suggesting ultimately that it is unwise to base one's humanitarian view of the world on the reading of sentimental stories. "Am I so liberal, so socially aware, so solicitous of my fellow man as I think I am," asks the reader, "if all I am doing is shedding tears over fictional match girls? If Bykov is the father of Pokrovsky, Jr. and Varvara is a prostitute, if I don't see that Devushkin is absurd in the role of the White Knight, hadn't I better reestablish my sense of the boundaries between literature and life?" An unexceptional Stylization is, thus, a challenge to the epistemology of the complacent bourgeois. In a sustained grotesque like *The Nose* or *The Double*, on the other hand, the philosophical implications of the assault on the reader have been raised by one power. It is his ontology which is called into question, his identity. We are disoriented by an ordinary Stylization because we do not always make the appropriate figurative interpretation; our sentimentalized response imposes an attendant set of literal demands on the narrator or plot which these constructs will not tolerate. But we *must* play the literal games of a sustained grotesque. We cannot enter into the figurative play of the story. The pricniple of the pun, applied at every structural level of the narrative, blocks our access. At every point where we might make a figurative interpretation of some component in the narrative, the ambiguous identity of that component compels us to effect a literal projection of it onto the non-fictive world.

One final comparison: In the case of a contained Stylization, if we can relate to the fictional narrative on its own figurative terms, we can and should project ourselves into it. The secret is not to try to project the fiction onto life. But in the case of a sustained grotesque, every time we approach the narrative, we are compelled to project it onto life, and this leads to an irreversible confounding of ourselves and the fiction. We are drawn into a vortex of confused identities, ours and the fictive ones. And when the narrative dematerializes we cannot extract ourselves. We cannot make our way back. The system of violated literary conventions, like a boat abused on the outward voyage, will not get us back to home port. The temporary loss of identity we experience in *The Double* becomes, in the hands of Dostoevsky the mature novelist, a formidable tool and constitutes his real capitalization on the legacy of Gogol.

University of California, Los Angeles

THE NIGHTMARISH QUEST
OF JERZY KOSINSKI

Geoffrey Green

It is well known that Freud in his 1908 essay, "Creative Writers and Day-dreaming," relates the creative writer to the person who concocts dreams during the day: the artistic constructions of the writer parallel the dreams that are dreamed while awake. Like a child at play, the creative writer formulates his own reality or else reorders the aspects of his world so that the resultant vision appeals to him. Both the fantasies evoked through language as fiction and the fantasies perceived in our waking thoughts have, as their basis, the unfulfilled wishes, conscious and unconscious, which lurk within us; the expression of these fantasies, through art or through daydreams, creates satisfying versions of our inner wishes. So it is that a writer's fiction may exist as the projection into language of the unfulfilled wishes which precipitate daydreams: characters may, to a certain extent, be envisioned as alternative conceptions of the author and his life circumstances.

Jerzy Kosinski's fiction has consistently explored the realm in which literature exists as the reflection of our desire for (and propensity toward) order in our lives. Memory recalled is thus reordered and fashioned anew. The human imagination strives to transcend its own situation through art just as that art is rooted in the reality which necessitates imaginative functioning. Accordingly, Kosinski proposes that his novel, *The Painted Bird* (1965), "could be the author's vision of himself as a child; a *vision*, not an examination, or a revisitation of childhood."[1]

Central to this notion is the often elusive demarcation between the authorial self and his created vision; what is created as an artistic dream may loom threateningly when the barriers which separate it from functional reality are erased or confused. In Kosinski's novel, *Cockpit* (1975), the protagonist Tarden recalls his university days in Eastern Europe:

---

[1] Jerzy Kosinski, "Interview," in *The New Fiction: Interviews with Innovative American Writers*, ed., J. D. Bellamy (Chicago: University of Illinois Press, 1974), p. 159.

I began to experiment with my memory. I found that it automatically intensified while I slept. If I misplaced something, such as a set of keys, I took a nap. It was as if I were dreaming a film about losing the keys that was being run backwards in slow motion. By the time I woke up I recalled where I left them. During exam periods, when my fellow students were staying up all night to study, I slept, to their disgust, twice as much as usual. In my sleep I reviewed all the texts which I had originally only skimmed, and by exam time had total recall of the necessary material.[2]

Soon after writing *Cockpit*, Kosinski discussed his own powers of memory and dreams:

My dreams are incorporated into my life. My dream-life has always been a direct extension or reflection of my daily problems, predicaments, and interests. When I want to make certain that I memorized something well, I go to sleep. While asleep, I review the whole text, making certain I remember it. If not, then, still in sleep, I "mark" the passages I couldn't remember and check them again when I awake. My dreams are exact: they are replicas of daily situations with one difference—I am asleep."[3]

The distinction between Tarden's achievements and Kosinski's own aspirations is hazy and suggestive.

Although Kosinski the author and Tarden the character are endowed with similar traits, Kosinski's emphasis is that Tarden's qualities—while obviously built upon Kosinski's own—are not Kosinski's qualities since they have been reformed within a fictional context. For Kosinski, recollection is a matter of creating anew; to remember one's past is to will it into existence and gaze upon it as an other. But the individual self who imagines, dreams, and creates operates within the encompassing structure of society and culture. Thus, Kosinski's fictions dwell upon the self and its relationship to the communal forces of society: "Language connects us not only with our primary reality, with the reality of the self, with the reality of the emotion; it also connects us with a certain social reality outside us."[4] To dream and create (through language) art which emanates from life and the fantasies suggested by life is to synthesize a new vision of life through the process of selectively ordering and organizing imaginary versions of once actual events; according to

[2] Kosinski, *Cockpit* (Boston: Houghton Mifflin, 1975), p. 91.
[3] Geoffrey Movius, "A Conversation with Jerzy Kosinski," *New Boston Review*, 1, No. 3 (Winter 1975), p. 6.
[4] *The New Fiction*, p. 159.

Kosinski, "a 'lower-class' experience is different from the 'upper-class' not only in terms of the content of the actual experience but in terms of its organization, its ordering by language at the time when it had occurred."[5]

Dreams or fictions develop from the unfulfilled wishes of the self; Kosinski's work incorporates these projected dreams into what he terms a vision of his life; his principal mode of organizing and ordering this fictional vision of his life is through his conception of the picaresque. I will discuss Kosinski's version of the picaro and explore his utilization of the picaresque form in a number of his fictions. But since Kosinski's life and his fictional vision of his life are so closely related, and since he holds that language connects not only with our self but with our social reality, I will consider Kosinski's work in terms of the circumstances of his life. I will attempt to establish that Kosinski's use of the picaresque as an organizational structure changes throughout his novels and that this alteration of form corresponds to a fundamental change in Kosinski's life circumstances and social perspective. His ability to order and organize what he calls 'upper-class' and 'lower-class' experiences evolves along with his personal progression up the ladder of social and economic privilege. If we avail ourselves of Claudio Guillén's notion that the picaro is a "half-outsider"[6] involved in an "economic and social predicament of the most immediate and pressing nature,"[7] it may well be that Kosinski the author began as a half-outsider whose dreams projected into novels constituted modern picaresque structures; but as he increasingly has adopted an insider's role and stance, the nature of the dreams which he projects into his novels has resulted in an inherent incongruity between his mode of organization and the fictional material drawn from life which he wishes to bring to order.

Kosinski described his version of the picaro as "the type or the character who is constantly in a stage of becoming. Picaros dot—rather highlight—literary history. Odysseus, Don Quixote, Tom Jones, Gil Blas, Moll Flanders, Felix Krull—the freelancers, the freebooters who played out their whims and caprices and lived their lives rather than considering their condition. . . . The picaro is the last champion of selfhood."[8] It is clear that Kosinski's predominant enthusiasm for the genre stems from his identification of the picaro as "the last champion of selfhood"—in other words, as a figure consistent with his own fictional preoccupation. But the characteristics of the picaro are not

---

[5] *The New Fiction*, p. 159.

[6] Claudio Guillén, *Literature as System: Essays Toward the Theory of Literary History* (Princeton, N.J.: Princeton University Press, 1971), p. 80.

[7] Guillén, p. 77.

[8] Movius, p. 4.

quite so unconfined as Kosinski claims, nor would it be reasonable to accept all of Kosinski's examples as valid picaros.

The picaresque form appeared in the middle of the sixteenth century, embodying elements of the emerging Catholic-Protestant rivalry and representing an alternative to the romance pastorals and chivalrous novellas. The narrative centered upon the picaro, or rogue, a scoundrel who existed on the fringe of society, frequently engaging in illicit deeds, but meaning no one any harm; at first a trusting innocent, the picaro proceeds, episode by episode, through the lower regions of society, aspiring to nothing but basic subsistence. Slowly he is initiated into the depravities of humanity, which he sees from "the worm's eye view." By wandering, the picaro is able to reflect upon and evaluate the elements of society. But what distinguished the picaresque genre from bawdy comedy was the fact that the authenticity and verisimilitude, the humor, the honesty and cynicism existed within a satiric context: the rogue is "at odds" with a corrupt humanity; when he ultimately is reconciled with the masses, the irony is wielded against the society itself. The picaresque form, then, included the rogue as autobiographical narrator (or anti-hero) in a situation that minimized standard plot in favor of random episodic narrative. The narrator could be unreliable while the landscape remained realistic. In the picaresque, Kosinski was presented with a vehicle that would enable him to dispense with certain novelistic elements (such as sympathetic protagonists and formal plot progression) while maintaining a relevant and pointed view towards society.

Kosinski's first novel, *The Painted Bird*, is both his most fully realized work of fiction and the one with the most extensive use of the picaresque form. It relates the personal narrative of a six-year old boy who was forced to wander from village to village throughout Eastern Europe during the second World War. Kosinski's utilization of an innocent narrator who gradually becomes acquainted with the brutality of the world, the episodic progression of the narrative from incident to incident, the boy's precarious search for food, shelter, and warmth (and his punishment for seeking even that much), the violence, the revenge, the simple prose—all of this is firmly grounded in the picaresque tradition. But naturally, Kosinski is using the form for his own artistic purposes; he emphasizes the qualities and elements that best suit his particular vision—those dreams drawn from life and projected into fiction. So we find practically none of the picaresque humor or sarcasm; instead, we are exposed to an almost relentless focus upon the grotesque and brutal aspects of the picaro's quest. By working with a child narrator, Kosinski allows events to assume a dominant position, thus diminishing character and emphasizing the ironic vision. And by eliminating an elaborately structured plot, Kosinski is able to enter the realm of repetitive image, motif, and patterned landscape. The combination of the primal world of the child and the unfettered, plotless narrative progression creates a nightmarish vision of a child's world, where objects and events can be suddenly and horrifically vitalized, without reason, purpose, or meaning. The episodes, though random, take on a significance when viewed in sequence, so that although Kosinski is sure to remain within the limits of realistic prose and description, he is also able to depict a distorted and bloated landscape, a landscape where unconscious fantasies are liberated and horror escapes repression. The intent, of course, is to strive for an exaggeration so bizarre that the danger and terror of the actual are undermined. The reader is exposed to scenes of extremely disturbing violence and brutality as the boy is mercilessly and sadistically tortured or deprived, or else, witnesses the sufferings of other characters. The violence is not only graphic and physical; it functions symbolically as well, on a psychosexual level. For instance, after the boy is forced to act as the "lover" of Ewka, a peasant girl, he is ordered by her father, Makar, to kill and skin a large rabbit. In the midst of being skinned, the rabbit, not dead but only stunned, suddenly comes to life, and in a compulsively prolonged scene, hysterically bleats and runs around the yard until it is killed by Makar's ax. The farmer nearly beats the boy to death in punishment and afterward, the boy witnesses the daughter Ewka coupling with a goat. His disgust and revulsion combine the unnatural qualities of the act with his vision of himself as a rejected lover; the rabbit's tormented squirmings are associated on some level with the premature and distorted sexuality of the boy. Throughout the book, the Nazi dimension is clearly minimized, yet we witness the germination of violence and perversity in the small boy, his victim's desire for lurid revenge, his mechanisms of identification with his tormentors that manipulate his own personal dynamics of barbarism.

The effect is consistent with the moralistic criticism of the society that exists with the picaresque. We sympathize with the boy's innocence and his poignant quest to discover his parents; this quest or brutal initiation provides the narrative impetus for our journey through scores of brutal scenes, each more horrifying than the one before; as we continue it is with the awareness that our numbing process (and perhaps, our innate cruelty) permits us to accept violence. From our "worm's eye view," we see a humanity stripped of its trivial organizations, devoted to a rampant, sadistic brutality. Like the picaro, the small boy is ultimately reintegrated into the society, but though we are pleased that he will be cared for, we no longer view this humanity as decent and desirable. At the end of *The Painted Bird*, the boy (long mute as a result of a traumatic shock) finds that suddenly he can speak; but as he gropes for words, his "eyeballs swelled for a moment, as though trying to pop out onto the floor,"[9] reminding us of an earlier bloody revenge scene: a miller scoops out the eyes of his plowboy

[9] Kosinski, *The Painted Bird* (Boston, 1965; rpt. New York: Pocket Books, 1970), p. 213.

to avenge the flirtation between the plowboy and his wife. Our sense of affirmative resolution is tempered by our ironic knowledge of cruelty and evil.

Steps (1968) in some ways could be viewed as the continuing adventures of the small boy from *The Painted Bird*, now an adult. The rural Eastern European terrain remains, although we now find cities as well. The first person narrator recalls incidents that could have been included in the earlier work. The notion of revenge, particularly, remains powerfully situated in the picaresque:

> It became clear to me that the peasants' love for their children was just as uncontrollable as an outbreak of fever among the cattle. Often I saw a mother touching her child's soft hair, a father's hands flinging the child into the air and catching it safely again. . . .
>
> Then one day I saw a sheep writhing convulsively in a slow death, its desperate bleating bringing terror to the entire flock. The peasants claimed that the animal must have swallowed a fishhook or a shard of glass in its feed.
>
> Months passed. One morning a cow from the herd in my charge strayed onto a neighbor's property, damaging the crops. This was reported to my master. Upon my return from the fields, the farmer was waiting for me. He pushed me into the barn and whipped me until the blood oozed from my legs. Bellowing with rage he finally hurled the leather thong in my face.
>
> I began to collect discarded fishhooks and bury them behind the barn. After the farmer and his wife left for church I slipped them into my hiding place and kneaded a couple of fishhooks and crushed glass into balls of fresh bread which I had torn out of the day's newly baked loaves. . . .
>
> One day the little girl [the farmer's youngest child] hugged me. I dampened a ball of bread with my saliva and asked her to swallow it in one piece. When she hesitated, I took a piece of apple, put it into the back of my mouth, and pushing it with my forefinger, instantly swallowed it. The girl imitated me, swallowing the balls, one after another. I looked away from her face, forcing myself to think only of the burning of her father's whip.
>
> From then on I gazed boldly into my persecutor's eyes, provoking their assault and maltreatment. I felt no pain. For each lash I received my tormentors were condemned to pain a hundred times greater than mine. Now I was no longer their victim; I had become their judge and executioner.[10]

Let us compare this scene with a revenge sequence from *The Life of Lazarillo*

---

[10] Kosinski, *Steps* (New York, 1968; rpt. New York: Bantam, 1969), pp. 35-36.

de Tormes (1554), an early picaresque novel. Lazarillo's master, a blind beggar, hoards the common wine jug. The picaro at first steals a few sips, then secretly uses a straw; both tricks are discovered by his master:

> . . . Since the straw trick no longer worked, I decided to make a little bunghole in the bottom of the jug, and delicately cover it with a thin wafer of wax. When it came time to eat, pretending I was cold, I would crawl between his legs to warm myself by the tiny fire we built; and when the heat of it had melted the small amount of wax, a trickle would begin to run into my mouth, which I put in such a position that never a drop was lost. When the old fellow went to drink, he found nothing there. . . .
>
> By turning and feeling the jug, he finally found the opening and caught on to the trick; but he did not let on, as though he had not discovered it.
>
> The next day, I was letting the jug leak into my mouth as usual without thought of the harm in wait for me, nor that the wicked man knew anything, and was seated in my usual position, receiving those sweet drippings with my face skyward and my eyes half-shut the better to savor the delightful nectar. The blind man felt that the moment had come to take his revenge on me, and raising that sweet and bitter jug with both his hands, he brought it down upon my mouth with all his strength so that . . . it truly seemed that the heavens and all they held had fallen. . . .
>
> The affectionate little tap left me dazed and senseless, and the blow with the jug was so great that pieces of it cut through my face in many places, and knocked out my front teeth, without which I have remained to this very day. From that moment I took a dislike to the cruel blind man. . . . He washed with wine the cuts that he had inflicted with the jug, and said smiling:
>
> "What do you think of this, Lázaro? The very thing that brought on your illness cures you and restores your health," and other quips not at all to my liking.
>
> When I was half recovered from my nasty punishment and bruises, thinking to myself that the cruel blind man would get rid of me for good, I decided to get rid of him; but I bided my time so I could do it with greater safety and effect.

[The two are attempting to return to the inn during a rain storm and the picaro tells the beggar they must cross a brook. The blind man asks him to lead to the narrowest part so that he can hop across. Lazarillo leads him instead to "a pillar or post of stone, which stood in the square."]

> . . . I brought him squarely in front of the pillar, gave a jump and got

> behind the post; and like a person awaiting the rush of a bull, I said
> to him:
> "Come on! Give a big jump so you will land on this side of the
> water."
> The words were not out of my mouth when the poor old fellow
> charged like a goat, taking a step back to get a running start and leap
> farther. He jumped with all his strength, landing headfirst against the
> pillar, which echoed as though it had been hit with a big squash;
> then he fell backward, half dead and with his head split open.[11]

The comparison emphasizes several points. We can readily notice the similar
sparse prose styles of each passage, the cautious, compulsive attention to
detail, the attempt at equating the revenge with the punishment. But we also
spot the comic irony of the picaresque piece and the grim determinism of the
Kosinski passage: beyond this, the picaresque revenge is reciprocal ("an eye
for an eye") in that the punishment is leveled against the master; in Kosinski,
the dream of vengeance is turned into a nightmare: the revenge has become
quite sophisticated in its execution, opting for the sadistic pleasures of a
premeditated, extended indirect suffering. But the picaro, after tricking his
master, flees the scene. We never actually discover whether the blind man has
died. This does not suit Kosinski's purpose: the anguished death of the child
is predicted by the careful attention to the death of the sheep; the narrator
not only wishes to exact revenge but to *exceed* the pain he received. To the
extent that the girl's pain (or future suffering) is documented more completely than the provocation, we lose our identification with the narrator;
this never occurs with Lazarillo and we remain sympathetic. But this change
in emphasis points to a difference between *Steps* and *The Painted Bird*: in
the earlier book, the small boy causes the death of the carpenter who had
planned on killing him by pushing the man into a pit filled with ravenous
rats; but this violence is primarily defensive. The sophisticated (and brutal)
indirect revenge of the small boy in *Steps* underscores the movement away
from the basic good-natured qualities of the picaro. The narrator of *Steps*
rather whimsically kills a man, causes a woman to be violated by a gang of
men, among other sadistic diversions. We can no longer remain aligned with
this narrator.

Beyond this, we can find evidence of Kosinski dispensing with other
picaresque standards. The incidents are episodically linked together, but we
have no quest or search to provide a context. The narrator is never more or
less innocent. We are only faced with a series of vignettes which could be

[11] Harriet de Onís, trans. *The Life of Lazarillo de Tormes* (New York: Barron's,
1959), pp. 9-18.

overheard in a bar, told by a stranger. Since we cannot identify with the narrator, his occasional moralistic concerns (with the rape and torture of a brain-damaged girl) are puzzling and strange; the effect is not to condemn the society as a mass, but rather to probe the inner recesses of the individual psyche, the thin line between reality and dream. The concerted violence of the earlier book frequently extended symbolically to sexual and psychic realms. In *Steps*, Kosinski moves aggressively into the regions of sexuality and political totalitarianism; but instead of using the violence and sexuality to bear upon the psychic flaws of the society (from the picaresque), he now uses the violence and psychic abnormalities to explore the common ground between sexual and political brutalities.

The narrator of *Steps* is considerably beyond searching for food, shelter, and clothing, and most of the time is financially stable. This, of course, is another movement away from the picaro; it is interesting to note that at certain moments, to provide a change in effect, Kosinski will deprive his narrator of the basic necessities. We can see that in *Steps*, Kosinski continues to utilize the picaresque (in a modern context) by focusing still more obsessively upon violence and revenge, by using a non-plot that is completely episodic (heightening the visionary landscape effect), and by exploring the realms of an unreliable and morally problematic autobiographical narrator. But he has begun to be more interested in the regimental, bureaucratic medium realms of society: no longer do we have the "worm's eye view." Kosinski explores the terrain of the distorted and monstrous nightmare landscape, the psychic injuries of a singular detached narrator as metaphor for a universal disturbed consciousness.

It is at this point that we need to consider the fact that Kosinski's fictions are not purely imaginative but represent the conversion into fiction of actual autobiographical experiences; the events of his life correspond closely to the events of his novels. Born in Poland in 1933, he was the son of a philologist father and a pianist mother. As a small boy, he was also separated from his parents and wandered alone from village to village in Eastern Europe during the war. But unlike the boy in *The Painted Bird* who lost his trauma-induced muteness after about three years, Kosinski remained mute for over six years. As a young man (like the narrator in *Steps*) he was a photographer, a university student, a member of the student militia—in short, active within the collective structures that are described in his novels. He graduated with advanced degrees in History and Political Science, and from 1955 to 1957, he served as Associate Professor at the Polish Academy of Sciences in Warsaw. In December of 1957, Kosinski arrived in the United States with no knowledge of the English language. He views the writing of *The Painted Bird* as the result of a "slow unfreezing of a mind long gripped by fear."[12] He devoted several years to learning the English language, supporting himself by working as a truck driver. It was only after he had written two works of nonfiction—on the "collective behavior" of the Soviet bloc peoples [*The Future is Ours, Comrade* (1960) and *No Third Path* (1962), both under the name, "Joseph Novak"]—that he began work on *The Painted Bird*. Many of the anecdotes included in the nonfiction books are also present—somewhat altered—in the fictions. He has frequently been confronted about the possibility of his novels being nonfiction. A characteristic answer was:

> Well, to say that *The Painted Bird*, for example, is nonfiction, or even autobiographical, may be convenient for classification, but it's not easily justified. What we remember lacks the hard edge of fact. To help us along we create little fictions, highly subtle and individual scenarios which clarify and shape our experience. The remembered event becomes a fiction, a structure made to accommodate certain feelings. This is obvious to me. If it weren't for these structures, art would be too personal for the artist to create, much less for the audience to grasp. Even film, the most literal of all the arts, is edited.[13]

This underscores our earlier recognition of Kosinski's belief that the ordering and organization of the memory function, combined with the conversion of psychic impulses into language, constitutes a valid creative process—relative to the context formed by the circumstances of the memory's reconstruction. What looms significantly is the role Kosinski's actual life experiences play in determining the form and mechanisms of his artistic expressions. We find that Kosinski moved away from the modern picaresque as an artistic method of organization when the material he was transforming into fiction changed from individual to collective, when the sexual and political began to emerge as perceptual equivalents to the violent. Although Kosinski the artist exploited the picaresque to fictionally dramatize his childhood, it could also be suggested that Kosinski's childhood wanderings embody the fictional picaresque genre.

After *The Painted Bird* and *Steps*, Kosinski began to deal in his books with American life. This corresponded to a change in his life which had occurred some years earlier. In 1962, he married the steel heiress Mary Hayward Weir, "a wealthy, white Anglo-Saxon Protestant who grounded me

---

[12]George Plimpton and Rocco Landesman, "Interview with Jerzy Kosinski," *The Paris Review*, No. 54 (1972), 190.

[13]Plimpton and Landesman, p. 189.

very definitely in purely American experience."[14] She died in 1968. By 1969, Jerzy Kosinski had lived for over a decade as an American, had won the National Book Award for *Steps*, and had fictionally depicted his life up until 1957. He has noted that: "English helped me sever myself from my childhood, from my adolescence. In English I don't make involuntary associations with my childhood."[15] Kosinski credits his writing in an adopted language as an aid in his ability to detach himself from his life by projecting his reassembled memories into fiction. No doubt the remarkable and compelling esthetic distance in *The Painted Bird* and *Steps* results, in part, from the attempt to reconceive materials from a different time, place, and certainly, language. But it is questionable as to whether Kosinski's marriage to Mary Hayward Weir provided him with a firm context for an American literary sensibility that would operate in accordance with a picaresque mode of order.

Being There (1970) is Kosinski's first book that is set in the United States. It also completely departs from the picaresque tradition, moving squarely into the realms of fable and allegory. Basically, he has constructed an ironic version of the American Dream. The novel outlines the life of a brain damaged orphan who, adopted by an old man, is brought up to tend garden and watch television. Upon the old man's death, the orphan, Chance, enters the world; his simplistic mutterings about television and gardens are viewed as astute, sophisticated metaphors of the modern predicament. He is befriended by a rich, powerful industrialist, whose young wife falls in love with him; at the novel's end, still empty-headed, he is being considered as a candidate for the Vice Presidency. The rhythmic, measured prose remains, but what is noticeably missing here is any reference to the violence of the earlier novels. Obviously, this novel is more purely fictional than the earlier ones. But in presenting an ironic version of the American Dream, Kosinski nonetheless defines it in a peculiar way, considering his stated affinity for the picaresque as an organizational structure for his fiction: what is bizarre for him is that the Dream is qualitatively non-discriminating; the process, the act of moving oneself from the bottom to the top of the American social and economic ladder is, for him, a reality. What would be viewed with suspicion by most American writers oriented toward the picaresque is the assertion that a man could, in contemporary society, fulfill the Horatio Alger dream and actually rise from "a newsboy to become President"; what disturbs Kosinski is that this newsboy might not be a man of talent or worth. Surely, this concept of America is not "grounded very definitely in [the] purely American experience" which remains in harmony with a picaresque "worm's eye view." Rather, it is rooted in the Weir family's American experience. But Kosinski,

---

[14] Plimpton and Landesman, p. 184.
[15] Plimpton and Landesman, pp. 193-94.

the small Jewish boy alone in hostile Eastern Europe, the individual in the
oppressive collective system, has, in acclimating himself to America, identified his dreams with the American wealth, industrialism, and ideals of an elite
upper stratum of society. In *Being There*, he studiously avoids all conspicuous opportunities to "re-make" the society; he avoids all descriptions of
television, radio, and the inner workings of the political system. What should
be evident is that Kosinski's conceptualization of his fiction—that it uses the
picaro as "the best champion of selfhood"—is at odds with his projected
dreams that are entwined with the wealthy industrialist affinities of his
American family.

Yet curiously, in *The Devil Tree* (1973), Kosinski moves again in the
direction of the picaresque, attempting to combine it with his individualized
vision of America. Earlier, he published an essay, "The Lone Wolf," devoted
to discussing the career of his relative through marriage, Ernest T. Weir; in it,
Kosinski praised the maverick qualities of the steel industrialist, which the
author considered exemplary. He concluded that "as long as this country is
founded on private enterprise, and regardless of our personal likes or dislikes
of that system, an American businessman remains a central figure in the
trinity of politician, businessman, and union leader."[16] Kosinski also discusses what he calls "the painful predicament of the American businessman":

> The American ethos credits him with the creation of the American
> Way of Life while denying him a direct share in this life as expressed
> by the political process. Unlike a politician's responsibility to an
> amorphous electorate the businessman's responsibility is concrete. If
> and when his business fails, he must hold himself primarily respon-
> sible.[17]

And according to Kosinski, Weir, who "in a lifetime of nearly eighty-two
years ... turned a rolling mill into a billion-dollar steel empire, founded
Wierton, a town bearing his name ... took on the most powerful adversaries—
the federal government, presidents, organized labor ... the steel industry
itself,"[18] and who, in 1953, to make his views known, "privately printed"
and then "distributed, at his own expense, over three hundred thousand
copies"[19] of a pamphlet he wrote—typified this "painful predicament" of
businessmen having only a "peripheral political role"; indeed, perhaps

---

[16] Kosinski, "The Lone Wolf," *The American Scholar*, 41, No. 4 (Autumn 1972),
p. 519.

[17] Kosinski, "The Lone Wolf," p. 518.

[18] Kosinski, "The Lone Wolf," p. 513.

[19] Kosinski, "The Lone Wolf," p. 517.

Kosinski equates Weir's dominant individuality and relentless motivation for success with the "champion of selfhood" attributes he emphasizes in the picaresque.

Out of this intense admiration for and identification with Ernest T. Weir emanate many of the materials cultivated in *The Devil Tree*. The millionaire business industrialist becomes a pivotal figure in the novel: he is the father of Jonathan Whalen, the protagonist. Whalen is the young heir to one of the largest fortunes in America; still, he is alienated: a former hippy, an ex-drug addict, he struggles through the pain of his love affairs and his encounter group to penetrate to his real essence. Once again, we find an episodic narrative, a "stringing together" of random scenes. Again we are faced with violence, though here it is not so much a physical violence but the institutional barbarism of the American society. Whalen, the protagonist, is in some sense an anti-picaro: he views the society from a "bird's eye view"; he is alienated in the upper fringes of American life; he struggles, not for necessities, but for spiritual truths, for essences. But unlike the picaro, though like the narrator of *Steps*, he is cruel, spoiled, sadistic, an actual murderer, as well as a lonely and sympathetic person. Whalen is the least likeable of all Kosinski's characters; indeed, Kosinski himself seems to have ambivalent feelings about him and feels the need to alternate between Whalen's first person account and a fairly standard third person narration, to no ostensible stylistic advantage: perhaps this shifting of narrative perspective exemplifies the conflict between Kosinski's preoccupation with "upper-class" subject materials and his inclination toward the picaresque form—with its intrinsic "lower-class" vantage point—to structure them. It is perplexing to envision how an American reader would have any sort of positive response to a protagonist who is a spoiled-wealthy-American-hipster-drug-addicted murderer. Certainly, the picaresque elements of *The Devil Tree* serve to alienate the reader from the narrator and therefore, hinder Kosinski's desired effect.

The language itself, however, reveals the change in Kosinski's sense of identity and the altered quality of the dreams he wishes to project into fictional manifestation. In an interview, he spoke of the "disadvantages" of writing in an adopted language: "The main one for me is that I am never certain whether my English prose is sufficiently clear. Also, I rarely allow myself to use English in a truly spontaneous way and therefore, I always have a sense of trembling—but so does a compass, after all."[20]

It is not difficult to conceive how the non-spontaneous English prose of *The Painted Bird* and *Steps* works to evoke a lean, rhythmic language that is reminiscent of Eastern Europe. In this instance, Kosinski's spare, decimated language serves to enhance the effect of a specific regional milieu:

[20]Plimpton and Landesman, p. 196.

> In the villages people laughed at Lekh. They said that Stupid Lud-
> mila had cast a spell over him and put fire in his loins, a fire that
> would drive him insane. Lekh protested, hurling the most evil curses
> at them and threatening to send birds against them that would peck
> out their eyes. Once he rushed at me and struck me in the face. He
> shouted that my presence scared his woman off because she was
> afraid of my Gypsy eyes. For the next two days he lay ill. When he
> arose he packed his knapsack, took along a loaf of bread, and went
> into the forest, ordering me to keep setting new snares and catching
> new birds.[21]

This versatile and evocative prose is consistent with the atmosphere and
derivation; its effectiveness depends upon the careful understatement, the
balanced use of image-centered and atmospheric nouns. Kosinski describes
the effect: "I wanted to make the language of my fiction as unobtrusive as
possible, almost transparent, so that the reader would be drawn right away
into each dramatic incident. I suppress in my prose any language which calls
attention to itself."[22] And yet, considering this statement of intent, how are
we to deal with derivative passages such as these from *The Devil Tree*?

> Look, man, I'm just being friendly, that's all. I was standing
> behind you in the line at the bank. I saw you writing something on
> that little piece of paper, right? You gave it to the cashier and then
> he handed you all those travelers checks. Not even a check. Man,
> you have some sonofabitch of a contact in this bank. That's doing
> it better than the tellers do it.
>   You know what they've got going on the side, don't you? They
> take down the name and address of every old lady and widower and
> faggy loner and other rich bastard who comes in with a fat little
> savings or check book. Then they sell the creep's name to certain
> guys in this town who want to know where those kind of rich num-
> bers live. Some of these guys pay up to a hundred bills for one good
> name. A hundred bucks for a lousy address![23]

The curious fact in this passage is that the person speaking with young Whalen has just identified him as a wealthy individual, or at least, as a man with
contacts at the bank; he then proceeds to inform him what some people do
to "creeps" with "fat little savings or check books": it is reasonable to posit
that this peculiar instantaneous attitudinal change from the admiration to the

---

[21] Kosinski, *The Painted Bird*, p. 45.

[22] Plimpton and Landesman, p. 196.

[23] Kosinski, *The Devil Tree* (New York: Harcourt, Brace, Jovanovich, 1973), pp.
10-11.

resentment of wealth mirrors the pervasive conflict existent in Kosinski's recent work between his dreams and his vehicle for projecting them into fiction. In addition, the compulsive use of slang and idiomatic adjectives is excessive and contrived.

> I want to enjoy life, even model. Be free to dash off to Paris, to go to Morocco for Christmas, to ski in Austria and Switzerland. To meet German, French, Italian men. To sip warm beer in Dublin pubs, and invite friends for dinner at my apartment in Rome. Now I have the chance and it won't come again. I don't want to waste time being miserable over an adolescent love affair. [24]

Again, the frequent and compressed use of banality and cliché results in a voice that is distorted, or artificial; phrases such as "I want to enjoy life," "be free," "now I have the chance," "it won't come again," "adolescent love affair," when combined in a few lines of speech evoke the sort of language that is found in advertising copy. But further, this impulsive and privileged wandering transcends any meaningful interaction with society of the sort contained in the picaresque which Claudio Guillén regards as "a process of conflict between the individual and his environment"[25]—the fanciful narrator described here is able to control her own environment, certainly to the extent of determining the setting for her life experiences.

> Before I left America there were other men around Karen; particularly there was David. His being an actor gave him a larger-than-life, star quality: Stick your dick out the window and screw them all, on the table, on the carpet, against a wall, hump and jump and kick and lick—that was David. Once, in front of me, Karen said to him, "I would like to fuck you, baby, until, until—" Then she dragged him into the bathroom and slammed the door. When she came out, she said to him, "Will I see you again?" and he answered, "I don't know. That depends on how bad you want it."[26]

In this passage, the unlikely use of internal rhyme in graphically detailing the crude eroticism of David, combined with his bloated, mundane response tend to focus attention upon the incident and to question its likelihood, rather than to precipitate our involvement in the situation. Rather than conveying a sense of detachment and objectivity, the dominant feeling is of Kosinski's aloofness to the crude manner of communication of his characters—thus,

[24] Kosinski, *The Devil Tree*, pp. 24-25.
[25] Guillén, p. 78.
[26] Kosinski, *The Devil Tree*, p. 41.

what is meant to be a colloquial expression of sexual conflict among the children of the very rich descends to the level of an unintentionally humorous caricature.

In *Cockpit*, Kosinski devises a conceit to enable him to deal with contemporary American themes and yet work within the Eastern European milieu in which he is so accomplished. Tarden, the protagonist, is an ex-spy, an immigrant to America, a former C.I.A. operative. In relating the story of Tarden's life in random episodic fashion, Kosinski returns to a more picaresque-centered, entirely first person narrative, a narrative that includes modern American urban scenes as well as incidents that recall the young boy of *The Painted Bird* in Eastern Europe. The change is dramatic: Kosinski is no longer attempting to capture American language idioms, but instead, vividly strives to depict through visual scenes the stark lowlife of pimps, whores, hustlers, and street pornographers—certainly the realm of a modern picaro.

Yet Kosinski still retains his exalted and isolated stance towards society, viewing it from above. Tarden, as a plain C.I.A. agent—or even an agent hunted by the C.I.A.—might conceivably function in a modern picaresque manner. But Kosinski's Tarden is no ordinary fugitive from the secret service: not a lowly man-in-hiding, but the world's richest ex-spy, a superstar of fugitives, with penthouse apartments in every major city of America and Europe, each flat equipped with elaborate electronic detection devices. Tarden finances his life through the sale of ancient antique snuff boxes, which he hides in obscure places such as toilet tanks, and sells whenever he requires a few million dollars. Though presumably he is depicted as a man-in-hiding, because he has erased all trace of himself in official transcripts and dossiers, the effect is of a man in control. For amusement, Tarden "descends" to the street world: to briefly work at a petty job, to photograph prostitutes, to induce guilt and trauma in the lives of the bourgeois inhabitants of a rural town, to visit pornography shops, to talk with victims of depravity. Tarden's enormous array of secret devices, hidden cameras, crafty resources, his tremendous wealth and absolute lack of occupation effectively destroy our empathy for him as a wanted man, or as a "half-outsider"; also destroyed is any connection with contemporary American themes as approached from a picaresque perspective, since by linking the spy with the affluent and powerful members of American society, Kosinski provides an ambivalent context for any social applications to contemporary America. Tarden remains a privileged anti-picaro, viewing his society from above in a manner that reflects Kosinski's own lofty perspective and personal identification.

If the creation of fiction is akin to the formulation of daydreams, then it is evident that the nature and quality of our lives will influence our dreams and those dream materials which are recalled and projected into fictional form. The traumatic circumstances of Jerzy Kosinski's early years prompted him to create novels which transform dreams of wish fulfillment into nightmares of horror and torment; as a means of expressing the content of these "'lower-class' experiences," he appropriately conceived of the picaresque genre (with its "worm's eye view") as the prevailing mode of organization for his work. But when he strove to convert into fiction the materials derived from his move to America and his entrance through marriage into the upper econo-mic and social realms of American society, his themes altered to represent "'upper-class' experiences"; yet he has not reconceived his notion of the picaresque as a functional mode of ordering his fictional vision. Thus, when Kosinski attempts to reassemble his American experiences into fictional form, the result reveals a fundamental conflict between the author's dreams—in the form of his social and economic inclinations—and his method of structure—in the form of the picaresque and its affinity for movement through the squalid depths of society.

The effect of this conflict is to deny the novels as self-contained works and to focus our attention instead upon Jerzy Kosinski, the circumstances of his actual life, and his dramatic attempt to convert his wishes and dreams into the essence of fiction—or rather, on the *process* by which Kosinski creates novels from out of his own life experiences: Kosinski himself becomes the object of our gaze and the subject of his fiction. Just as, in memory, Kosinski the subject seeks to perceive his recalled self as an other, through his work he becomes for us the subject—of an ongoing literary text which threatens to eradicate the boundaries between our coherent and unconscious selves, between the dream of realizing our lives, and our lives as realized dreams.

University of Southern California

THE DREAM-LIKE TECHNIQUE
IN *IL DESERTO DEI TARTARI*:
THE READER'S DELIGHT AND THE CRITIC'S NIGHTMARE

Franca Schettino

Some works of art, like some people, are endowed with a special charisma. Whoever comes into contact with them falls under a powerful spell. Generally speaking, such works are of a kind that appeals to the senses rather than to the intellect, and they all have in common an extremely facile form of communication. This is a quality that renders them far easier to *consume* than to evaluate. They excite, at best, only the emotions, and do not thwart one's expectations of entertainment. Thus, they are greatly favored by ordinary consumers, who, most often, are seeking entertainment when they approach art forms. These same properties, however, arouse questions in the minds of more sophisticated consumers, such as critics, who grow wary because they, too, find themselves falling under the spell. The critics know that this will prevent them from doing a proper job of judging the material. Those critics who fail to notice the imperviousness of 'charismatic works' to analysis, unwittingly end up simply paraphrasing their content. Others, who recognize how unavoidably they are caught up by the charismatic influence, take a simplistic stance, either expelling the concerned works from the elite of the art, or condemning them as banal, or merely ignoring them. Finally, critics who cannot come to a decision admit their enchantment, but confess also an inability to explain the mystery of the spell, and thereby 'mythify' the works.

Thus, on the whole, critics have a general feeling of helplessness in the face of charismatic works. But the helplessness may be due less to the works than to the critics themselves, who are often psychologically unprepared to be sufficiently flexible in the application of available theories, methods, and approaches. A sort of critical *inertia* results, then, precisely in those cases where the object of study probably would best be treated as an unknown entity, as a phenomenon requiring *ex novo* observation. Rather than leave such works in limbo, it would be preferable to pass beyond this inertial stage, not just in order to identify the nature of the problematic works and explain their existence, but also to define and refine the types of elements that can be used to form new critical tools for the study of similar cases.

Most of the literary works of Dino Buzzati share the same sort of charisma described above, and the same divergent/inertial overall status of related criticism. The main problem with Buzzati criticism seems connected to the fact that it has not yet recognized that the 'mystery' of Buzzati's works lies in the peculiar facile mode of communication which characterizes them and makes them align easily with popular literature. Whether or not one acknowledges it, Buzzati's facile communication is the major stumbling block to any analysis of his works, regardless of the critical approach angle. The *Deserto dei Tartari*, Buzzati's most famous book, is endowed with an unusual share of charismatic charm. Since its first publication in 1940, this book has been the delight of readers, but has been surrounded by an aura of mystery for many critics.[1] For me, the *Deserto* remained a delight as long as I stayed a plain reader, but it became a nightmare the instant I assumed the critic's role and tried to establish with it a rational rapport and to unveil the source of its spell. As a reader, I grew conscious very early of its charisma and its pronounced ease of reading. As a critic, what I most desired to learn was what makes the reading such an unforgettable experience, in spite of the essentially banal story. I wanted to know what made the text so highly readable, and to discover where this readability leads, in terms of the *Deserto*'s function or significance in the literary narrative system at large. Previous studies on the book had never concerned themselves seriously with examining the *Deserto*'s 'readability,' and I wondered whether they had thus missed a key to its true meaning and significance. In setting out to try to elucidate all these things, I had, without knowing it, engaged in a far more complex undertaking than I could ever have imagined. Eventually I was able to accomplish this task I had set for myself, and the results of my investigation will form the subject of this essay. But before my efforts met with success, I traversed numerous stages of perplexity with regard to what method or approach I should use. As I have

[1] For a general overview of the criticism and bibliography on all of Buzzati's works, see the following: F. Gianfranceschi, *Dino Buzzati* (Torino: Borla, 1967); A. Veronese Arslan, *Invito alla lettura di Buzzati* (Torino: Mursia, 1974); I. Crotti, *Dino Buzzati*, "Il Castoro," No. 129 (Firenze: La Nuova Italia, 1977). For recent re-considerations of Buzzati, see the *Cahiers-Dino Buzzati*, published annually (since 1977) by R. Laffont, under the auspices of the "Association Internationale des Amis de Dino Buzzati." For a re-consideration of the *Deserto*, see, for example, M. Carlino, *Come leggere* "Il deserto dei Tartari" (Milano: Mursia, 1976), which proposes a reading of the work along V. Propp's lines.

hinted, it can be useful to future investigations of charismatic works to develop as clearly as possible a functional critical method to which they are amenable. Therefore, it seems relevant to sketch briefly, at least, my 'search for a method' in this instance, in order to give some background for the rationale which determined the approach I finally selected for the study of the *Deserto*. A trail beginning at one point may fork and end up in more than one place; in a similar sense, sharing some of the 'method search' experience can be of use as groundwork, either for the development of a similar approach or of a different one based on related principles, for the purpose of examining problematical works like the *Deserto*. It is my hope that by presenting, together in this essay, both an outline of my 'method search' and the results of my analysis, I can offer an example of what sort of work may be done with narrative literature of the so-called "popular" variety. The value of investigating such literature seems, after all, to be worthy of consideration, in spite of a frequently-held belief. I refer to the view that considers such literature trivial and not "productive" from a critical point of view because it proposes nothing "new" in content or form.[2] My recent experiences with Buzzatian texts and texts by other "popular" authors have strongly convinced me otherwise. For the above reasons, then, I will now summarize my arrival at a working approach, before presenting the investigation proper.

At some point after reading the book for the first time, I conceived the notion that the lasting impression it leaves in the reader's mind is a deep, peaceful feeling—a highly hedonistic experience culminating in a sense of pleasant awe. This thought seemed to be supported by the fact that one emerges from the completed reading enchanted, as one does from certain dreams or films, which may have an extremely banal content, yet nevertheless exert an unforgettable spell.[3] But I found, unexpectedly, that this after-reading sensation and lasting experience of the *Deserto* stood in sharp contrast to a certain sense of unease that could be felt during the actual reading. The uneasy feeling seemed associated with the presence of an anxious-fantastic subject in the book. I grew very puzzled when I failed to find any logical connection between this actual reading experience and the book's final effect of pleasant awe. The absence of a link between the two impressions was what

[2] See, for example, W. Iser, *The Act of Reading: A Theory of Aesthetic Response* (Baltimore: Johns Hopkins Univ. Press, 1978), and *The Implied Reader: Patterns of Communication in Prose Fiction from Bunyan to Beckett* (Baltimore: Johns Hopkins Univ. Press, 1974). Iser regards art manifestations which tend to maintain the prevailing norms of form and content as being "inferior" to those which do not confirm traditional values.

[3] On the subject of how dreams affect memory, see, for example, R. Caillois, "Problemi logici e filosofici del sogno," in *Il sogno e le civiltà umane*, trans. and intro. by I. Molinari, ed. E. de Martino (Bari: Laterza, 1966), pp. 29-59.

first made me wish to question the validity of conclusions reached by previous criticism on the *Deserto*. In general, the pre-existing studies reflected
critical readings that seemed to have stopped at the experience occurring
during the reading. These studies widely accepted, on the whole, a classification of the *Deserto* as a work belonging to the "new fantastic" genre—a
work portraying Modern Man's anxiety, which often derives from unspeci-
fiable threats.[4] I attempted to be convinced by this view, but was unable to
repeat the investigative modes of the previous criticism, or rather, failed to
obtain the same results. When face-to-face with the text I discovered, to my
great surprise, that the anxious-fantastic subject was actually not present in
the *Deserto* in palpable form, even though I had somehow felt its presence
during the reading. This disappearance of the anxious-fantastic subject was
total, and did not in the least resemble the loss which normally occurs upon
a second reading of a fantastic tale. Unable to explain this enigma readily, I
entertained the idea that the *Deserto*'s anxious-fantastic subject was only a
by-product of the book, not its essence, and that for this reason it could not
lend the book the kind of significance attributed to it by previous criticism.
This idea, as well as the existence of the above-mentioned serene, final effect
(the after-reading enchantment and sense of awe) gradually led me to believe
that the true significance of the *Deserto* was somehow tied to the final effect
of the instinctive, non-critical first reading. Reflecting upon this, I came at
last to a vague intuition that the final effect derives from an *atypical reading
perception* linked to an exceptional *visuality* of the text's writing. This
decided me to examine the text's structure, but the text was resistant to
conventional critical methods, such as stylistic or structuralistic analysis. It
was at this point, after various failures, that I realized that the only way I
could hope to penetrate it was to use a type of examination following the
dictates of my instictive, pre-critical, first reading. I would have to recover
this kind of reading almost step by step, by first freeing myself as much as
possible from any preconceived critical notions (including my own) about the
text and about the reading process in general. I felt that I would have to
'recapture' my *reader*-self—that part of me that is at work when I read a
book only for the sake of enjoying the story. By thus studying the phenomenology of the pre-critical reading act, I believed I would be able to trace the
receptive-perceptive route I must have followed unconsciously. I hoped that
this would help me to explain the text's structure, and the enigmatic lack of
consistency between the reader's response during the actual reading of the
text and his lasting memory of it. This process of recapture was not easy. It

---

[4]On the subject of "fantastic literature," see, especially: T. Todorov, *Introduction
à la littérature fantastique* (Paris: Editions du Seuil, 1970); and J.-B. Baronian, *Un
nouveau fantastique* (Lausanne: L'Age d'Homme, 1977).

must be a difficult process in any similar case, when one may require to study one's own instinctive reading, especially when attempting to do so in such a way as to allow others to repeat the experiment. Given this situation, the present study should be considered as an experiment in criticism. Because of the inadequacies I found in other known methods of criticism when I tried to apply them to this work, I have had to perform an *ad hoc* investigation, using a variety of tools I custom-made from scratch, so to speak. In building these tools, I have used theoretical notions from various fields, including the theories of information communication, reader-response, film criticism, semiotics, aesthetics of perception, Gestalt psychology, psychology of art, and several others.[5] I did not willfully choose this eclectic approach; it was imposed upon me by the complex structural physiognomy of the text. However, what I think has made it possible for me to follow a phenomenological line of investigation is my own educational background. My former training in biological and medical sciences and my original formation as a critic along Leo Spitzer's lines of psychological and stylistic criticism predisposed me toward 'diagnostic' types of criticism, which approach objects inductively, through the observation, collection, and evaluation of 'symptoms.' Critical trends that study the phenomenology of the reader-text relationship belong to this group, and it is these trends I have followed in

[5] Following is a minimal list of references consulted: A. Moles, *Théorie de l'information et perception esthétique* (Paris: Flammarion & Cie, 1958); M. Merleau-Ponty, *Phénoménologie de la perception* (Paris: Gallimard, 1945); R. Arnheim, *Art and Visual Perception: A Psychology of the Creative Eye* (Berkeley-Los Angeles-London: Univ. of California Press, 1971); *Visual Thinking* (Berkeley-Los Angeles-London: Univ. of California Press, 1972); R. L. Gregory, *Eye and Brain: The Psychology of Seeing* (1966; rpt. New York-Toronto: McGraw-Hill Book Co., 1971); *Memory and Attention: An Introduction to Human Information Processing*, ed. D. A. Norman (New York-London-Sydney-Toronto: J. Wiley & Sons Inc., 1969); *Reader-Response Criticism: From Formalism to Post-Structuralism*, ed. J. P. Tompkins (Baltimore and London: Johns Hopkins Univ. Press, 1980); W. Iser, *The Act of Reading: A Theory of Aesthetic Response* (Baltimore: Johns Hopkins Univ. Press, 1978); N. Holland, *The Dynamics of Literary Response* (New York: Oxford Univ. Press, 1968); G. Steiner, "'Critic'/'Reader'," *New Literary History* 10 (Spring 1979), 423-52; A. Rothe, "Le rôle du lecteur dans la critique allemande contemporaine," *Littérature* 32 (Décembre 1978), 96-109; U. Eco, *Lector in Fabula: La cooperazione interpretativa nei testi narrativi* (Milano: Bompiani, 1979); J. Kristeva, *Desire in Language: A Semiotic Approach to Literature and Art*, trans. Th. Gora, A. Jardine, and L. S. Roudiez, ed. L. S. Roudiez, (New York: Columbia Univ. Press, 1980); R. Huss and L. Silverstein, *The Film Experience* (New York: Dell, 1978); E. H. Gombrich, *Art and Illusion: A Study in the Psychology of Pictorial Representation* (Princeton: Princeton Univ. Press, 1972); G. Zaccaria, *Il romanzo d'appendice: Aspetti della narrativa* "popolare" *nei secoli XIX e XX* (Torino: Paravia, 1977); A. Bianchini, *Il romanzo d'appendice* (Torino: ERI, 1969); L. Pacini Savoj, "Arte e 'letteratura amena'," *Belfagor* 2 (1979), 141-55.

this investigation. As I will endeavor to show, I believe that this approach has given satisfactory results.[6]

A preliminary review of my ordinary reading of the *Deserto* gave me some clues that the *visuality* of the book's writing was linked to a dominant structural pattern of *pictures* or *tableaux*. General examination of the reading process revealed that this design constantly forces the reader to *look*, subliminally transforming his reading into an act of *seeing*. Closer examination made it clear that the *à tableau* pattern and its global effect result from a cumulative effect exerted on the reader by specific narrative 'microstructures,' which give a unique semantic aspect to the syntactical fabric. The narration has a chain-like or epic progress. Concepts are first announced and then expressed, allowing step-by-step reception of both denotative and connotative information. This facilitates the mnemonic-synthetic processing of the information. But what aids the reader's reception most of all is a balanced distribution of frequent, interposed-punctuating and spatial pauses in the narrative discourse. The skillful use of these pauses makes the text's writing, and the reading of it, proceed with coordination and order, from image to image, scene to scene. The step-by-step reception of the information makes the reader experience the effect of a capillary matrix of *tableaux*, which gradually develop within one another, proceeding from the smallest ones (the sentences) through the mid-sized ones (the paragraphs), to the largest ones (the chapters). This is a *contemplative* kind of writing, producing a similar kind of reading, because it permits the reader to contemplate an image formed in a just-completed sentence, paragraph, or chapter, while preparing to contemplate the next image in the discourse. This iconic continuity keeps the mental eye in constant progressive movement, favoring uninterrupted reception. The principal roots of this contemplative writing/reading process are found in a *parataxical organization* of paragraphs.

The *Deserto*'s parataxical narration most often results from a *gaze*, either a character's or the narrator's. This is certainly not a new mode of narration in literature. What makes it noteworthy, here, is the fact that the gaze unfolding the parataxical description is conceived *cinematically*; it seems built upon the general theoretical principle of the "partial illusion," which aims at

---

[6]These results are part of a larger investigation on Buzzati. I presented portions of it in two other public communications: "La tecnica narrativa nel *Deserto dei Tartari*," paper read at the IIe Colloque International on "La creation littéraire chez Dino Buzzati," organized by the Association Internationale des Amis de Dino Buzzati, XIIe Festival International du Livre, Nice (France), May 9-11, 1980, and forthcoming in *Cahiers-Dino Buzzati* No. 5; and "Il potere della terza persona narrativa in *Un amore* di Buzzati," read at the Italian Section, Meeting of the Philological Association of the Pacific Coast (PAPC), University of California, Berkely, November 7-9, 1980.

intensifying the reader's illusion of reality, as a film intensifies a cinema spectator's illusion of reality.[7] The two segments[8] in Example 1 exemplify an application of this principle:

> Drogo si voltò indietro a guardare la città contro luce; fumi mattutini si alzavano dai tetti. *Vide di lontano* la propria casa. *Identificò* la finestra della sua stanza. *Probabilmente* i vetri erano aperti, le donne stavano mettendo in ordine.
>
> (I, pp. 25-26)

> In uno spiraglio delle vicine rupi, già ricoperto di buio, dietro una caotica scalinata di creste, a una lontananza incalcolabile, immerso ancora nel rosso sole del tramonto, come uscito da un incantesimo, Giovanni Drogo *vide allora un nudo colle* e sul ciglio di esso una striscia regolare e geometrica di uno speciale colore giallastro: il profilo della Fortezza.
>
> (I, p. 28)

Example 1

Both of these *tableaux* not only have an essentiality of description, but are also *filmic* because they are structured like *panoramic long shots*[9]—two photographs of distant objects (Drogo's house and the fort) seen in a partial context. Both are also rendered cinematically dramatic by a *close-up*. In the first segment, the word *identificò* acts as a sort of *zoom-freeze*; it brings the long shot abruptly from a distance, to proximity, as though by a camera lens adjustment. Consider the sequence *vide di lontano* followed by *identificò*, which ends with a kind of *still shot* of a detail, namely, *la finestra*. Next, *i vetri erano aperti* is juxtaposed with *le donne stavano mettendo in ordine*, following a verbal *cut*—the word *probabilmente*. This cut may appear to be one of the conventional expedients of narrative literature used to pass from the external reality to the internal reality of the character's thoughts. Yet,

---

[7]For the "partial illusion" principle, see R. Arnheim, *Film as Art* (Berkeley-Los Angeles-London: Univ. of California Press, 1971), pp. 8-180.

[8]All quotations from the text are from Dino Buzzati, *Il deserto dei Tartari* (Milano: Mondadori, 1976; 6th rpt. of the 1966 Oscar edition).

[9]For the terminology and general principles of film technique, cf.: *Vocabulaire du Cinéma*, comp. S. I. van Nooten (La Haye, Pays-Bas: n.p., n.d.); T. C. Jordan Jr., *Glossary of Motion Picture Terminology* (Menlo Park, Calif., Pacific Coast Publishers, 1968); Huss and Silverstein, *The Film Experience*; and R. Spotiswoode, *A Grammar of the Film: An Analysis of Film Technique* (Berkeley-Los Angeles: Univ. of California Press, 1950).

here, the reader not only overlooks the transition, but perceives the scene directly, without loss of continuity. In the second segment of Example 1, the *tableau* results from a kind of *pan shot* that resolves into a *long shot* represented by *vide allora un nudo colle*. The long shot gradually slows down by means of a *zoom-freeze*, namely the colon (:), ending in a *close-up still shot* represented by *il profilo della Fortezza*.

Observations of this kind lead us to the intuition that the *Deserto* was conceived as though it were a *film*. The intuition gains certainty when we contemplate a picture like that in Example 2:

> *E si avvicinava la sera.*
>   *Guardateli, Giovanni Drogo e il suo cavallo, come piccoli sul fianco delle montagne* che si fanno sempre piú grandi e selvagge. Egli continua a salire per arrivare alla Fortezza in giornata, ma piú svelte di lui, dal fondo, dove romba il torrente, piú svelte di lui salgono le ombre. A un certo punto esse si trovano proprio all'altezza di Drogo sul versante opposto della gola, sembrano per un momento rallentare la corsa, come per non scoraggiarlo, poi scivolano su per i greppi e i roccioni, *il cavaliere è rimasto di sotto.*
>   *Tutto il vallone era già zeppo di tenebre violette ...* quando Drogo si trovò improvvisamente davanti ... una costruzione militaresca che sembrava antica e deserta.
>
>   (I, p. 27)
>
>   Example 2

Here we encounter a real and proper series of filmic shots, so to speak. Another panoramic shot is involved. It is inserted between the phrase *e si avvicinava la sera* (a *fade-out* from the preceding scene) and *Tutto il vallone era già zeppo di tenebre violette* (a *fade-in* for the next scene). It has its own *fade-in* and *fade-out*, represented, respectively, by the phrases *Guardateli, Giovanni Drogo e il suo cavallo* and *il cavaliere è rimasto di sotto*.[10] This paragraph is a way to abbreviate, in space and time, the description of Drogo's journey from the city to the fort. Condensing devices of this sort are used often in narrative literature. But this one here is a condensing technique

[10]This panoramic long shot is an *objective zoom* onto a segment of a long *panoramic tracking shot* (I, pp. 24-27), which is detectable in the text as a trail of enunciatory phrases marking out the paragraphs of Chapter I, in the same way that titles of a *storyboard* mark out the sketches forming the shooting plan for a film. Interestingly, in an interview granted to A. Sala, Buzzati said that the *Deserto* was constructed on the basis of a schematic outline ("scaletta") of the various episodes.

typical of film, rather than of literature. Consider how the phrase *il cavaliere è rimasto di sotto*, which appears to interrupt the description of Drogo's journey, actually allows the reader to continue it mentally instead, as though in a film. In other words, contrary to appearances, there is no break in the line of iconic continuity, and this permits the reader to continue the journey subliminally, until he, like Drogo, finds a military construction before him (*Drogo si trovò improvvisamente davanti . . . una costruzione militaresca*).

The techniques exemplified above confirm the cinematic quality of the *Deserto*. They not only intensify the effect of the text's visuality for the reader, but they also make the reader subliminally conscious that he is part of an 'audience' *watching* a 'spectacle.' The elements responsible for this additional effect are explicit in some exhorting and demonstrative addresses made to the reader by the narrative voice. The first and most important of these is the address *Guardateli*, in Example 2. The plural imperative verb form has the power to inform the reader with a single magic stroke, that the reading is a *vision*; it seats the reader in a film audience and makes him watch the action on a *screen*. In considering this authoritative exhortation, we realize that the pronouncing voice is distinct from the voice in narrative segments such as those of Example 1. We also note that the 'exhortative voice' speaks in the present indicative, whereas the other one uses past tenses. This is extremely important. Through association with other similar passages in the present indicative (scattered throughout the text), we can identify the exhortative voice (that says *Guardateli*) as the voice of a *commentator*. And from this, through various back-and-forth readings, we can discern the co-existence of two texts within the book: (1) a *text-film*, and (2) a *text-comment*. Awareness of these two texts and their implications points to the following basic narrative situation:

(1) A *screen*, on which the text-film is projected, implied by the exhorting verb forms.

(2) A *text-film*, consisting of a story and its background, detectable in the past perfect and imperfect third-person narration.

(3) A *text-comment*, concerning the text-film, and detectable in the exhorting verb forms and present indicative, third-person narration.

(4) An *audience*—the reader turned spectator—also implied by the exhorting verb forms.

This new knowledge of the text's organization allows us to examine the act of reading more systematically, analyzing separately the reading directives imparted by the text-film and the text-comment. The first part of this examination is a reading of the text-comment.

Our discovery of the commentator gradually leads us to realize that the text-film (the story of Drogo and the fort) is an *abridged* story, edited by the commentator. The reader is shown only some episodes of the last thirty years of Drogo's life, the ones spent at the fort. These episodes are precisely selected by a clear, expository, didactic plan. They are salient events, ordered according to the principle of cause and effect, and connected with one another by a technique resembling that of a folk tale. The didactic exposition is documented by the recurrence of implicitly-causal phrases, which often stand at the beginnings of key paragraphs of the text-comment. Examples of these phrases are: *nominato ufficiale, appena arrivato, sepolto che fú, cessata la neve.* They give the narration a sense of order and prevent the reader from losing the story's thread. As we seek out these implicitly causal phrases, we find that they form only one part of a vast *actualization* process, which the text-comment applies to the text-film. The commentator operates this process by employing a capillary network of various expedients at strategic points of his text-comment. These expedients are, specifically, certain items in his discourse, including the following: the temporal adverbs for the present tense (e.g., *adesso, oramai, ora, per ora,* etc); the various demonstrative adverbs (e.g., *ecco, cosí,* etc.); the verbal forms imitating sounds or movements (e.g., *cioc, ploc,* "le teste dei due cavalli che facevano *sì sì* ad ogni passo," etc.); and the addresses to characters (e.g., *guardalo Lagorio*; *cosa aspetti, signor colonnello*; *coraggio Drogo*, etc.). All of these items produce a dramatic 'now' effect. They help maintain the film-screen illusion announced by the first address to the reader (the *Guardateli* mentioned above) and cause the reader to become *absorbed* in the text-film, thus obscuring the fact that the story is not continuous, by hindering the reader's awareness of the breaks. The support of the film-screen illusion by the dramatic actualization also explains why the commentator's extensive work goes unnoticed during the reading. The actualization of the text-film (and the resulting absorption of the reader) reach maximal levels at specific points, especially in chapters XIII, XIV, XVII, XXI, and XXV. I will not describe in detail the writing/reading process in each of these chapters. It suffices to say, in general, that the skillful use of actualization expedients at these points places the reader *inside* the text, as occurs with film when the techniques of tension or suspense merge a spectator visually and emotionally with a situation on the screen. In retrospect, the commentator actually seems to act in a dual fashion at some points, as both a *camera man* and a perspicacious *viewer-guide* for the reader. He underlines the 'camera effects,' enhancing the reader's appreciation of the picture, without the reader knowing it. The commentator's dual role as camera man and guide is best seen in the *montage* experienced in

Chapter XVII (pp. 165-69). Here, unwittingly, we simultaneously experience both the creation of a filmic montage and a commentator-guided appreciation of the effects generated by the 'camera movements.' The commentator's own 'analysis' of the complex series of shots in this montage gradually leads us to an aesthetic appreciation of that exhilarating psychological state evoked in mankind by the passage from winter to spring. I will briefly trace the sequence of shots just to sketch out the picture's complexity and the commentator's elaborate activity. The sketch will not suffice to show, in full, the film-illusion effect of the montage, but it will aid the readers of this essay to make their own 'photogrammatic' analysis, in the portions of the text to which I shall refer them.

The first part of the sequence in question is a series of *panning* (p. 165) and *cross-cutting* shots (p. 166). They take us from the outside to the inside of the fort, then outside again, finally ending in a *close-up* of the fort—a shot which summarizes epigrammatically the first tract of a long psychological and physical journey the 'camera' has made. Still guided by the commentator, we begin the second part of the sequence. A *tracking shot* of an unspecified officer (perhaps Drogo) replaces us within the fort, where the tracking shot resolves into a *pan shot* (of the lavatory rooms the officer traverses) and then into a *subjective close-up* (of the officer looking at the high window). Two *wipes* centrifugally expand the subjective close-up toward the fort's exterior, becoming a *panoramic long shot* that takes us far from the fort. Another *wipe* makes us appreciate a *close-up* of the green fields, unfolding in the character's mind, but visualized as though upon a screen. Another *cross-cut* shifts once more into the fort, concretizing the character's gaze with another *subjective close-up*. Another *wipe* moves us out of the time-space of the scene in progress, lengthening into a *long shot* of the distant city in the springtime, with people strolling the streets in their spring clothes. A *lighting*-change in the picture alerts us that this is a *flash-back*—a faded print of memories of times past. Then, another *cross-cut* returns us to the lavatories, to experience another *subjective close-up*—again the officer's gaze. A slow *wipe* extends it into a *partial long shot* of the fort—a short we soon recognize as a *flash-back* of a faded still photograph. There follows a rapid cascade of *cross-cuts*, taking us on a *panning* tour inside/outside/inside the fort, and describing its inhabitants as they attend to various chores. Another *cross-cut* leads to a *tracking shot* of Drogo on horseback, descending toward the city (*Corri, allora, cavallino*). And the tracking shot becomes another *pan shot* (pp. 168-169), in a physical-psychological key, structured like a litany of pictures whose anaphoric skeleton can be detected in a chain of chanting refrains ("E allora addio . . . addio . . . addio . . . Un saluto . . . un saluto . . . l'ultimo saluto . . . ," etc.). The complex sequence of shots is closed by a *panoramic long shot* (the chapter's last paragraph, p. 169), of Drogo on the edge of the "sassoso pianoro." He is seen from the back, spurring his horse toward the valley.

Aided by the commentator's elaborate analysis of the whole, we can appreciate the rhythmic and tonal shades of the description. In retrospect, we can detect in it some structural and content elements of the folk *ballad* (e.g., dramatic description of the action, incremental repetition, etc.) and can perceive undertones evoking the music and scenery of a film Western. These undertones have a subtle parodic effect for the reader, revealing an ironic vein in the chant accompanying Drogo's descent toward the city. By association, we recognize, now, that a similar vein subliminally tinges other points of the narration. And recollecting this feeling, we see that a sort of overall musical accompaniment or *leitmotif* enhances the reader's emotions at various peak points of the story. Other *ballads* are detectable in the book, such as the "Ballad of soldier Lazzari's death." Its meditative allure—more than its real-istic picture—transforms the Life/Death struggle into an ironic-pathetic spectacle, somehow satirizing the whole convention-ruled life at the fort. A similar 'ballad motif' reappears at the death of Lieutenant Angustina, and finally at that of Major Drogo, at the end of the book. All these ballads are perfectly integrated into the text's general structural pattern *à tableau*, and contribute to the contemplative writing/reading process discussed earlier.

The more conscious we become of the ironic-pathetic undercurrent trav-ersing the text from beginning to end, the clearer it becomes that the text-comment's territory within the book is much larger, and its role far more complex, than suspected at the start of the analysis. Thus, we gradually take notice of those extended meditative segments that open or close various chapters; they back-shadow or fore-shadow Drogo's existential misadventure, projecting it against the thematic background of Life's brevity and Time's passage. During the ordinary reading, we do not really think about these segments, and their function seems to be to arouse our empathy for the character's misfortunes. Their meditative and somewhat elegiac tone enhances the effect of a *tableau*-spectacle contemplated at a distance, favoring in the reader a compassionate feeling for Drogo's 'doom.' The commentator's elegiac tone guides us, as readers, to *view* past and future events of Drogo's life, flashed-back or flashed-forward during the course of the main action. This creates in our minds a gentle iconic *collage* of what is happening *now* and what *did* or *will* happen to Drogo. The effect is so successful that the reader fails to notice the tricks played on him by the commentator's intru-sions, and it explains why, during the plain reading, we are not disturbed by those long digressions on Drogo's impending fate. Also, our absorption with the iconic redundancy of images on our mind-screen prevents us from notic-ing consciously the numerous negative shadings that the commentator casts on Drogo's image. This masked perception during our reading is what makes us accept, on one hand, the dreamlike, hallucinatory atmosphere produced by Drogo's own anxious state, and, on the other, the belief that Drogo is a truly unfortunate man worthy of our compassion. Our new knowledge of the text-comment, and of the mechanics of its reception by the reader, suggests that what the commentator says about Drogo is not what he actually means. This impression can be confirmed by an attentive re-examination (omitted here for economy) of the overall receptive-perceptive process through the entire text, along a 'Drogo wavelength' (everything pertinent to Drogo, said by the commentator). In essence, from such an examination, we learn that the image of Drogo fashioned by the text-film is varied constantly during the 'film-projection.' And the variations result, as we have seen, from the undermining nature of the 'musical score' and/or 'lyric chorus' generated by the text-comment. Ultimately, this negative modulation explains why the anxious-fantastic subject which the reader 'feels' during the ordinary reading (and which belongs almost entirely to Drogo's crumbling image) does not survive to leave residues of anxiety or pathos in the book's lasting impression. Thus, contrary to what one might at first believe, the reader does not take Drogo seriously, in the end, primarily due to the commentator's ironic treatment of the character. Recognition of the commentator's ironic tone now permits us to review or reject a great deal of what seemed at first sight to be "clear" and "obvious" in the *Deserto*.[11] But not everything that seemed obvious needs to be revised in our minds: the commentator's ironic shadings appear linked only to Drogo's own anxious state (and to that of other inhabitants and to the general life at Fort Bastiani). They seem to leave everything else intact and pure, as will become clearer later.

We can conclude, then, that the text-comment plays a determining role in the technical economy of the *Deserto*. It establishes the basic reading situation: 'seated comfortably' in a position like a film spectator's, the reader 'looks attentively' at the 'screen', and his mind faithfully registers all the information on it. But the commentator's intermittent flash-backs and flashforwards of the action produce an iconic redundancy which hinders the reader's clear perception of the commentator's voice and its impact. Because he is unaware of the commentator's extensive manipulations, the reader actually 'watches' and 'sees' the story in a manner completely different from that in which he *thinks* he does. It should now be clear that the way in which the reader perceives what happens on the 'screen' is intrinsic to the text-comment. But, on the other side of the coin, the *essence* of the reader's acts of 'looking' and 'seeing' is intrinsic to the text-film. This will

---

[11]On the function of irony in literature, see, for example: W. C. Booth, *A Rhetoric of Irony* (Chicago and London: Univ. of Chicago Press, 1974); and G. Guglielmi, *Ironia e negazione* (Torino: Einaudi, 1974).

be demonstrated by an examination of the *text-film* itself, to which we have now come.

The text-film—Drogo's story—seems at first to have been 'shot' completely from an objective point of view; the filmed material is presented in a straight-forward, impersonal manner. This results from a dominant, declarative syntax, consisting of sentences which state the text-film's overall content in definite terms. The ideas, thoughts, circumstances, facts, actions, and objects of the story all seem to present themselves explicitly, assertively, and autonomously, without any intermediary, rendering the text-film's content authentic and credible. But a second look at the text-film's narrative 'grammar' shows that the point of view often appears to *shift* from an objective to a subjective angle. In normal circumstances, this would imply that at such points the reader should 'see' things from the character's viewpoint. Yet, the effect on the reader does not confirm this second impression. Instead, our perception of the *Deserto*'s world seems to remain basically impersonal, even when the 'camera movements' suggest that we should see through Drogo's eyes. In short, the character's gaze is depersonalized. This is well exemplified by Drogo's contemplation of the spectacle of the fort, from Dr. Rovina's office window (Chapter IX). This scene appears to be the most classical *subjective shot* in the whole text-film, but the reader perceives it as though Drogo were absent. Thus, in terms of the effect on the reader, there is no difference between what is 'photographed' in a straight objective fashion and what seems to be 'shot' from the character's viewpoint. The character appears to serve only as a reference point for the 'camera,' as though he has no role but to fulfill the traditional "objective requirement of continuity." The reason for this impression is not immediately obvious to us, because the text-film employs no 'unorthodox camera techniques' and because the reader is unaware of the shifting viewpoint. These facts might suggest, by themselves, that we are dealing with the classical shifting techniques in films, called "the look of the outward regard" (the character looking at something) and "the eye-line shot" (what the character sees). Yet the principle of these techniques would imply that the "eye-line shots" in the *Deserto*, in spite of their discreetness, are still subjective. Therefore, we continue to face the apparent paradox of subjective shots that have an impersonal, objective effect. A closer examination (omitted here) of the 'film's' content, relative to its effect on the reader-spectator, reveals a 'shooting style' (use of angling, object framing, footage, etc.) that does not aim, after all, only at satisfying the traditional objective requirement of continuity. The whole text-film seems, instead, to be based on what I'd like to call an *audience-oriented* style. Its general effect is that of a film shot from the audience's viewpoint—as though the 'camera' were placed beside the reader-spectator. Expanding this thought, we realize that although Drogo's numerous "looks of outward regard" are followed in traditional fashion by "eye-line shots" (views of what he sees), each eye-line shot is actually transformed into a peculiar *blend* of both objective and subjective shots. What seems to happen, in effect, is that the object which the character begins to see ends up fascinating the 'film-maker' intensely, to such a point that the 'film-maker' injects his own admiration into what is filmed, totally superseding Drogo's admiration. What we thought as Drogo's gaze is really the 'film-maker's,' and ultimately the reader's. The final result resembles a Cinerama presentation, which reflects neither the character's viewpoint nor the 'film-maker's,' but gives the spectator the illusion of experiencing the action himself.

This new perception of the text-film's 'shooting mechanics' permits us to see that the use of the usually-subjective eye-line shot is deceptive: it does not serve to give the reader-spectator Drogo's perception of the world, but serves to channel the reader-spectator's gaze through that of the 'film-maker,' without the reader-spectator realizing the 'film-maker's' presence. From this perspective, Drogo's eye-line shot of the fort from Rovina's office is a strong example of how the reader is skillfully transformed into a direct-viewer of what is outside the window. Many elements are used to perform the trick, but one in particular is responsible for the reader's 'metamorphosis.' I am referring to the anaphorical use of the verb morpheme *vide*. Repeated four times, *vide*, although it seems to indicate each eye-movement of the character, emphasizes instead the 'film-maker's' surprise, and that of the reader, at what they both discover (as if by chance) outside the window, while focusing along Drogo's eye-line. In the end, the incremental repetition of *vide* loses any subjective quality (linked to either the character or the 'film-maker'), and becomes the track along which the reader himself builds the view of the fort, from inside Rovina's office.

Many different expedients are responsible for the overall 'shooting style' of the *Deserto*, but I cannot give here a detailed analysis of all of them. It will suffice to outline briefly the basic material that allows the above-described *audience-oriented* style to exist, namely, the basic technical material forming much of the foundation for the filmic visuality of the writing/reading of the *Deserto* as a whole. This basic technical working material, which renders the text's effect so Cinerama-like, can be identified with the third-person narration in the past perfect and imperfect tenses: specifically, those supportive narrative verb forms which tell the factual story. The choice of past-tense, third-person verbs is very important, because the narrative fabric which it generates exerts psycho-visual effects on the reader that other possible choices of grammatical persons and tenses would not permit. In order to illustrate properly what I mean, I would have to provide hypothetical verb-versions of parts of the text-film of the *Deserto*, using persons and tenses differing from the original's, and compare them with the original text. But lack of space does not allow me to do so. Thus, I must ask my readers to perform a brief experiment, to test the validity of my statement. I propose that they do the following: (1) Read the two textual passages given below in Example 3:

> *Si fece* svegliare ch'*era* ancora notte e *vestì* per la prima volta la divisa di tenente. Come *ebbe finito* ... *si guardò* nello specchio, ma senza trovare la letizia che *aveva sperato*.
>
> (I, p. 23)

> Drogo *capiva* di voler bene ancora a Maria e di amare il suo mondo: ma tutte le cose che nutrivano la sua vita di un tempo si *erano fatte* lontane; un mondo di altri dove il *suo* posto *era stato* facilmente occupato. E lo *considerava* oramai dal di fuori, pur con rimpianto ... *Quella* non *era* più la *sua* vita, *lui aveva preso* un' altra strada, tornare indietro *sarebbe stato* stupido e vano.
>
> (XIX, p. 181)

Example 3

(2) Construct three verb-versions of each of these passages, using (a) the first person present indicative, (b) the third person present indicative, and (c) the first person simple perfect (for Example 3's first passage) and the first person imperfect (for Example 3's second passage); (3) Place all three versions in the specified order, in front of each of the original passages, thus forming two four-unit sets; and (4) Read each set in progressive order. This reading experiment should permit one to feel changes occurring in the reader's perception of the subject. The changes I myself have experienced are as follows. In versions (a) and (b) of each passage, the visual perception of 'image contours' is less clear than it is in version (c) and much less clear than in the original passage. This seems due to a decreased 'distance' between reader and object, and an increased 'speed of reception' relative to version (c) and to the original passage. In version (c), perception of images is ambiguous compared to that of the original passage, due to an excessive 'nearness' of the narrative voice to the reader. This causes the reader to pay more attention to the voice *per se* than to what is narrated. Furthermore, the subjective-reflective element (present in all first-person narrations) disturbs the reader's reception of the information, causing a subliminal alteration of images. A vision constantly contaminated by subjective reflection is a retouched vision of the object. The *original* passages in Example 3, compared to their hypothetical versions, reveal an exceptional sharpness of images and a maximal clarity of perception, which seem to result from a knowing use of 'distance' and from a balanced 'speed' in the 'shooting' and 'projection.' A general illusion of

slowed-down narration is created in the reader, as if materials were projected at 'middle-speed' onto a flat surface, at some distance. The illusion has grammatical roots. I am referring to the basic 'auditory' characteristics of the third-person verb morphemes of the simple past perfect and imperfect tenses of the Italian language. These characteristics include the following: (1) the particular incisiveness of given syllables in the morphemes of the past perfect, third-person singular (as in *fé ce, dì sse, á ndò*, etc.); (2) the syllabic extension of the morphemes indicating the third person of the past imperfect tense (as in *á ndáva, fá cēva*, etc.) and the ones indicating the third person plural for both simple past perfect and imperfect (as in *fé cero, dì ssero, facé vano, dicé vano*, etc.); and (3) the tonal accentuation which the abundance of these temporal morphemes creates in the prosodic syntax of the text-film. Once aware of these characteristics, we can grasp how a skillful manipulation of the inherent qualities of the basic language contributes to generating in the reader the 'film experience' outlined at various points of this essay, namely: (1) the slow, contemplative, and incisive writing of the text-film; (2) the clear perception of object contours; (3) the continuous reception of the material; and (4) the illusion, in the reader, of actually *seeing* what is written. Much of the visuality of the *Deserto* is thus fundamentally built upon the prosodic specificity of the Italian narrative verb forms. This explains, in part, why the filmic quality of the book is lost in most translations, especially translations into non-Romance languages.[12]

It should now be clear that the text-film forms the underlying basis of the *Deserto*'s visual properties. They are built up from a foundation of specific language material and further elaborated with 'camera work.' On the basis of the data collected or alluded to here, we can now safely speculate that whatever other basic set of materials might have been selected for the 'shooting' of the text-film, the visual impact of the *Deserto* would not have been of the type displayed by the work in its present form. Ultimately, the book would have lacked the charismatic power that characterizes it, since this power arises largely from the exceptional visuality of the writing.

As we have seen from the above separate examinations of the text-comment and text-film, each one has a distinct role. Generally speaking, the text-film sets up a fundamental visuality or filmic quality of the book, which is modified or enhanced by the contributing influences of the text-comment. But a basic premise of this investigation is that the filmic visuality of the *Deserto* is what ultimately gives rise to the text's enigmatic contrast between the experience during the reading and its final, lasting effect; this relationship

---

[12] See, for example, the English versions of the passages of Example 3 in *The Tartar Steppe*, trans. S. C. Hood (New York: Avon Books, 1980), pp. 1 and 145-46.

can be explored clearly only by a deeper consideration of the *concerted* work of the text-comment and text-film. The *Deserto* is, of course, an integrated work, and the text-comment and text-film *collaborate* toward a common, final effect. We can now reflect in greater detail on this collaboration and its consequences. Looking retrospectively at the results obtained from this investigation, our examination of the *Deserto*'s reading mechanics has allowed us to see that the peculiar, binary narrative mode places the reader at a 'physical' and psychological distance from the subject matter, generating an overall 'dramatic irony' situation, wherein the reader knows (and/or feels) things that the characters do not. Drogo's anxious state is degraded to one of petty anxieties, downgrading the reader's original empathy for him to indifference, and the mysterious features of the environment are reduced to banal dimensions, changing the reader's sense of eeriness to one of plain curiosity. The most active influence in this erosive process is that of the text-comment, which alters the main line of information by injecting ambivalent shades of empathy and irony. The text-film, on the other hand, introduces a special 'shooting style' which pretends to focus the 'camera' on Drogo but actually aims at the background, making the character's presence lose importance. In conclusion, therefore, the *Deserto* has, at the bottom of its communicative system, a process that nullifies the anxious-fantastic subject even as it is being formed. The book is not, in the end, a fantastic tale, nor it is a moral, existential, existentialist, or realistic tale, as it has led many critics to believe. In other words, the dramatic irony does not generate any lasting uncanny feeling, and does not reflect, except in passing, modern existential anxiety or mankind's condition in general. The text-reader distance produced by the binary mode of narration ultimately leads, instead, to the formulation of a totally different message. It serves to build a comfortable atmosphere, one in which the reader gradually develops a tension-free, contemplative state of mind. This state of mind, on one hand, and the overall, impressive filmic 'photography' of the text on the other, cause the reader's attention to shift from the insignificant foreground to the significant background; from the literal and allegorical story (Drogo/Mankind's misadventure in the context of Drogo/Mankind's life) to the natural, spatial, and temporal spectacle of life. Predisposed by the restful atmosphere, the reader (through the 'filmmaker') marvels at eye-catching sights such as dawns, wild mountains, yellow plains, etc. Together, the phasing-out of all the thematic subjects (especially the anxious-fantastic one) and the enhancing of the serene subject explain how and why the reader is impressed only with a remembered sense of pleasant awe: the powerful, dreamlike effect which the binary mode of narration exerts on the reader simply 'steals the show' from the apparent meaning(s) of the book. In the end, we recall neither the *what* nor the *why* of what we have read, but only *how we have seen*. Our engrossment in the text's visual adventure is responsible both for the book's charisma and for its general imperviousness to critical reading.

The above reflections clearly point out that the *Deserto*'s real significance and importance is the form in which the text communicates information. The text's structural and thematic fabrics are no more than means employed in the service of an exceptional aesthetic 'event:' the realization of a 'film experience' in narrative literature. The fact that the reader reads-sees, perceives and consumes the *Deserto* as if it were a film, makes the reader totally dependent on the text, because his attention is involved entirely with following images 'moving' on a 'screen'. The result is a sort of hypnotic sleep-vision or dream, like the waking dream experienced by a film spectator. Examples of cinematic effects are scattered everywhere throughout modern narrative literature, following individual techniques inspired by the film medium. But the film techniques and film experience in the *Deserto* are *pervasive*, rather than just occasional elements of its narrative structure. Thus, we have a narrative work that totally subverts the norms of narrative literature. Both the unusual textual construction and the reader's response to it give the *Deserto* a significance which surpasses the limits of its own system—literature —and acquires connotations of sociological, historical, and art-psychological nature. The mode in which we experience the 'film' in this work makes the written text a case of *pseudomorphosis* of literary narration. That is, the *Deserto* enables narrative literature to do something 'other' than it normally does, but without altering its original characteristics. The reader unwittingly gets a perceptive experience different from the one he normally obtains from a book; instead of 'seeing' in the usual literary fashion, by interpreting the writing, he sees *cinematically*, finding the text's written reality to be ready-made, as though in a film print. All this points to a 'modification' within the literary narrative system, namely, to a *new* form of literary narration. The *Deserto*'s matching of the communicative faculties of film allows one to discover, in literature, some unsuspected potential faculties, thus proving that narrative literature can act like film and simply be a medium, if it wishes. In so doing, this text declares itself as an "avant-garde" work, because it leads one to use a new code of reading, thus placing in question the *normality* of narrative writing, as well as our preconceived notions about the act of reading and about the social function of fiction writing in general.[13] By proposing a code normally held to belong to audio-visual media, the *Deserto*'s text presents narrative literature with an example of how to progress toward other forms, which will help it to regain part of the entertainment power it once possessed, and which is today almost completely monopolized by

[13]On the concept of *avant-garde*, see, for example: R. Poggioli, *Teoria dell'arte d'avanguardia* (Bologna: Il Mulino, 1962).

cinema and TV. In our modern, paroxysmally-consumeristic civilization, where the reading of literature (and reading in general) has become an ever more difficult endeavor and an ever less sought-for pastime, the new *modus percepiendi* which the *Deserto* has brought to literature is of extreme interest. It has foreseen the altered sensitivity of today's reader, who is audio-visually ultra-conditioned—addicted to prefabricated images—and who is no longer a traditional reader, but a habitual 'spectator.'[14]

At the basis of this achievement are elements of Buzzati's professional training, consumeristic habits, and literary concepts and theories, all working together in the laboratory of a peculiar type of mind. Buzzati's journalistic training undoubtedly had much to do (as recognized by Buzzati) with his way of writing. Perhaps also because he was a journalist and writer, he must have felt an increasing competition from film, as a means of mass entertainment. But as a consumer of film he must have felt a fascination with its form. The *Deserto* reflects this, as well as Bontempelli's concept that literature should learn to emulate mass entertainment media, such as film and theater. The *Deserto* reflects, most of all, Buzzati's own consistent respect for the reader, and his concept of what it is that a writer should do for the reader. Buzzati felt that a writer's first duty is to recall that a written work can never achieve its aim unless it lets itself be read with pleasure.[15] However, further contemplation of the *Deserto*'s construction, as it has been recovered through our investigation, indicates that the conception of the *Deserto* as if it were a film seems to have derived more from instinct than from reason. A pertinent clue is the fact that the *poesis* reflected by the text recognizes no boundaries between art forms; it incorporates and fully integrates elements from literature, visual arts, architecture, and even performing arts. The perfect blending of all these elements points to a mind with exceptional sensory integration powers. Such a mind does not interpret reality but *feels* it, so to speak, retaining the essential traits of the minds of primitives and children. I believe that the activity of such a mind must have generated Buzzati's "wish-to-create-a form" (*Kunstwollen*); a form that excites the reader's audiovisual faculties more than the intellectual-perceptive ones. The fact that the *Deserto*

[14] On the general subject of reading in an audio-visual culture, see, for example: M. McLuhan, *Understanding Media: The Extension of Man* (New York: McGraw-Hill Book Co., 1964); *Mass Media and Mass Man*, ed. A. Casty (New York: Holt, Rinehart, and Winston, Inc., 1968); *Media Culture*, ed. J. Monaco (New York: Dell, 1978); *La fatica di leggere*, eds. S. Piccone-Stella and A. Rossi (Roma: Editori Riuniti, 1976).

[15] For Buzzati's ideas about narrative literature and many other topics (including the "fantastic"), see Y. Panafieu, *Dino Buzzati: Un Autoritratto. Dialoghi con Y. Panafieu*, luglio-settembre, 1971 (Milano: Mondadori, 1973), passim. For Massimo Bontempelli's innovative program, cf. A. Saccone, "Il Novecentismo di Massimo Bontempelli: 'realismo magico' e società di massa," *Lavoro critico* 13 (1978), 41-82.

does not seem to be the only Buzzatian text engaged in such a wish suggests that we are dealing with more than just a socio-cultural influence on the creative process. In other words, the 'film' in the *Deserto* is not merely the result of the mass-communication media's influence on the creative process, but is a natural outgrowth of the use of the media characteristics by an already audiovisual mind.

All of these observations bring to light the astonishing significance of the *Deserto*, one that could not be detected by previous criticism, given the general inadequacy of the critical approaches used. As I said at the beginning of this essay, I used an *ad hoc* critical approach to investigate the *Deserto*, one that concentrated on the phenomenology of the reader-text relationship. I do not claim that this is the sole valid approach. Yet, with regard to the *Deserto*, I now believe that no other method could have led me, personally, to the results I have obtained. If I am in any way mistaken in this belief, I would like to say what Boccaccio said about his work on Dante: "Se io in parte alcuna ho errato, darò materia altrui di scrivere per dire il vero, del nostro [Buzzati]."

University of Southern California

NIGHTMARE AND THE HORROR FILM:
THE SYMBOLIC BIOLOGY OF FANTASTIC BEINGS*

Noel Carroll

> And believe me, Sir,
> dreams are of such stuff
> that if you sleep on them you
> will come to see things as I
> see them; and you will wish them
> to be as I relate them.
>
> Quevedo, *Visions*

> Dreams seem to be spurred on not
> by reason but desire, not by the
> head but the heart.
>
> Dostoevsky, *The Dream
> of a Ridiculous Man*

Whereas the Western was the dominant genre of the late 60s and early 70s, horror and science fiction are the reigning popular forms of the late 70s and early 80s. Launched by blockbusters like *The Exorcist* and *Jaws*, the cycle has flourished steadily; it seems as unstoppable as some of the demons it has spawned. The present cycle, like the horror cycle of the 30s and the science fiction cycle of the 50s, comes at a particular kind of moment in American history—one where feelings of paralysis, helplessness and vulnerability (hallmarks of the nightmare) prevail. If the Western worked well as an open forum for debate about our values and our history during the years of the Vietnam war, the horror and science fiction film poignantly expresses the sense of powerlessness and anxiety that correlates with times of depression, recession, Cold War strife, galloping inflation and national confusion.

The purpose of this paper is to examine the basic structures and themes of these timely genres by extending some of the points made in Ernest Jones'

*Another version of this paper was published after the Symposium in *Film Quarterly* (Spring, 1981), pp. 16-25.

On the Nightmare.[1] Jones used his analysis of the nightmare to unravel the
symbolic meaning and structure of such figures of medieval superstition as
the incubus, vampire, werewolf, devil, and witch. Similarly, I will consider
the manner in which the imagery of the horror/science fiction film is constructed in ways that correspond to the construction of nightmare imagery.
My special, though not exclusive, focus will be on the articulation of the
imagery of horrific creatures—on what I call their symbolic biologies. A
less pretentious subtitle for this essay might have been "How to make a
monster."

Before beginning this "unholy" task, some qualifications are necessary.
Throughout this paper I will slip freely between examples drawn from horror
films and science fiction films. Like many connoisseurs of science fiction
literature, I think that, historically, movie science fiction has evolved as a
sub-class of the horror film. That is, in the main, science fiction films are
monster films, rather than explorations of grand themes like alternate socie-
ties or alternate technologies.

Secondly, I am approaching the horror/science fiction film in terms of a
psychoanalytic framework, though I do not believe that psychoanalysis is
a hermeneutic method that can be applied unproblematically to any kind of
film or work of art. I would argue that it is appropriate to use psychoanalysis
in relation to the horror film, however, because within our culture the horror
genre is explicitly acknowledged as a vehicle for expressing psychoanalytically
significant themes such as repressed sexuality, oral sadism, necrophilia, etc.
Indeed, in recent films, such as Jean Rollin's *Le Frisson des Vampires* and
La Vampire Nue, all concealment of the psychosexual subtext of the vampire
myth is disgarded. We have all learnt to treat the creatures of the night—like
werewolves—as creatures of the id, whether we are spectators or filmmakers.
Socially, psychoanalysis, more or less, is the *lingua franca* of the horror film
and, thus, the privileged critical tool for discussing the genre. In fact, horror
films often seem to be little more than bowdlerized, pop psychoanalysis, so
enmeshed is Freudian psychology with the genre.

Nor is the coincidence of psychoanalytic themes and those of the horror
genre only a contemporary phenomenon. Horror has been tied to nightmare
and dream since the inception of the modern tradition. Over a century before
the birth of psychoanalysis Horace Walpole wrote of the *Castle of Otranto*,

> I waked one morning, in the beginning of last June, from a dream,
> of which all I could recover was, that I had thought myself in an
> ancient castle (a very natural dream for a head like mine filled
> with Gothic story) and that on the uppermost bannister of a great

[1] Ernest Jones, *On the Nightmare* (London: Liveright, 1971).

staircase I saw a gigantic hand in armour. In the evening I sat down, and began to write, without knowing in the least what I intended to say or relate. The work grew on my hands and I grew so fond of it that one evening, I wrote from the time I had drunk my tea, about six o'clock, till half an hour after one in the morning, when my hands and fingers were so weary that I could not hold the pen to finish the sentence.[2]

The assertion that a given horror story originated as a dream or nightmare occurs often enough that one begins to suspect that it is something akin to invoking a muse (or an incubus or succubus, as the case may be). Mary Shelley's *Frankenstein*, Bram Stoker's *Dracula* and Henry James' "The Jolly Corner" are all attributed to fitful sleep as is much of Robert Lewis Stevenson's output—notably *Dr. Jekyll and Mr. Hyde*.[3] In what sense these tales were caused by nightmares or modeled on dreams is less important than the fact that the nightmare is a culturally established framework for presenting and understanding the horror genre. And this makes the resort to psychoanalysis unavoidable.

A central concept in Jones' treatment of the imagery of nightmare is conflict. The products of the dreamwork are often simultaneously attractive and repellent insofar as they function to enunciate both a wish and its inhibition. Jones writes

> The reason why the object seen in a Nightmare is frightful or hideous is simply that the representation of the underlying wish is not permitted in its naked form so that the dream is a compromise of the wish on the one hand and on the other of the intense fear belonging to the inhibition.[4]

The notion of the conflict between attraction and repulsion is particularly useful in considering the horror film. Too often, writing about this genre only emphasizes one side of the imagery. Many journalists will single-mindedly underscore only the repellent aspects of a horror film—rejecting it as disgusting, indecent and foul. Yet this tack fails to offer any account of why people are interested in seeing such exercises.

On the other hand, defenders of the genre or of a specific example of the

---

[2] From a letter by H. Walpole, as quoted in an introduction by W. S. Lewis, to Horace Walpole's *The Castle of Otranto* (London: Oxford Univ. Press, 1964), p. ix.

[3] M. Katan claims that *The Turn of the Screw* also originated in a nightmare. See "A Causerie on Henry James's *The Turn of the Screw*" in *Psychoanalytic Study of the Child* 17:473-93, 1962.

[4] Jones, p. 78.

genre will often indulge in allegorical readings that render their subjects wholly appealing and that do not acknowledge their repellent aspects. Thus, we are told that Frankenstein is really an existential parable about man thrown-into-the-world, an "isolated sufferer."[5] But if *Frankenstein* is part *Nausea*, it is also nauseating. Where in the allegorical formulation can we find an explanation for the purpose of the unsettling effect of the charnel house imagery? The dangers of this allegorizing/valorizing tendency can be seen in some of the work of Robin Wood, the most vigorous champion of the contemporary horror film. About *Sisters*, he writes

> *Sisters* analyzes the ways in which women are oppressed within patriarchal society on two levels which one can define as professional (Grace) and the psychosexual (Danielle/Dominique).[6]

One wants to say "perhaps but. . . . " Specifically, what about the unnerving, gory murders and the brackish, fecal bond that links the Siamese twins? Horror films cannot be construed as completely repelling or completely appealing. Either outlook denies something essential to the form, Jones' use of the concept of conflict in the nightmare to illuminate the symbolic portent of the monsters of superstition, therefore, suggests a direction of research into the study of the horror film that accords with the genre's unique combination of repulsion and delight.

As a hardline Freudian, Jones suffers from one important liability; he overemphasizes the degree to which incestuous desires shape the conflicts in the nightmare (and, by extension, in the formation of fantastic beings) and he claims that nightmares always relate to the sexual act.[7] As John Mack has argued, this perspective is too narrow;

> the analysis of nightmares regularly leads us to the earliest, most

[5] Frank McConnell, *Spoken Seen* (Baltimore: Johns Hopkins U. Press, 1975), p. 76.

[6] Robin Wood, "Sisters," in *American Nightmare* (Toronto: Festival of Festivals Publication, 1979), p. 60.

In his analyses of horror films, Wood has cited the concept of ambivalence. Specifically, he uses this idea to characterize the situation in which audiences regard monsters as heroes. And, for Wood, of course, monsters are heroes because they represent what society, in the name of normality, unconscionably represses. This use of the concept of ambivalence, a predictable outcome of Wood's particular *parti pris*, differs from the idea of conflict presented in this paper. I am not saying that monsters are heroes *despite* their repugnant ("abnormal") packaging but that monsters are composed of mixtures of attractive *and* repelling attributes. The rudimentary task of criticism is not to find the hero *within* the monster but to discover *both* the positive and negative elements that make up the symbolic biology of such creatures.

[7] Jones, p. 79.

profound, and inescapable anxieties and conflicts to which human beings are subject: those involving destructive aggression, castration, separation and abandonment, devouring and being devoured, and fear regarding loss of identity and fusion with the mother.[8]

Thus, modifying Jones, we will study the nightmare conflicts embodied in the horror film as having broader reference than simply sexuality.

Our starting hypothesis is that horror film imagery, like that of the nightmare, incarnates archaic, conflicting impulses. Furthermore, this assumption orients inquiry, leading us to review horror film imagery with an eye to separating out thematic strands that represent opposing attitudes. To clarify what is involved in this sort of analysis, an example is in order.

When *The Exorcist* first opened, responses to it were extreme. It was denounced as a new cultural low at the same time that extra theaters had to be found in New York, Los Angeles and other cities to accommodate the overflow crowds. The imagery of the film touched deep chords in our national psyche. The spectacle of possession addressed and reflected profound fears and desires never before explored in film. The basic infectious terror in the film is that personal identity is a frail thing, easily lost. Linda Blair's Regan, with her "tsks" and her "ahs," is a model of middle-class domesticity, a vapid mask quickly engulfed by repressed powers. The character is not just another evil child in the tradition of *The Bad Seed*. It is an expression of the fear that beneath the self we present to others are forces that can erupt to obliterate every vestige of self-control and personal identity.

In *The Exorcist*, the possibility of the loss of self is greeted with both terror and glee. The fear of losing self-control is great, but the manner in which that loss is manifested is attractive. Once possessed, Regan's new powers, exhibited in hysterical displays of cinematic pyrotechnics, act out the imagery of infantile beliefs in the omnipotence of the will. Each grisly scene is a celebration of infantile rage. Regan's anger cracks doors and ceilings and levitates beds. And she can deck a full-grown man with the flick of a wrist. The audience is aghast at her loss of self-control, which begins fittingly enough with her urinating on the living room rug, but at the same time its archaic beliefs in the metaphysical prowess of the emotions are cinematically confirmed. Thought is given direct causal efficacy. Regan's feelings know no bounds; they pour out of her, tearing her own flesh apart with their intensity and hurling people and furniture in every direction. Part of the legacy of *The Exorcist* to its successors—like *Carrie*, *The Fury*, and *Patrick*, to name but a few titles in this rampant subgenre—is the fascination with telekinesis, which is nothing but a cinematic metaphor of the unlimited power of repressed rage.

[8] John Mack, *Nightmares and Human Conflict* (Boston: Little Brown, 1970).

The audience is both drawn to and repelled by it—we recognize such rage in ourselves and superstitiously fear its emergence, while simultaneously we are pleased when we see a demonstration, albeit fictive, of the power of that rage.[9]

Christopher Lasch has argued that the neurotic personality of our time vacillates between fantasies of self-loathing and infantile delusions of grandeur.[10] The strength of *The Exorcist* is that it captures this oscillation cinematically. Regan, through the machinations of Satan, is the epitome of self-hatred and self-degredation—a filthy thing, festering in its bed, befoulling itself, with fetid breath, full of scabs, dirty hair and a complexion that makes her look like a pile of old newspapers.

The origins of this self-hatred imagery is connected with sexual themes. Regan's sudden concupiscence corresponds with a birthday, presumably her thirteenth. There are all sorts of allusions to masturbation: not only does Regan misuse the crucifix, splattering her thighs with blood in an act symbolic of both loss of virginity and menstruation, but later her hands are bound (one enshrined method for stopping "self-abuse") and her skin goes bad (as we were all warned it would). Turning the head 360 degrees also has sexual connotations; in theology, it is described as a technique Satan uses to sodomize witches. Regan incarnates images of worthlessness, of being virtually trash, in a context laden with sex and self-laceration. But the moments of self-degradation give way to images that express delusions of grandeur as she rocks the house in storms of rage. She embodies moods of guilt and rebellion, of self-loathing and omnipotence that speak to the Narcissus in each of us.

The fantastic beings of horror films can be seen as symbolic formations that organize conflicting themes into figures that are simultaneously attractive and repulsive. Two major symbolic structures appear most prominent in this regard: fusion, in which the conflicting themes are yoked together in one, spatio-temporally unified figure; and fission, in which the conflicting themes are distributed—over space or time—among more than one figure.

Dracula, one of the classic film monsters, falls into the category of fusion. In order to identify the symbolic import of this figure we can begin with Jones' account of vampires—since Dracula is a vampire—but we must also

[9] Rage is always an important component in horror films. Nevertheless, in the present horror cycle—given its fascination with telekinesis and omnipotent, Satanic children (and including the "psychoplasmic" imagery of *The Brood*)—rage has an unparalleled salience. In the America of Nixon, Ford and Carter, the recurring cine-fantasy seems to be of pent-up, channel-less anger, welling-up, exploding, overwhelming everything.

[10] Christopher Lasch, *The Culture of Narcissism* (New York: Norton, 1979). Both Lasch's and my concepts of narcissism are roughly based on Otto Kernberg, *Borderline Conditions and Pathological Narcissism* (New York: Jason Aronson, 1975).

amplify that account since Dracula is a very special vampire. According to Jones, the vampires of superstition have two fundamental constituent attributes: revenance and blood sucking. The mythic, as opposed to movie, vampire first visits its relatives. For Jones, this stands for the relatives' longing for the loved one to return from the dead. But the figure is charged with terror. What is fearful is blood sucking, which Jones associates with seduction. In short, the desire for an incestuous encounter with the dead relative is transformed, through a form of denial, into an assault—attraction and love metamorphose into repulsion and sadism. At the same time, via projection, the living portray themselves as passive victims, imbuing the dead with a dimension of active agency that permits pleasure without blame. Lastly, Jones not only connects blood sucking with the exhausting embrace of the incubus but with a regressive mixture of sucking and biting characteristic of the oral stage of psychosexual development. By negation—the transformation of love to hate—by projection—through which the desired dead become active, and the desiring living passive—and by regression—from genital to oral sexuality—the vampire legend gratifies incestuous and necrophiliac desires by amalgamating them in a fearsome iconography.

The vampire of lore and the Dracula figure of stage and screen have several points of tangency, but Dracula also has a number of distinctive attributes. Of necessity, Dracula is Count Dracula. He is an aristocrat; his bearing is noble; and, of course, through hypnosis, he is a paradigmatic authority figure. He is commanding in both senses of the word. Above all, Dracula demands *obedience* of his minions and mistresses. He is extremely old—associated with *ancient* castles—and possessed of incontestable strength. Dracula cannot be overcome by force—he can only be outsmarted or outmaneuvered; humans are typically described as puny in comparison to him. At times, Dracula is invested with omniscience, observing from afar the measures taken against him. He also hordes women and is a harem master. In brief, Dracula is a bad father figure, often balanced off against Van Helsing who defends virgins against the seemingly younger, more vibrant Count.[11] The phallic symbolism of Dracula is hard to miss—he is aged, buried in a filthy place, impure, powerful and aggressive.

The contrast with Van Helsing immediately suggests another cluster of Dracula's attributes. He does appear the younger of the two specifically because he represents the rebellious son at the same time that he is the violent father. This identification is achieved by means of the Satanic imagery that

---

[11]This opposition is encapsulated perfectly in a shot in Browning's *Dracula*. The camera is set up behind the parlous Count in such a way that he appears enormous while in the background a seemingly much smaller Van Helsing stands in front of the virgin Dracula is menacing.

contributes to Dracula's persona. Dracula is the Devil—one film in fact refers to him in its title as the "Prince of Darkness." With few exceptions, Dracula is depicted as eternally uncontrite, bent on luring hapless souls. Most importantly, Dracula is a modern devil which means, above everything else, that he is a rival to God.[12] Religiously, Dracula is presented as a force of unmitigated evil. Dramatically, this is translated into a quantum of awesome will or will-fulness, often flexed in those mental duels with Van Helsing. Dracula, in part, exists as a rival to the father, as a figure of defiance and rebellion, fulfilling the oedipal wish via a hero of Miltonic proclivities. The Dracula image, then, is a fusion of conflicting attributes of the bad (primal) father and the rebel-lius son that is simultaneously appealing and forbidding because of the way it conjoins different dimensions of the oedipal fantasy.

The fusion of conflicting tendencies in the figure of the monster in horror films has the dream process of condensation as its approximate psychic proto-type. In analysing the symbolic meaning of these fusion figures our task is to individuate the conflicting themes that constitute the creature. Like Dracula, the Frankenstein monster is a fusion figure, one that is quite literally a com-posite. Mary Shelley first dreamt of the creature at a time in her life fraught with tragedies connected with childbirth.[13] Victor Frankenstein's creation—his "hideous progeny"—is a gruesome parody of birth; indeed, Shelley's description of the creature's appearance bears passing correspondences to that of newborn—its waxen skin, misshapen head and touch of jaundice. James Whale's *Frankenstein* also emphasizes the association of the monster with a child; its walk is unsteady and halting, its head is outsized and its eyes sleepy. And in the film, though not in the novel, the creature's basic cognitive skills are barely developed; it is mystified by fire and has difficulty differentiating between little girls and flowers. The monster in one respect is a child and its creation is a birth that is presented as ghastly. At the same time, the monster is made of waste, of dead things, in "Frankenstein's workshop of filthy crea-tion." The excremental reference is hardly disguised. The association of the creature with waste implies that, in part, the story is underwritten by the infantile confusion over the processes of elimination and reproduction. The

[12] Freud—in "A Neurosis of Demonical Possession in the Seventeenth Century"—identifies the Devil as a father substitute, but I think that Jones—in his chapter "The Devil"—is more correct when he interprets the figure as a composite of aspects of both father and son. Dracula inherits a great many of the features that Jones isolates in the Devil.

[13] Ellen Moers, *Literary Women* (Garden City, N.Y.: Anchor, 1977), pp. 140-51.

The novel *Frankenstein* may also support a feminist, autobiographical interpreta-tion. The monster—seen as standing for Mary Shelley—is an intelligent, (autodidactically) educated individual, ultimately excluded from the circle of *man*kind (Godwin? Shelley? Byron?) on the basis of *biological difference*.

monster is reviled as heinous and as unwholesome filth, rejected by its creator
—its father—perhaps in a way that reorchestrated Mary Shelley's feelings of
rejection by her father William Godwin.

But these images of loathesomeness are fused with opposite qualities.
In the film myth, the monster is all but omnipotent (it can function as
a sparring partner for Godzilla), indomitable and, for all intents and purposes, immortal (perhaps partly for the intent and purpose of sequels).
It is both helpless and powerful, worthless and godlike. Its rejection spurs
rampaging vengeance, combining fury and strength in infantile orgies of
rage and destruction. Interestingly, in the novel, this ire is directed against
Victor Frankenstein's family. And even in Whale's 1931 version of the
myth the monster's definition as outside (excluded from a place in) the
family is maintained in a number of ways: the killing of Maria; the juxta-
position of the monster's wandering over the countryside with wedding
preparations; and the opposition of Frankenstein's preoccupation with
affairs centered around the monster to the interest of propagating an heir
to the family barony. The emotional logic of the tale proceeds from the
initial loathesomeness of the monster, which triggers its rejection, which
causes the monster to explode in omnipotent rage over its alienation from
the family, which, in turn, confirms the earlier intimation of "badness,"
thereby justifying the parental rejection.[14] This scenario, moreover, is predi-
cated on the inherently conflicting tendencies—of being waste and being
god—that are condensed in the creature from the start. It is, therefore,
a necessary condition for the success of the tale that the creature be repellent.

One method for composing fantastic beings is fusion. On the visual level,
this often entails the construction of creatures that transgress categorical
distinctions such as inside/outside, insect/human, flesh/machine, etc.[15]
The particular affective significance of these admixtures depends to a large
extent on the specific narrative context in which they are embedded. But
apart from fusion, another means for articulating emotional conflicts in
horror films is fission. That is, conflicts concerning sexuality, identity,
aggressiveness, etc. can be mapped over different entities—each standing
for a different facet of conflict—which are nevertheless linked by some
magical, supernatural or sci-fi process. The type of creatures that I have
in mind here include *doppelgängers*, alter-egos, and werewolves.

[14]The use of mythic types of fantasies to justify parental behavior is discussed in
Dorothy Block, *So the Witch Won't Eat Me* (Boston: Houghton Mifflin Co., 1978).
[15]The slave creatures in *This Island Earth* are examples of the fusion of inside/out-
side and insect/human while the last apparition of the monster in *Alien*—with its spring-
mounted iron maw—is an example of the fusion of flesh and machine, as is the alien's
stranded spaceship.

Fission has two major modes in the horror film.[16] The first distributes the conflict over space through the creation of doubles, e.g., *The Portrait of Dorian Gray*, *The Student of Prague* and *Warning Shadows*. Structurally, what is involved in spatial fission is a process of multiplication, i.e., a character or set of characters is multiplied into one or more new facets each standing for another aspect of the self, generally one that is either hidden, ignored, repressed or denied by the character who has been cloned. These examples each employ some mechanism of reflection—a portrait, a mirror, shadows—as the pretext for doubling. But this sort of fission figure can appear without such devices. In *I Married a Monster from Outer Space*, a young bride begins to suspect that her new husband is not quite himself. Somehow he's different than the man she used to date. And, she's quite right. Her boyfriend was kidnapped by invaders from outer space on his way back from a bachelor party and was replaced by an alien. This double, however, initially lacks feelings—the essential characteristic of being human in 50s sci-fi films—and his bride intuits this. This basic story—sci-fi elements aside—resembles a very specific paranoid delusion called Capgras syndrome. The delusion involves the patient's belief that his or her parents, lovers, etc. have become minatory *doppelgängers*. This enables the patient to deny his fear or hatred of a loved one by splitting the loved one in half, creating a bad version (the invader) and a good one (the victim). The new relation of marriage in *I Married a Monster.* . . . appears to engender a conflict, perhaps over sexuality, in the wife that is expressed through the fission figure.[17] Splitting as a psychic trope of denial is the root prototype for spatial fission in the horror film, organizing conflict through the multiplication of characters.

Fission occurs in horror films not only in terms of multiplication but also in terms of division. That is, a character can be divided in time as well as multiplied in space. *Dr. Jekyll and Mr. Hyde* and the various werewolves, cat people, gorgons and other changelings of the genre are immediate examples. In the horror film, temporal fission—usually marked by shape changing—is often self-consciously concerned with repression. In *Curse of the Werewolf* one shot shows the prospective monster behind the bars of a wine cellar window holding a bottle; it is an icon of restrained delirium. The traditional

[16]Robert Rogers, *A Psychoanalytic Study of the Double in Literature* (Detroit: Wayne State University Press, 1970).

[17]*I Married a Monster from Outer Space* belongs to a subgenre of space-possession films including *Invasion of the Body Snatchers*, *It Conquered the World*, *They Came from Beyond Space*, *Creation of the Humanoids*, *Man from Planet X*, *Invaders from Mars*, *Phantom from Space*, *It Came from Outer Space*, *Killers from Space*, etc. Depending on the specific context of the film, the possessed earthlings in these films can be examples of either spatial or temporal fission. For an interpretation of *Invasion of the Body Snatchers*, see my "You're Next" in *The Soho Weekly News*, Dec. 21, 1978.

conflict in these films is sexuality. Stevenson's *Jekyll and Hyde* is altered in screen variants so that the central theme of Hyde's brutality—which I think is connected to an allegory against alcoholism in the text—becomes a preoccupation with lechery.[18] Often changeling films, like *The Werewolf of London* or *The Cat People*, eventuate in the monster attacking its lover, suggesting that this subgenre begins in infantile confusions over sexuality and aggression. The imagery of werewolf films also has been associated with conflicts connected with the bodily changes of puberty and adolescence:[19] unprecedented hair spreads over the body, accompanied by uncontrollable, vaguely understood urges leading to puzzlement and even to fear of madness. This imagery becomes especially compelling in *The Wolfman*, where the tension between father and son mounts through anger and tyranny until at last the father beats the son to death with a silver cane in a paroxysm of oedipal anxiety.[20]

Fusion and fission generate a large number of the symbolic biologies of horror films, but not all. Magnification of power or size—e.g., giant insects (and other exaggerated animalcules)—is another mode of symbol formation. Often magnification takes a particular phobia as its subject and, in general, much of this imagery seems comprehensible in terms of Freud's observation that "the majority of phobias ... are traceable to such a fear on the ego's part of the demands of the libido."[21]

Giant insects are a case in point. The giant spider, for instance, appeared in silent film in John Barrymore's *Jekyll and Hyde* as an explicit symbol of desire. Perhaps insects, especially spiders, can perform this role not only

[18] Aside from the Jekyll and Hyde split, movie versions of the Stevenson story, as early as the Barrymore variant, also add the opposition between Muriel and Ivy, the mother and the whore. From the matrix of Jekyll/Hyde and Muriel/Ivy, the core of the film story can be generated through a simple set of combinations. Scenes of Jekyll with Muriel are followed by ones of Jekyll with Ivy followed by Hyde with Ivy, then Jekyll with Ivy and then Hyde with Muriel.

[19] Daniel Dervin, "The Primal Scene and the Technology of Perception in Theater and Film," in *Psychoanalytic Review*, 62, no. 2, (1975), 278.

[20] In regard to shape changing figures, like werewolves, it is important to note that metamorphosis in and of itself does not indicate a fission figure. Consider vampires; they readily shed human form to become bats and wolves. Yet, vampires are not fission figures. They are allotropic, varying their physical properties while remaining the same dirity in substance. But with werewolves the change in shape betokens a change in its nature.

Another, though connected, difference between werewolves and vampires hinges on the issue of will. Werewolves—most often futilely—resist their fate while vampires, especially Dracula, prefer theirs. This is a crucial reason for having the two different myths.

[21] Sigmund Freud, *The Problem of Anxiety* (New York: Norton, 1963), p. 39.

because of their resemblance to hands—the hairy hands of masturbation—but also because of their cultural association with impurity.[22] At the same time, their identification as poisonous—indeed stinging—and predatory—devouring— can be mobilized to express anxious fantasies over sexuality. Like giant reptiles, giant insects are often encountered in two specific contexts in horror films. They inhabit negative paradises—jungles and lost worlds—that unaware humans happen into, not to find Edenic milk and honey but the gnashing teeth or mandibles of oral regression. Or, giant insects or reptiles are slumbering potentials of nature released or awakened by physical or chemical altecations caused by human experiments in areas of knowledge best left to the gods. Here, the predominant metaphor is that these creatures or forces have been unfettered or unleashed, suggesting their close connection with erotic impulses. Like the fusion and fission figures of horror films, these nightmares are also explicable as effigies of deep-seated, archaic conflicts.

So far I have dwelt on the symbolic composition of the monsters in horror films, extrapolating from the framework set out by Jones in *On the Nightmare* in the hope of beginning a crude approximation of a taxonomy. But before concluding, it is worthwhile to consider briefly the relevance of archaic conflicts of the sort already discussed to the themes repeated again and again in the basic plot structures of the horror film.[23]

---

[22] The spider, of course, has polyvalent associations. It figures importantly as a phobic object because of its ruthlessness—i.e., its use of a trap—its oral sadism—it sucks its prey—and, for men, because of its sexual practices—some female spiders feast upon their mates. In much of the psychoanalytic literature the spider is correlated with the oral, sadistic mother; its body is associated with the vagina; its legs are sometimes glossed as the fantasized penis that the mother is believed to possess. Some references concerning spider imagery include: Karl Abraham, "The Spider as a Dream Symbol" in *Selected Papers*, trans. Douglas Bryan and Alix Strachey (London: Hogarth Press, 1927); Ralph Little, "Oral Agression in Spider Legends," *American Imago* 23: 169-80, 1966; R. Little, "Umbilical Cord Symbolism of the Spider's Dropline," *Psychoanalytic Quarterly*; Richard Sterba, "On spiders, hanging and oral sadism" *American Imago* 7:21-28. There is also an influential reading of "Little Miss Muffet. . . ." in Ella Freeman Sharpe, "Cautionary Tales," *International Journal of Psychoanalysis* 24:41-45. In the preceding text I have also connected spiders to masturbation. I have done this not simply because spiders somewhat resemble hands but because that resemblance itself is part of our literary culture. Recall the legend of Arachne who was punished by Minerva by being reduced to a hand which becomes a spider. Thomas Bulfinch writes that Minerva sprinkled Arachne "with the juices of aconite, and immediately her hair came off and ears likewise. Her form shrank up, and her head grew smaller yet; her fingers cleaved to her side and served for legs. All the rest of her body, out of which she spins her thread, often hanging suspended from it, in the same attitude as when Minerva touched her and transformed her into a spider." Thomas Bulfinch, *Mythology* (New York: Dell Publishing Co., 1959), p. 93.

[23] Some typical science fiction plots are outlined in the opening of Susan Sontag's

Perhaps the most serviceable narrative armature in the horror film genre is what I call the Discovery Plot. It is used in *Dracula*, *The Exorcist*, *Jaws I & II*, *It Came From Outer Space*, *Curse of the Demon*, *Close Encounters of the Third Kind*, *It Came From Beneath the Sea*, and myriad other films. It has four essential movements. The first is onset: the monster's presence is established, e.g., by an attack, as in *Jaws*. Next, the monster's existence is discovered by an individual or a group, but for one reason or another its existence, or the nature of the threat it actually poses is not acknowledged by the powers that be. "There are no such things as vampires" the police chief might say at this point. Discovery, therefore, flows into the next plot movement which is confirmation. The discoverers or believers must convince some other group of the existence and proportions of mortal danger at hand. Often this section of the plot is the most elaborate, and suspenseful. As the UN refuses to accept the reality of the onslaught of killer bees or invaders from Mars, precious time is lost, during which the creature or creatures often gain power and advantage. This interlude also allows for a great deal of discussion about the encroaching monster, and this talk about its invulnerability, its scarcely imaginable strength, and its nasty habits endows the off-screen beast with the qualities that prime the audience's fearful anticipation. Language is one of the most effective ingredients in a horror film and I would guess that the genre's primary success in sound film rather than silent film has less to do with the absence of sound effects in the silents than with the presence of all that dialogue about the unseen monster in the talkies.

After the hesitations of confirmation, the Discovery Plot culminates in confrontation. Mankind meets its monster, most often winning the debacle, but on occasion, like the remake of *Invasion of the Body Snatchers*, losing. What is particularly of interest in this plot structure is the tension caused by the delay between discovery and confirmation. Thematically it involves the audience not only in the drama of proof but also in the play between

---

"The Imagination of Disaster" in *Film Theory and Criticism* (New York: Oxford U. Press, 1979). Sontag's first model plot is like the Discovery Plot described in this paper. However, the problem with Sontag's variant is that she does not give enough emphasis to the drama of proving the existence of the monster over skeptical objections. This, I feel is the crux of most horror/sci-fi films of the Discovery Plot variety.

The benefit derived by producing abstract idealizations of horror film plots is that they enable us to zero-in on the particular qualities of specific horror films in terms of their adaptation of the basic plot. The original (*cum* framing story) version of *Invasion of the Body Snatchers* is intensely paranoid. We can see why when we catalogue it as an imperfect instance of the Discovery Plot. It foregoes the issue of onset entirely and only implies the final confrontation, spending all of its estimable energies on the matter of discovery and confirmation.

knowing and not knowing,[24] between acknowledgment versus nonacknowledgment, that has the growing awareness of sexuality in the adolescent as its archetype. This conflict can become very pronounced when the gainsayers in question—generals, police chiefs, scientists, heads of institutions, etc.—are obviously parental authority figures.

Another important plot structure is that of the Overreacher. *Frankenstein*, *Jekyll and Hyde* and *Man with the X-Ray Eyes* are all examples of this approach. Whereas the Discovery Plot often stresses the short-sightedness of science, the Overreacher Plot criticizes science's will to knowledge. The Overreacher Plot has four basic movements. The first comprises the preparation for the experiment, generally including a philosophical, popular-mechanics explanation, or debate about the experiment's motivation. The overreacher himself (usually Dr. Soandso) can become quite megalomaniacal here, a quality commented upon, for instance, by the dizzingly vertical laboratory sets in *Frankenstein* and *Bride of Frankenstein*. Next comes the experiment itself, whose partial success allows for some more megalomania. But the experiment goes awry, leading to the destruction of innocent victims and/or to damage or threat to the experimenter or his loved ones. At this point, some overreachers renounce their blasphemy; the ones who don't are mad scientists. Finally, there is a confrontation with the monster, generally in the penultimate scene of the film.

The Overreacher Plot can be combined with the Discovery Plot by making the overreacher and/or his experiments the object of discovery and confirmation. This yields a plot with seven movements—onset, discovery, confirmation, preparation for the experiment, experimentation, untoward consequences, and confrontation. (Confirmation as well as discovery may come after or between the next three movements in this structure.) But the basic Overreacher Plot differs thematically from the Discovery Plot insofar as the conflicts central to the Overreacher Plot reside in fantasies of omniscience, omnipotence and control. The plot eventually cautions

[24] The theme of knowing/not knowing is important to horror films along many different dimensions. In terms of cinematic technique, it can influence the director's choice of formal strategies. For example, in recent horror films, there is a great deal of use of what I call unassigned camera movement in the context of stories about demons, ghosts and other unseen but all-seeing monsters. In *The Changeling*, the camera begins to move around George C. Scott in his study. It is not supplying new narrative information nor is its movement explicitly correlated within the scene to any specific character. It has no assignment either in terms of narrative or characterological function. But it does call attention to itself. The audience sees it. And the audience cannot help postulating that the camera movement *might* represent the presence of some unseen, supernatural force that is observing Scott for devilish purposes. The audience cannot know this for sure; but the point of the camera movement is to provoke the spectator into a state of uncertainty in which he/she shifts between knowing and not knowing.

against these impulses, but not until it gratifies them with partial success and a strong dose of theatrical panache.

In suggesting that the plot structures and fantastic beings of the horror film correlate with nightmares in terms of presenting archaic conflicts composed of concurrently attractive and repulsive materials, I do not mean to claim that horror films are nightmares. Structurally, horror films are far more rationally ordered than nightmares, even in extremely disjunctive and dreamlike experiments like *Phantasm*. Moreover, phenomenologically, horror film buffs do not believe that they are literally the victims of the mayhem they witness whereas a dreamer can quite often become a participant and a victim in his/her dream. We can and do seek out horror films for pleasure, while someone who looked forward to a nightmare would be a rare bird indeed. Nevertheless, there do seem to be enough thematic and symbolic correspondences between nightmare and horror to indicate the distant genesis of horror motifs in nightmare as well as significant similarities between the two phenomena. Granted, these motifs become highly stylized on the screen. Yet, for some, the horror film may release some part of the tensions that would otherwise eruct in nightmares. Perhaps we can say that the aforesaid horror film fans go to the movies (in the afternoon) perchance to sleep (at night).

School of Visual Arts, N.Y.

COCTEAU, CAUCHEMAR, CINEMA

Lindley Hanlon

Extending the analogy between the individual and the epoch, one can say that a literary trend is to its time what a dream is to man: an activity propelled by an unconscious design, which rebels against limits imposed by the conscience only in order to enlarge the scope of the conscience and the literature that inspires it. . . . [Literature drawing on the orphic tradition] is diametrically opposed to realism. . . . These works therefore take advantage of everything in the dream that is undefined, ambiguous, in the sense that, just as it is difficult to find out whether the content of a dream is desired or feared, passionately longed for or violently recoiled from.

In tracing the place of the myth of Orpheus in the French literary tradition of the last one hundred years, Eva Kushner suggests three periods which reflect increasingly pessimistic visions of man's power and potential. The first period encompasses the writers of the 1885 generation (Grandmougin, Delorme, de Launay, Mallarmé) for whom Orphée was an inspiration, a guide whose heroic actions represented the first triumph of the free spirit over the forces of fate, over the Bacchantes.[1] For this pre-World War I visionary company, faith in man, goodness, and progress seemed to thrive on the most optimistic images of a dreamlike world. However, the writers of the post-World War I world saw Orphée as more limited, stressing his role as a poet and treating art as a religion. This generation (including Gide, Apollinaire, Valéry, Segalen, Maurras, Barzun) demonstrated the increasingly psychological concerns of French thought freed of illusions, what she terms "a scrupulously sincere analysis of the self, the ego."[2] Gide, she points out, idealizes Orphée as the singer whose marvelous influence alone can put an

---

[1] Eva Kushner, *Le Mythe d'Orphée dans la littérature française contemporaine* (Paris: A. G. Nizet Publishers, 1961), p. 21.

[2] Kushner, p. 22.

end to the eternal torments of the Shadows of Hell.[3] The world of Hell, which is the world of nightmares, threatens to erupt and consume, but at this stage can be tamed.

The third period, including Dada and surrealism, reveals the influence of Freud and provides yet another revision of the myth which stresses the importance of the mysterious figure of Eurydice.[4] Orphée and Eurydice come to represent two poles: Orphée embodies truth and spirit and is tempted to the realm of Hell or instinct by Eurydice. The myth no longer affirms the grandeur of man. This generation suggests that Orphée (unconsciously) wished to be rid of his wife, who for him is the obsessive image of the Mother, the obstacle to the free development of Man. Woman becomes a symbol of Death and a perpetual menace to the creative spirit of Orphée. Or, Orphée becomes a man divided against himself in whom light and darkness cohabit.[5] It is to this generation that Cocteau belongs. Cocteau embroiders strands of the nightmare into the Orphic tale by inventing a tempting, Vampirish figure of Death—the very opposite of loving, domestic Eurydice.

Yet, as Kushner herself points out, the writers who chose to resurrect this classical myth were a company of solitaries: Victor Segalen, Cocteau, Anouilh, Pierre Jean Jouve, and Pierre Emmanuel. The works of Baudelaire, Sade, Lautréamont, and Rimbaud constitute a broader tradition in the history of French literature which prefigures the Surrealists' interest in eroticism and hellish underworlds. Many of these writers, and many of the Symbolist painters as well, share a passionate urge to enter, decipher, and depict a world of nightmares. For Cocteau, who rejected and was rejected by the Surrealists, the key to that world was opium during the day, his dreams at night. A great number of his works, but most especially his films, focus on the mirror-thin borderline between reality and dream, Earth and Hell, love and hate, life and death, banality and art which the poet strives to transgress.

From 1924-25 Cocteau was an opium addict, later a steady user, and spent much of his time in and out of sanitoriums where, when off opium, he transposed his opium visions.[6] At Villefranche he would smoke opium and spend his days sitting in front of the mirror "watching himself die."[7] Mirrors were the membrane "where Death comes and goes."[8] Opium for Cocteau was a transporting medium which, by causing the death of the exterior, allowed the interior to flourish. He said in *Secrets of a Professional* that "Life and death

[3] Kushner, p. 22.
[4] Kushner, p. 23.
[5] Kushner, p. 25.
[6] Arthur Evans, *Jean Cocteau and His Films of Orphic Identity* (Philadelphia: Art Alliance Press, 1977), pp. 38-39.
[7] Jean Cocteau quoted in Evans, p. 39.
[8] Cocteau quoted in Evans, p. 44.

are as far apart from one another as heads and tails of a coin, but opium goes through the coin."[9] In his films the mirror recurs again and again as the passageway between the worlds of Life and Death, between reality and dream.

In an interview with André Fraigneau he attributes the same power to dreams:

> I live intensely only in dreams. My dreams are detailed, terribly realistic. They involve me in innumerable adventures, in contact with places and people who do not exist in a waking state and who are made up for me by the phenomenon of dreaming down to the smallest word. I try to rub it all out in the morning, dreading to confuse the two worlds and add the incomprehensible to the incomprehensible.
>
> Naturally enough, I have no fear of death which seems to me a haven.[10]

In the same interview he confesses that film work becomes for him a similar addiction. He makes his first film in 1930, when he has given up opium.

> ... that [film] work, as I was saying, is so compact and takes one so far away from the world and its ways that it comes to resemble dreaming in that the people and the happenings of the film become the only things that matter.[11]

On the other side of addiction or obsession Cocteau feared the pull of the void; he preferred the somnambulist's living death to the banality and emptiness of the mundane. Possession is the *sine qua non* of the poet. "Unless I happen to become the vehicle of an unknown force, which I then clumsily help to take shape, I cannot read, or write, or even think."[12]

Death then is Cocteau's passion, and it is from his imaginings and dreams of that world that he claims that the figures and decor of certain of his plays and films are fabricated. He often spoke of Death as an Angel, who, like the poet, shuttles back and forth between life and death, between the visible and the invisible.[13] Further elaborating the rituals of his writing,

---

[9] Cocteau quoted in Evans, p. 36.

[10] André Fraigneau, *Cocteau on Film: Conversations with Jean Cocteau* (New York: Dover, 1972), pp. 25-26.

[11] Cocteau in Fraigneau, p. 26.

[12] Cocteau in Fraigneau, pp. 22-23.

[13] Evans, p. 32.

he spoke of five successive deaths which were required to transfer his poetry from his self to the world: [14]

1. the death of "opium consciousness."
2. the death of traditional art forms.
3. the death of the poet during actual creation.
4. the death of the purity of the original vision as it is adapted and transformed.
5. the death of the poet's presence with the finished work of art.

Cocteau felt that he died after each poetic passage, and became another "I." [15] Narcissus was as frequent a visitor to the world of his works as Orpheus.

Cocteau's obsession with death was certainly a result of his acquaintance with death at an early age, an acquaintance that returned all too often. His father committed suicide when Cocteau was nine years old in 1898. His love of Raymond Radiguet ended with his death at age twenty in 1923, a grief eased with the help of opium. In 1944 he lost two other close friends at the hands of the Germans: Max Jacob at the Drancy camp; Jean Desbordes tortured by the Gestapo; *La Belle et la Bête* opened in 1946. [16] His mother died before he began work on the film *Orphée*; his sister died before his creation of *Le Testament d'Orphée*. His fascination with the population of the world of death suggests his deep desire to join these lost loves there. Opium and art were his ways of entering that world.

Is this world of opium and dreams a nightmare world for Cocteau? Although the figures who populate that world, from his necessarily unverifiable accounts, resemble those of classical nightmares, Cocteau claims an inverted relationship of pleasure to that world, dreading, fearing, avoiding the ordinariness of the everyday world of light. Rather than using writing and filming to tame those worlds, he needed to keep those worlds alive and vivid as his primary source of imagery. John E. Mack has claimed in *Nightmares and Human Conflict* that creativity and madness are alternatives. [17] Although I think it would be very difficult to psychoanalyse Cocteau at this distance from the realm of Death to which he was finally permanently delivered in 1963, it certainly seems that creativity and a kind of madness were divided

[14] Evans, p. 49.

[15] Evans, p. 52.

[16] Jacques Brosse, *Jean Cocteau: Orphée*, Extraits de la tragédie d'*Orphée* ainsi que des films *Orphée* et *Le Testament d'Orphée*. (Paris: Bordas, 1973), pp. 6-9.

[17] John E. Mack, *Nightmares and Human Conflict* (Boston: Houghton Mifflin Company, 1974), p. 99.

in Cocteau's life by a very fragile line indeed. The contours and characters of Cocteau's world of Death will be traced here.

Nightmares occur in various works throughout Cocteau's career: the prophetic, somnambulist nightmare of Elisabeth in *Les Enfants terribles* (1925); the dream of Jocaste in *La Machine infernale* (1934) in which a mass of matter that sticks to her acquires a mouth as had the hand of the poet in *Sang d'un poète* (1930). Yet it is in the film work of Cocteau that the dream achieves its greatest hegemony and clarity, so permeating each shot of the film that we begin to wonder when the dream begins and ends. Most attractive of film's virtues to Cocteau was the freedom with which time and space could be manipulated, freeing man from his physical limitations.[18] It is this flexibility of movement backward and forward, slow and fast, far and near which characterizes the dreamers in Cocteau's films who traverse mirrors at the bequest of a female temptress and float forward and backward in time and space. Early on Cocteau realized that vagueness would not suffice for the depiction of a dream world. He says of his friend and technical director Berard:

> He was the only one to understand that the marvelous cannot be evoked through vagueness, and that mystery exists only in precise things. He also knew that nothing is easier to create than false fantasy in the film world.[19]

It is obvious in this statement that Cocteau does not clearly distinguish his states of mystery, fantasy, dream, poetry, intoxication, and nightmare, states which seem to exist on one flowing continuum of intensified experience. Similarly it is rather difficult to label just what is dream and what is nightmare in his films, or who is the dreamer and what is dreamed. The interpretation of a sequence as nightmare seems paradigmatically a function of point of view. The points of view of the author (from written accounts, cinematic treatment, and voice-over texts), characters (from actions, reactions, and dialogue) and spectator (who matches these images with her own and with psychological paradigms) often diverge. Pleasure and pain, desire and repulsion, dream and nightmare are very closely wedded in Cocteau's imagery, as I will show in three films: *Le Sang d'un poète, Orphée,* and *Le Testament d'Orphée.* The overwhelming terror, helplessness, paralysis, and threat of extinction which the dreamer experiences in the classic nightmare rarely occur in full force in Cocteau's world, where death is seen as a refuge from

[18] Evans, p. 46.
[19] Evans, p. 41.

the world of the ordinary.[20] I will concentrate here on the figure of Death
in her many incarnations, for it is she who controls the life of the dreamer.

The three main incidents in *Le Sang d'un poète* are framed by two shots
of a tower's collapse, suggesting that the events of the film take place in an
instant, although the events within each incident are slow and attenuated.
This framing event is both wondrous and terrifying, with clear connotations
of castration, a proper metaphor, one can argue, for the poet's tormented
relationship with his controlling muse. There is no dreamer specifically
posited, although we hear the disembodied voice of Cocteau. The next
sequence involving the hand-mouth dramatizes the frightful, devouring
orality characteristic of certain nightmares, yet also makes clear the poet's
pleasure in this self-seducing body part, even as he tries to resist temptation.
The artist, drawing a portrait, discovers that the mouth of his figure is a
real one, attempts to erase it, and finds the mouth embedded in his hand
(vaguely resembling the deep ovoid scar that marks his naked shoulder).
He discovers the hand as it sends bubbles up from a basin of water; he tries
deperately to shake it off. In alternate shots plaster body parts are substi-
tuted, introducing the theme of the inanimate. The mouth pleads for air,
which the artist gives it at the window.

Here the anxiety of the artist wanes and his erotic encounter begins.
He raises those lips to his lips, and slips them over his body, resting at each
breast in masturbatory ecstasy, his eyes painted wide-open on his closed
eyelids, suggesting the illusory wide-awake state of the dreamer whose
eyes are really closed. Traces of moisture are left as the hand-mouth moves
over his body as his hand moves down. An incident which had seemed comic
at first turns more serious and sensual. The next morning, as the voice-over
informs us of the passage of time, we see the artist asleep, his hand-lips
uttering the incoherent sputters of the dreamer. He awakens. We infer that
the previous episode was not a dream, because the mouth is still there.
His anxiety and anger censor the sensuality he had experienced before.
He viciously approaches a statue from behind and holds the mouth over
hers, transferring it to her in a gesture of triumph. The statue in her mono-
dic, hypnotic voice refers to the mouth as a wound.

Reticent about inflicting any one interpretation, Cocteau nevertheless
offers one in the form of a talk given at a showing of the film in 1932: "I
could say:

> The solitude of the poet is so great, he lives out his creations so
> vividly that the mouth of one of his creations is imprinted on his
> hand like a wound; that he loves this mouth, that he loves himself,

in other words; that he wakes up in the morning with his mouth against him like a chance acquaintance; that he tries to get rid of it, that he gets rid of it, on a dead statue—that this statue comes to life—that it takes revenge; that it sends him off into terrible adventures. I could tell you that the snowball fight represents the poet's childhood and that he plays the card game with his Glory, with his Destiny, he cheats by drawing from his childhood instead of from within himself. I could tell you that afterwards, when he has tried to create a terrestrial glory for himself, he falls into that "mortal tedium of immortaliy" that one always dreams of when in front of famous tombs.[21]

The symbolic objects in the film we can infer to be projections and personifications of his emotions and thoughts, exhibiting all the characteristics of primary process thinking: symbolization, condensation, displacement, distortion, and projection.[22] The actions of this sequence suggest an enactment of the mechanisms of repression of both erotic and poetic urges, which Cocteau shows us are one.

The problematic and transitional figure here is the statue-woman, who, like the Princess in *Orphée* and *Le Testament d'Orphée*, invites or orders the poet to enter through the mirror to the world beyond and resembles in many of her aspects Ernest Jones' paradigm of the vampire. In *Le Sang d'un poète* the statue is less hostile and bitter than she will become in the later films. When the poet awakes she is in the form of a classical plaster statue, armless, with short hair and an androgynous head that resembles the poet's, but with the body and features of a woman. After the lovemaking Cocteau had cut in a strange plaster mask that rotates back and forth with a suggestion of disapproval, preparing us for the arrival of the female figure. She also resembles the figure in the drawing whose lips become embedded in his hand. It is the voice of a woman that, through those lips, beseeches him for air. In the second sequence Cocteau specifically represents the figure of the hermaphrodite which is already suggested here. Cocteau wrestles with what he seems to consider the female aspects of his nature.

The poet approaches the statue as if half-afraid of waking her and clamps the hand-mouth over hers, which wakes her. She laughs and warns him that it is not so easy to get rid of a wound. The poet gropes along the walls of the set seen from high above and reaches a mirror which he beseeches her to open for him, as a child would ask his mother. Maternally she urges him to try. He ends up in the Hôtel des Folies Dramatiques where a series of voyeuristic

---

[21] Jean Cocteau, "Postscript" in *Jean Cocteau: Two Screenplays*, trans. Carol Martin-Sperry (New York: Orion Press, 1968), p. 65.

[22] Mack, p. 65.

adventures unfolds. This muse of poetry seems to represent inspiration and work which hold him in a love-hate relationship. The violent and voyeuristic nature of the next scenes suggest the loosely connected episodes of a dream.

The motion of the dreamer through the hallways of the Hotel of Dramatic Follies resembles the paralyzed efforts we experience in nightmares. Yet the motion is endowed with sensuality as the half-bare torso strains in slow motion against physical odds as he moves against gravity from door to door on this voyage of discovery. Like the lascivious, sadistic stare of the man in *Un Chien Andalou*, the poet seems to enjoy what he sees through the keyhole; yet to the spectator the images seem nighmarish: a Mexican is shot and reconstructed in reverse motion; a girl is kept hanging from the wall and ceiling to avoid the whip lashes and raised fist of a spinsterish woman; Chinese eyes stare out from an opium den; a Hermaphrodite raises a loincloth revealing a pillow warning: Danger of Death. The poet's responses to these views seem charged with eroticism as he quite literally climbs the walls to gain a better viewpoint. Freed from the mechanisms of repression, the poet experiences pleasure at these sights, but is subsequently punished: he shoots himself with a gun handed to him at the end of the hallway.

Returning through the mirror, he must encounter the imperious figure of the statue who is a perfect, neutral, white plaster screen for the projection of guilt feelings and who provides remonstrances as well. This repressed hostility, which Jones considers central in the incarnation of a vampire figure, is unleashed on her as he smashes the statue wildly, blaming her for his perilous journey.[23] The plaster dust from the smashed statue covers him so that he looks like a statue himself, and the voice-over warns: "by breaking statues one risks turning into one oneself." This warning throws the story back to a childhood incident which begins with schoolboys pelting a statue with snowballs, suggesting the psychological genesis of the violence and initiating the scene which is most clearly nightmarish: the gagging on blood of a fallen comrade.

The statuesque woman reappears in this scene as a cosmopolitan woman who deals out the destiny of the poet in a cardgame: again, his death at his own hands. She sits opposite the poet at a cardtable that rests on the body of the schoolboy. They nonchalantly play cards as an audience of elegantly dressed aristocrats watches them from the stone loges above. Stealing his life away, the poet takes the ace of hearts from the little boy's pocket. The haughtiness of this elegant company is contrasted with the benevolent appearance of a supernatural creature: a polished, black, angel-man who lies over the little boy and envelops him in a cape. The guardian angel spirits the body

---

[23] Ernest Jones, *On the Nightmare* (New York: Liveright, 1971), p. 113.

of the boy up the stairs, taking the ace of hearts from the poet's hand. The homosexuality of these actions is evident.

We return to the woman who scornfully stares at the poet and warns him that he is lost if he does not hold the ace. The poet again shoots himself, which the audience applauds, confirming Cocteau's statement that glory and fame are reserved for dead poets. The woman becomes a statue again, wearing black gloves up to the place where her arms had been broken off. She walks off in a trance, slowly and deliberately, her eyes painted on her eyelids, accompanied by a mythological bull with a map of Europe as a saddle. We finally see her lying down with orb and lyre, her facial features outlined in black. Opium smoke emanates from her mouth; the factory chimney completes its fall.

The figure of the woman represents poetic inspiration and death, which in Cocteau's alchemy are one and the same. She is a cold, controlling temptress who leads him on the road to death and fame. As Cocteau stated in his talk at the Vieux Columbier:

> The poet's work defeats and devours him. There isn't room for both the poet and his work. The work profits from the poet. Only after his death can the poet profit from the work. And anyway, the public prefers dead poets and they are right. A poet who isn't dead is an anachronism. [24]

She is an inanimate statue who comes to life to haunt him, luring him on a trance-like journey through voyeuristic experiences of torture and death, conforming closely to Ernest Jones' description of the figure of death:

> Even the idea of death itself may be used to represent this unknown being: dying is often depicted as an attack by a ruthless person who overpowers one against one's will. [25]

A benevolent figure is introduced as her male counterpart, the black angel-man whose gentleness and caring action contrast with her harsh, distant, stony visage. He is lithe, glistening, and sensuous. She resembles the surgically precise figure of Death in the play *Orphée* (1925-26) and the vampirish Princess in the film *Orphée*. He prefigures the guardian angel Heurtebise, the God among men whom Cocteau worshipped in poetry, plays, and film throughout his career. Jacques Brosse has suggested that the figure of Death first appeared to Cocteau during seances he held with friends, including

[24] Jean Cocteau, "Postscript," p. 67.
[25] Jones, p. 106.

Radiguet, in 1923 when a voice announced "Je suis la Mort."[26] Some months later Radiguet died, seeming to confirm the prophecy, and Cocteau took up opium. During a detoxification cure and creative flurry, Cocteau wrote the play *Orphée* in which he introduces the female figure of Death.

Going deeper than Cocteau's own analysis might, we can infer from various facts of Cocteau's life that this figure represents his mother, the Mother, whom other contemporaries, as Kushner suggests, embodied in the figure of Eurydice, giving the myth psychological overtones proper to this century. His mother supported Cocteau financially and emotionally, introducing him to her *salon* world. His letters to her, after he left the household at age nineteen, show a constant need to justify himself to her. When Cocteau presented a fiancée, Mademoiselle Carlier, to his mother, she intervened and Mlle. Carlier left Cocteau. Jean returned to live at home where Mme. Cocteau welcomed his homosexual friends. The Oedipal theme is made even more explicit in Cocteau's play *La Machine infernale* (1934), an adaptation of the story of Oedipus and Jocasta. As they sleep together in incestuous sheets, they are propelled into horrifying nightmares which awaken them from their restless sleep.[28]

In *Blood of a Poet* we could find potentially nightmarish images, but one could assert that Cocteau's personal images are overly hermetic; to use Mack's phrase: " . . . his capacity to relate to the world outside his own mind, must be sufficiently maintained to communicate the quality of shared illusion."[29] In *Orphée* the feeling of a nightmare is communicated more clearly and coherently. The rhythm of the editing, the pace of the dialogue, and the threatening harshness of drums, music, and mise-en-scène suggest the hurried sense of anxiety and torture which Orphée experiences. The sinister attire of the motorcyclists and the caustic iciness of the Princess who lashes out her orders affect the audience as well. In *Orphée* one sees that the nightmare world for Cocteau is never really a separate world except in its physical, spatial sense. It erupts in the domestic tranquillity of the home. In that sense Cocteau shows that the world of nightmare and dream is but a psychological extension of everyday emotions and actions. It is a metaphor for the tortures of the mind's interior from day to day.

The princess, played by Maria Casarès, first appears in the café scene where she is tending to the reputation and irritability of the young poet laureate Cégeste. She has arranged the publication of his book of poetry

---

[26] Brosse, p. 35.

[27] Brosse, p. 5.

[28] Jean Cocteau, *La Machine infernale* (Paris: Editions Bernard Grasset, 1934), pp. 153-56.

[29] Mack, p. 99.

Nudisme which contains blank pages, so that here as well she is linked irrevocably with the art of the poet. Orphée and the Princess exchange glances in which one senses their erotic attraction. He bitterly expresses his jealousy regarding the other poet's fame and following, and he is surprised when she beckons him to accompany her as a witness to the death of the young poet in an "accident" with the menacing motorcyclists. They drive off in a chauffeur-driven car on a journey reminiscent of *Nosferatu*. Negative images of the highway seem the landscape of a cloud world of the dream. The Princess orders him around fiercely, calling him stupid and berating him for asking questions. She is the figure of the Bitch personified, and as such, we feel, a projection of his own anger and frustration.

The dream-like quality of the actions as they unreel in a strangely lit space and hurried tempo is specified in the dialogue in which we discover that he sleeps and therefore sleep-walks:

> She: Dormez-vous debout?
> He: Je crois.
> She: Décidément vous dormez.
> He: Oui, je dors. C'est très curieux.
> She: Si vous dormez, si vous rêvez, acceptez vos rêves, c'est le rôle du dormeur.

He is in a trance, under her spell, and submits to her orders. She is the supreme Vamp, the seductress, who, like the statue, overpowers the man who is in her spell. Orpheus falls asleep, his face against a mirror which dissolves into an icy puddle on a sandy beach. Confused and anxious he awakens and returns home with Heurtebise. From then on his angers and obsessions become the nightmare of Eurydice.

In the next scene Orphée, like Juliette Janson's husband in Godard's *2 ou 3 choses que je sais d'Elle*, is obsessed with his radio transmissions from the Beyond which he copies down furiously. One detail from the play *Orphée* is worth mentioning here in tracing the morphology of Cocteau's nightmare world. In the play Orphée receives his messages through a horse who, like the wiseman Balthazar in Bresson's later incarnation, taps his hoof a number of times which Orphée translates into a letter. Orphée defends himself: "Ma nuit. Ce cheval entre dans ma nuit et il en sort comme un plongeur. Il en rapporte des phrases."[30] Jones's nightmare paradigm and etymology are almost perfectly expressed here. "My night. This horse enters my night and leaves like a plunger. He brings back phrases." A counterpart to the female figure of Death, this horse, figure of the father, communicates messages from

[30] Jean Cocteau, *Orphée*, p. 45.

the beyond, where his father's suicide had taken him. One of the messages the horse taps out is M-E-R-C-I, echoing Jones's etymology of the word "nightmare;" and one should not forget that the French word for mother is *mère*. In the film *Orphée* the litany of nightmare symbols is broadened. Maria Casarès' horse-like mane of hair and chin coincide with the replacement of the horse by a hearse-like car, inspired by Bresson's use of the same in *Les Dames du bois de Boulogne*. Death's accomplices ride through the night on motorcycles; surrogate, electrified horses. In *Le Testament d'Orphée* a man with a horse's head is reintroduced as a seductive figure whom Cocteau follows through a labyrinthine world. The homosexual overtones of the figure in this film are further foregrounded.

In *Orphée* the vampirelike sensuality of the Princess is contrasted with the simple domesticity of the wife, suggesting the Freudian paradigm of the nightmare as an expression of repressed sexual desires. His obsession with his transmissions is the extension of his trance-like subservience. In her second appearance the Princess resembles the classic succubus, watching Orphée sleep. Similarly Heurtebise watches over Eurydice. The anxious state of a nightmare is reintroduced as Orphée runs after the Princess who walks sternly through the frame in a series of disconnected spaces which constitutes a synthetic city. During this frustrating search for her, Orphée encounters the persons who will become the occupants of the world through which he travels to Hell in dreamlike motion: the angel-like figure of the *vitrier* carrying windowglass like wings (Heurtebise was the *vitrier* in the play *Orphée*). His fans follow, leer at, and attack him, a premonition of Fellini's haunted world in *8½*. The Princess visits his room a second time.

Her function as the mediator of the dead's journey to the underworld is clarified as she spirits Eurydice in reverse motion off the bed and through the mirror, ordering her fumbling assistants around in a petulant manner, demanding a meticulous discipline. She seems the very image of the superego detached from its integrating function, the accusatory image *par excellence*.[31] The judgmental quality is further elaborated as the characters appear before the judges of the underworld, who prefigure word for word Godard's depiction of computerized interrogation, a modern, totalitarian nightmare world, in *Alphaville*. In this court the tables begin to turn on the Princess as Orphée, with the help of Heurtebise, takes control of the journey and proceedings through the magic gloves. The Princess is accused of loving Orphée and entering his room without orders. Heurtebise is accused of loving Eurydice.

The phenomenon of incubation is made manifest in the room where the Princess and Orphée declare their passion to each other, a scene of ecstasy and pleasure, a fantasy fulfilled. At this point, the Princess suggests a key to

[31] Mack, p. 66.

the interpretation of the genesis of the nightmare depicted here. Orphée asks who gives the orders. She proposes an existentialist answer:

> Orphée: J'irai jusqu'à celui qui donne ces ordres.
> La Princesse: Mon pauvre amour . . . Il n'habite nulle part. Les uns croient qu'il pense à nous, d'autres qu'il nous pense. D'autres qu'il dort et que nous sommes son rêve . . . son mauvais rêve.[32]

God then is the primary dreamer; the existence of man his nightmare. The nightmare becomes in the modern tradition a metaphor for all of existence. Resnais' *Nuit et Brouillard* whose title clearly evokes this metaphor, is the prime example: the holocaust was a nightmare come true.

Orphée's return from Hell is assured by the vanquishing force of love, temporarily that is, inasmuch as the Princess is his Death and must finally claim him. The love of Orphée and Eurydice will be tested by a nightmarish ritual: Orphée may not look at Eurydice. Shot by the angry mob who accuse him of appropriating Cégeste's poetry, Death sends him back to earth again, to be able to claim him as an immortal later on. What has been done is undone. Reverse motion awakens them all from the nightmarish spell cast on them. The whole action of the voyage to Hell and back has taken place within an instant between the ringing of the bell by a postman and the deposit of a letter, repeating the extreme temporal condensation of *Blood of a Poet*.

The nightmare world is most vividly suggested, in these voyages to and from Hell, by the motionless motion through space of Heurtebise and the torturous flight along walls and slow-motion paralysis of Orphée. Occupants of the underworld float by aimlessly, deformed by professional narrow-mindedness. The mirror, where one can see Death at work on the surface of the face, is again the entryway to that world.

In *The Testament of Orpheus*, which begins with the closing images of *Orphée*, Cocteau, playing himself, takes a long, dream-like voyage, led by a man-horse. The scenes are disconnected and full of references to his whole life and work, like the last dream Cocteau might dream. The Princess reappears at the table of judges, incarnating yet again the accusatory voice. She accuses him of being a nightmare image:

> She: Don't forget that you are a nocturnal amalgamation of caves, forests, marshes, red rivers, populated with huge and fabulous beasts who devour each other.[33]

---

[32] Cocteau, filmscript of *Orphée*, p. 97.
[33] Cocteau, filmscript of *The Testament of Orpheus*, p. 108.

She condemns him to a life sentence. He ambles on and on, encountering himself whom he despises and wishes to kill, a voyage like that of the Professor's dream in *Wild Strawberries*. Other women appear as statuesque, mythological figures: a machine that eats autographs and turns out books, and Minerva, flanked by two horsemen guards. The Sphinx with her prominent breasts, horns, and feathery wings slides along a wall, a character from *La Machine infernale*. Like the insectoid, angel-man in *Blood of a Poet* the horsemen carry away his body, speared through the shoulders. The film returns to the disconnected syntax of *Blood of a Poet* in this retrospective film which reiterates the judgments and thoughts that haunted Cocteau's works and world.

Thus Cocteau's nightmare visions are paradoxical and ambiguous, demonstrating that dream and nightmare in his world are contiguous realms in which eroticism and creativity cohabit. The imagination, whether awake, drugged, or dreaming shuttles back and forth with an independence of spirit and will which led Cocteau to represent it as a mythical being, the classical, controlling muse. Above all, his images represent an attempt to domesticate and control his conception of death which intimately colored and determined much of his life and work. His highly symbolic, allegorical psychodramas represent in separate figures the conflicting impulses of the mind and body, battling, tormenting, and tempting each other. Well aware of the Freudian paradigm, Cocteau, in his films and literary works, attempts to project on the blank screen and page a host of fears and frenzies. Whether or not the images actually represent the troubled workings of Cocteau's self can only be left to speculation.

Yet as such his films greatly influenced his psychologically obsessed French contemporaries and especially the romantic visionaries of the American avant-garde. His free-wheeling conception of film space and time, his intrusive, subjective, and often literary narrations, his rejection of photographic realism in certain instances, and his imaginative annexation of symbolic objects juxtaposed freely in an original context greatly influenced the avant-garde who followed him on his labyrinthine subjective meanderings. Claiming that he merely documented scenes from another realm, Cocteau said:

> There is nothing we cannot convey in a film, provided we succeed in investing it with a force of expression sufficient for changing our phantasms into undeniable facts.[34]

Brooklyn College; The City University of New York

[34]Cocteau, *On Film*, p. ix. —I would like to thank Jean-Claude Martin and Steven Stockage of the Brooklyn College faculty for their helpful suggestions.

LOSS AND RECUPERATION IN SAURA'S
THE GARDEN OF DELIGHTS

Katherine S. Kovács

The fourteen feature films which Spanish director Carlos Saura has made over the past two decades bear witness to the experiences of his generation, those who were born in the 1930's and who came of age after The Spanish Civil War, in the 1940's and 1950's, when Spaniards lived isolated from the rest of Europe, still attempting to come to terms with the aftermath of that war both in economic and in psychic terms.[1] Saura's debut and development as a filmmaker coincide with another period of radical economic and social change in Spain, the 1960's and 1970's, when tourism, foreign investments and a drive towards industrialization dramatically transformed Spain from an underdeveloped rural country to an industrialized urbanized nation. Saura's films testify to the impact of both of these upheavals on his countrymen and point to some of the unresolved conflicts which they have generated. As he noted, "What interests me most in the Spanish middle class are the contradictions which can be observed. We are dealing with a country which is being quickly transformed, where technocracy has become important but where attitudes are still very close to what they were in the Middle Ages. The conception of religion, of family life, of the way in which a mother should bring up her children, the idea that the man is the head of the family ... none of these assumptions has been questioned."[2]

For many years under Franco it was not possible to confront these issues directly. All of the arts and especially the cinema were subject to close scrutiny. Film scripts had to be submitted before shooting was authorized and the final movie had to be approved by the censor before release. In the early

---

[1] Saura shot his first feature, *Los Golfos*, in 1959. At this writing he is shooting his fifteenth film in Mexico. The tentative title is *Antonieta*.

[2] Bernard Cohn, "Entretien avec Carlos Saura," *Positif*, No. 159 (mai, 1974), p. 30. This and all subsequent translations from articles in French or in Spanish are my own.

years of the Franco regime and especially during the 1950's, the few movies made which dealt with the past tended to glorify Spanish history; those with contemporary settings resolutely avoided any political or social commentary. In the 1960's the government began to encourage young filmmakers through the granting of subsidies and the much heralded "New Spanish Cinema" Movement was born. This movement reflected the Spanish government's search for a new image abroad; it did not really open up Spanish cinema. Saura and the other young filmmakers who debuted during this period were still severely restricted as to the subjects which they could present in their movies. Although themes of current or political interest such as the Opus Dei, the Civil War, or the Spanish Republic could be mentioned *en passant*, this was more for foreign rather than domestic consumption. While the films were shown in their entirety at film festivals, they were usually highly-censored or not even released at home.[3]

This situation started to change in the early 1970's, during the five years preceding Franco's death when a so-called *dictablanda* (soft dictatorship) replaced the *dictadura* and a number of outstanding films were made which dealt in an indirect often allegorical way with some of the attitudes, obsessions, problems, and life styles of Spaniards. These would include Victor Erice's *Spirit of the Beehive*, which describes a child's perceptions of real and imaginary worlds, José Luis Borau's *The Poachers*, a parable of sexual and political repression, and Jaime de Arminan's *My Dearest Señorita*, a black comedy on sex roles. During those five years, Saura himself directed four films: *The Garden of Delights* (1970), *Ana and the Wolves* (1972), *Cousin Angelica* (1973) and *Cría* (1975).[4]

In these films Saura presented protagonists who were in some way representative of the Spanish middle class, protagonists whose present situations attested to the impact of the past upon their lives—both their private past experiences and the collective past of Spain. Two themes recur with insistency in these works: childhood and the Spanish Civil War. For Saura the War

[3]On this period see Vicente Molina-Foix, *New Cinema in Spain* (London: British Film Institute, 1977), pp. 16-20.

[4]The first three of these films form a sort of trilogy on the consequences of the Spanish Civil War. Since Saura has developed the method of working with the same producer, actors, and creative team, he tends to elaborate his ideas from one film to the next. One often has the impression that each film is a consequence of the one that went before. Sometimes scenes, images or situations from one film will recur in a later one. For example as Saura himself has noted, the idea of a grotesque altarpiece which was first utilized in *The Garden of Delights* was his point of departure for *Ana and the Wolves*, where three brothers represent the three great powers in Spain, the church, the army, and the family. (See Enrique Brasó, "Post-scriptum sur *Ana y los lobos*," *Positif*, No. 159 [mai, 1974], p. 33).

is the central issue for all Spaniards: "It . . . had a decisive influence not only on those like us who lived through it . . . but also on later generations, on people born afterwards and who, while not experiencing it directly, suffered its consequences in the form of an entire political system, a repressive system of education, personal conflicts, and family losses (those who were executed, died in battle or went into exile)."[5]

Like Saura himself, a number of his protagonists were children during the 1930's. Their memories of the war are crucial to the way in which, as adults, they view themselves and respond to the world around them. In order to come to terms with their present conflicts and problems, some of them embark upon a search which is at once personal and collective, a search to resurrect their authentic past memories, to recapture what has been obliterated or falsified by the official interpretations which the victors have given to the events of the past. The first of Saura's searching protagonists is Antonio Cano in *The Garden of Delights*. This man who is virtually without memory, must recuperate it in his own way. He embarks upon a search which begins with The Civil War (referred to directly here for the first time in Spanish film) and eventually leads him to confront the conditions of life in modern Spain.[6]

Antonio's biography summarizes the history of Spain over the past forty years. Formerly a wealthy industrialist, "an intelligent man without scruples,"[7] Antonio is a member of the class of technocrats responsible for Spain's industrial transformation. In 1969, at the age of 45, he has a serious car accident which leaves him brain-damaged and partially paralyzed. The film begins after the accident, during the period of convalescence, when he and his family are attempting to cope with the fact that he is no longer "normal." Except for an occasional flashback to the period before the accident, throughout most of the film our attention remains resolutely fixed upon the new Antonio, a man without memory, without the ability to speak

[5] Enrique Brasó, "Nouvel entretien avec Carlos Saura," *Positif*, no. 162 (octobre, 1974), p. 33.

[6] Saura had a number of political problems with the film for this reason. It was not allowed to be shown in Spain for about seven months and was withdrawn as Spain's entry into a number of film festivals. An unauthorized copy was finally sent to the New York Film Festival where it received good reviews. As a result the Spanish censor allowed it to be released in Spain with a number of cuts.

[7] This notation and the biographical information on Antonio Cano found in this paragraph are taken from the unpublished shooting script of *The Garden of Delights*. It is found on the first page under the title "Essential Chronology of Antonio Martínez (sic)." All subsequent references to the script will be from this copy, which was Saura's shooting script (not the original screenplay). It contains a number of interesting drawings and handwritten notations by Saura. I am grateful to Professor Ramón Araluce for showing it to me.

or to act.[8] Antonio floats between objectivity and subjectivity, incapable of distinguishing between reality and dreams, past and present. He does not remember the past or understand the present, but merely watches as life unfolds before his eyes. Throughout the movie, the viewer watches Antonio watching. His role as spectator is stressed from the film's opening scene.[9]

The movie opens with a long traveling shot through a menacingly empty factory. From there we cut to a woman who is gazing into a mirror as she applies makeup. She compares her face to that of another woman whose photograph is placed next to her. An elderly gentleman by her side oversees the operation. In the manner of a stage or even of a film director, he instructs the woman on what to do, gives orders to the servants who are arranging the furniture and selects the music to be played on the victrola. The record which he chooses is a well-known song from the 1930's entitled, appropriately enough, *Recordar* (*Remembrance*). When a pig is inexplicably introduced into the room (shades of Bunuel), the preparations for the still-unrevealed ceremony are complete. Then we cut to a shot of Antonio who is noiselessly moving towards the camera. Saura focuses upon his eyes so that his role as spectator is established and then pulls the camera back so that we see him in a wheelchair. Then the action begins. What follows is a psychodramatic recreation of a traumatic incident from the childhood of Antonio. As if they were onstage (we have a long shot of the characters framed by the screen), the elderly gentleman who is his father shouts and gesticulates at the woman (an actress playing the part of his mother) who is dissolved in tears. They have decided to punish the five-year old Antonio for some unnamed action by locking him up with a pig. As they push Antonio towards the room where the pig awaits, we see a look of utter terror on his face. It is nevertheless clear that he does not understand what is happening, that he is confused and frightened by a scene with which he cannot identify, because without memory he does not recognize his own reflection in the mirror which the family holds up. When he is finally released from the room, he has fainted. Antonio's father has succeeded in frightening him without jarring his memory.

The purpose of the scene is to give Antonio back a memory, to impose it from the outside, in the hopes of eliciting a corresponding recollection which would transform him from spectator to participant in his own biography. Thus for the family the scene in an invocation, a magical rite in which, as in Buñuel's *Exterminating Angel*, everyone must return to his original place for the spell to be broken. For this reason, the father has gone to such lengths to recreate the period, the exact setting, the gestures, all

---

[8]The only real flashback in the film occurs near the end when Antonio remembers the day he went to his father's factory and told him he wanted to take over.

[9]Like Saint Anthony, Antonio must endure the temptations which assail him.

enacted in an histrionic acting style reminiscent of the films of the 1930's as well. This is the first of three recreations of scenes from the childhood of Antonio. Later we see his first communion, interrupted by Republican supporters who break down the church door; still later, there is the newsreel footage of Franco's troops entering Madrid, followed by a scene in which Antonio's mother (the same actress) dies. Each of these scenes is planned and performed by members of Antonio's family. By duplicating the experiences of Antonio the child, they hope to resurrect Antonio the adult who was destroyed by the car crash.

In all of these reenactments, Antonio's family and friends represent themselves as they were at different moments in time. They reveal their cruelty, indifference, and brutality both in the past, where we see the extent to which Antonio's upbringing was based upon guilt and fear, and in the present, for the experiences which they force him to relive are all negative ones which induce terror and pain. (Indeed his father chose the episode with the pig precisely because it was one which Antonio relived in his childhood nightmares). Ironically, the reenactments do not result in Antonio remembering himself. He is now an objective spectator, severed from his personal connections with his own biography, struck by the coercion and manipulation routinely practiced by these people onstage or off. He therefore resists accepting these visions of himself and of his life.

Thus the film opens with a recreated scene from the past. This is only one of five planes of action on which the movie unfolds. These five planes are described by Saura in his shooting script.[10] In the first category of "recreated past," he includes not only the decor, objects, and past scenes which Antonio's family recreates, but also newsreel footage, videotapes, photographs, newspapers and other sources which they use to document the facts of Antonio's life. The film is constructed in such a way that sequences taking place on these five different narrative levels are juxtaposed and combined in ever-new and startling combinations. The following diagram shows Antonio in relation to these different narrative levels:

1930's, Civil War, 1939, 1950, 1960's, 1969 (ACCIDENT)

RECREATED PAST	PRESENT	FUTURE

REALITY

———————————————————— ANTONIO ——————————————————

DREAMS

EVOKED PAST	ONEIRIC WORLD	FUTURE

1930's, Civil War, 1939, 1950's, 1960's, 1969 (ACCIDENT)

[10]This would be page 3 of Saura's shooting script.

Throughout the film, we move without transition from one realm of action to another, from reality to dreams and back again. Following the opening sequence, we switch to the second plane of action, set in the present. In present sequences, Saura realistically conveys the extent of Antonio's illness, his physical and mental limitations, and shows us the impact of his state upon his family in financial as well as in psychological terms.[11] The tone of the present sequences ranges from humor to real pathos as we see the comic and tragic contrasts between the present Antonio and the rather unpleasant but eminently capable man he once was. All of the present sequences depend for their impact upon the implicit contrast between the two Antonios. The characters in the movie have two distinct ways of responding to Antonio. They alternate between the two, sometimes within the same scene. Either they attempt to treat him as he used to be, a grotesquely inappropriate course of action which provides an ironic reversal (since the capable Antonio is no longer the real one) or they act as if he were a child.[12]

By reversing the roles and having someone treat an adult as if he were a child, Saura is offering a critique of the cruel restrictive method of child-rearing which we have already seen Antonio's father use on Antonio and which Antonio had in turn imposed upon his own son. This theme will receive extensive development in a number of Saura's subsequent films. As he once remarked: "I think that childhood is not the paradise which one always talks about, at least to the extent that my own childhood was not that way at all . . . in childhood the individual experiences nightly terrors and solitude because of the child's insecurity and lack of knowledge about what's going to happen. . . . There is also the conditioning in the system of education which claims to make the child a domesticated creature through a series of repressions. As a result, children feel weak and insecure."[13] Throughout *The Garden of Delights*, Antonio is reduced to the level of a defenseless child subject to society's efforts to educate, direct, control, and repress him.

This view of Antonio receives its richest elaboration in the film's second sequence when we watch the nurses prepare Antonio for bed, place a rubber sheet over the mattress, and tuck him in. As they turn out the lights and the camera focuses upon his face, one cannot help but think of Proust's Marcel,

---

[11] But as Saura tells us, we also see the progress which Antonio makes. (Saura, p. 3).

[12] This is illustrated in two juxtaposed scenes when Antonio wanders into his wife's room and then into that of his son's. His wife tries to get Antonio to act as he used to and then gives up in despair. His son, on the other hand, reverses the roles, playing the part of his father and repeating the angry words which Antonio had once used to humiliate him. Antonio flees from the room in terror.

[13] Augusto M. Torres and Vicente Molina-Foix, "Entretien avec Carlos Saura," *Ecran*, No. 49 (15 juillet 1976), p. 55.

the invalid who lies in bed at night and returns "without effort to an earlier stage of my life, now forever outgrown."[14]

In the following sequence, Antonio also returns to an earlier stage of his life. It is morning and as he lies in an outrageous 1930's seashell bed, a beautiful woman enters the room to awaken him. This is Antonio's aunt. As they begin to converse, the viewer has the impression that he is watching a beautiful film within a film. This might be a stylized rendering of one of Antonio's authentic childhood memories or the transposition of a scene from a movie he remembers having seen as a child. In any event, this dream-memory belongs to the third category of narration, which Saura calls that of the "evoked past:" isolated memories which Antonio still possesses of his former life. This memory seems to have been triggered by the song "Recordar," Antonio's "petite madeleine," played by his father in the first sequence and repeated here. In both scenes, we hear the voice of the famous Imperio Argentina, who had introduced "Recordar" in a movie made in 1931 entitled, *Su noche de bodas* (*Her Wedding Night*). The art deco setting of this sequence is therefore on one level a concrete parody of the Paramount Pictures style of that film and of other 1930's movies, an evocation (albeit in exaggerated form) of an atmosphere which prevailed in Spain during the 1930's and which is associated with the advent of the Spanish Republic.[15]

On another level the self-conscious nature of this parody leads the viewer to believe that these might also be memories which Carlos Saura himself has of the films which he saw or heard about as a child, films which provided an escape hatch from his real existence. Indeed, the movie is filled with allusions to other movies including *Alexander Nevsky*, *An American Tragedy* and others which Saura associates with incidents from his own childhood.[16] In *The Garden of Delights* certain scenes have special personal resonances for the director as well as for his protagonist.

In the case of Antonio, often his memories pivot upon the same period as those of his family's but interpret events in wholly different ways. Here for example Antonio resurrects the same era of the 1930's which his father

---

[14]Marcel Proust, *Swann's Way*, trans. C. K. Scott Moncrieff, (New York: Random House, 1956), p. 5.

[15]The aunt herself makes this association with the movies when she promises to take Antonio to see the movies which his mother won't allow him to see.

[16]In speaking of the cinematographic references found in *The Garden of Delights* Saura noted: "When I was a child, I always used to play with shields and balls of wool. I used to fight with my friends. The children in the film imitate adults by imitating the knights from (Alexander) *Nevsky*. As for the sequence in the boat, taken from *A Place in the Sun* (the title of the 1950's remake of *An American Tragedy*), I shot it because of the sound of the bird: "Ou, ou, ou." In fact I had a good time directing this film...." In "Entretien avec Carlos Saura," *Positif*, No. 159 (mai, 1974), p. 31.

had recreated in the film's opening but he offers a correction, or rather, a reversal of the earlier situation. Instead of being punished for some transgression, Antonio is now reliving a pleasurable erotic experience—his awakening and his sexual awakening by an aunt for whom he felt a vaguely incestuous attraction. The erotic nature of this feeling is underscored throughout the scene by the music, the decor, the curtains fluttering in the breeze, and by the fact that Saura presents Antonio as an adult who is being caressed by a beautiful woman. The latent content of this scene is manifested by a substitution. Both in the scene with his son and here with his aunt, Antonio the adult is placed in the position of a child. Here, however, as in all of Antonio's own memories, he is actively participating by playing the part of himself as a child. He uses his voice, facial expressions, and gestures to convey the difference in age. This novel technique in film is analagous to the perceptions of a patient in psychoanalysis who, in reliving a past moment, identifies totally with his former childhood self. He therefore does not see himself realistically in the form of a child but in the body of an adult as he appears at the moment when he is remembering.

This is the first scene in the movie when we see an event from Antonio's point of view. (Later this scene will be replayed and parodied when his former mistress Nicole wakes him up and stirs his memory of the accident while the spectator watches Antonio's family watching them on closed circuit t.v.). In the sequence with his aunt, we have entered Antonio's mind for the first time and watch him perform in a scene of his own creation. But it is only as the scene progresses that we realize that we are participating in a memory evoked by Antonio himself. In retrospect we realize that the doors and windows symbolize an opening into Antonio's mind and that the sounds of tennis balls which intrude as he embraces his aunt belong to the next scene.[17] In general Saura conveys the fact that a scene is not real through certain details of decor and acting style rather than by means of dissolves, cuts, or soft focus shots which are usually used in movies to indicate the passage from reality to memory, from present to past.

The same hold true for sequences which belong to the fourth category of narration, what Saura calls Antonio's "oneiric world."[18] Throughout the film Antonio has hallucinations, sees visions or images which do not have any

[17]When the scene shifts, Antonio is seated in the park next to the tennis court where his daughter is playing tennis with some friends. He is therefore not awakening in the morning from a dream (in which case he would be in his room) but from a vision which has been prolonged during the time when he dressed (or was dressed), ate, and was wheeled out into the park.

[18]In his shooting script Saura includes as part of Antonio's "oneric world: "—"Images evoked without apparent connection. —Fantastic or exaggerated images. —Dreamed images in the present or the past. —Mixture of recreated past-reality of Antonio, reality

apparent relation to his past or present life. Although they occasionally merge with visions from his evoked past, they tend to be more fleeting in nature. They appear without warning and are usually highly-charged, emotive and violent. They might correspond to obsessions or fears which Antonio is unable to articulate. In this category one finds the recurring motif of knights on horseback and combats with shields. Sometimes, in some undefinable way, these images seem to suggest that Antonio is attempting to come to terms with what has happened to him. The frequent shots of doors opening and closing and of long corridors which all seem to lead to a factory or attic filled with broken-down machinery might represent a mental landscape, the debris of Antonio's own brain through which he is painfully making his way. At other times these visions suggest that he is working through certain vaguely remembered experiences. At one point Antonio sees a child on a sled. This child immediately becomes Antonio himself moving rapidly towards the pool in his wheelchair. His bloodied hands attest to his efforts to stop himself, but to no avail. He plunges headlong into the pool. As we learn more about his accident later in the film, it becomes clear that the sensation of rolling uncontrollably is somehow associated with that event. In any case, Antonio's evoked memories, those images which we might call his daymares, are presented in a concrete and palpable manner. Our only hint that Antonio is about to "see" something is when the camera focuses upon his face as he gazes off into space.

Throughout the film there is a fluid passage from this world of daymares to reality and back again. This fluidity is suggested when we hear sounds in one scene which correspond to the image found in the next one. An example of the way in which dreams penetrate reality may be found in the sequence in the church, the recreation of Antonio's first communion. When he suddenly remembers the Civil War, he and we, hear the sound of airplanes passing overhead. In terror he calls out for his aunt who appears and saunters towards Antonio, making her way slowly through the crowd of real "extras" whom Antonio's father had assembled for the reenactment. A second time Antonio calls out for his aunt and again she makes her way through the crowd. This imaginary figure, invoked by Antonio to protect him, stands among the real actors as palpable as any of the other performers. Her presence is a graphic manifestation of the strength of the authentic imaginary when juxtaposed with the false real.

It is interesting to note that many of Antonio's visions tempt him in the garden. It is there that he spends most of his days, engaged in the painful, often frustrating, task of learning to write his name, a task from which he is

of the family, through fantasy (Antonio as a child—Antonio adolescent—Antonio adult—Antonio ill)." *The Garden of Delights*, p. 3.

easily distracted, by the sound of the wind in the trees, by the birds, and by the fantastic figures which act out scenes on his private stage. In spite of the fact that these hallucinations and phantoms often frighten him, he nevertheless finds comfort gazing at what Saura calls "the serene, friendly and beautiful expanse of his garden."[19]

In this context the title which Saura gave to his film is significant. It is a clear reference to the triptyque by Hieronymous Bosch which now hangs in the Prado. This altarpiece which is also known as *The Earthly Paradise*, has been in Spain since the time of Felipe 11 who placed it in the Escorial, admiring it as "a painted satire on the sins and ravings of man."[20] The title comes from the central panel situated between Eden on the left and hell on the right. Its meaning is still a subject of some debate. There are those for whom the garden of delights represents the childhood of the world, the golden age before the flood when men and beasts dwelt together satisfying all of their sensual appetites freely and without guilt. For Carlos Fuentes, who describes the painting in a chapter of *Terra Nostra*, Bosch was depicting the rites of the Adamite Christian sect who saw in carnal delights the road to paradise.[21] For other observers, however, Bosch's painting continues a long Medieval tradition which designates the garden as a false paradise which dazzles the eyes with an appearance of pleasure, promises instantaneous and complete gratification only to lead to ruin and the damnation of the soul.

Whatever interpretation one might choose to give to Bosch's giant strawberries, monstrous fish, and dismembered bodies, as Saura himself notes, "The title (of the painting) corresponds with what is narrated in the film. It is coherent with the painting ... the painting suggests something of the movie."[22] The painting suggests something of the movie because following his accident Antonio Cano finds himself in his private garden of delights, situated halfway between the innocent world of childhood and the purgatory of adult life. The style of Bosch's painting, a style developed for the scrupulous depiction of the here and now probably also appealed to Saura, who in his own *Garden of Delights* also presents the figures of dreams in an utterly realistic manner. Indeed throughout the film one finds a curious

---

[19] Ibid., *The Garden of Delights*, p. 46. (Written by hand.)

[20] Walter S. Gibson, *Bosch* (New York: Praeger Publishers, 1973), p. 156. The author goes on to note that "it was chiefly in Spain that Bosch's paintings were regarded with some of the same spirit which had conceived them. Not only did the largest porportion of his works find their way into Spain, but it was also here that the Medieval attitudes lingered long after they had disappeared in the rest of Europe. In the Escorial the cells of the monks were filled with his pictures."

[21] Carlos Fuentes, *Terra Nostra*, trans. Margaret Peden (New York: Farrar, 1976) pp. 580-581.

[22] Enrique Brasó, *Carlos Saura* (Madrid: Taller de Ediciones Josefina Betancor: 1974), p. 288.

reversal: while the dream figures possess a palpability and reality of their own, the purportedly realistic ones often seem stylized and false. This is in keeping with Saura's avowed intention to make of his film "a kind of grotesque altarpiece."[23] As he writes in the notes for his screenplay, this was to be "to a certain extent, a view of the last few years of Spain, a very special chronicle."[24]

The idea of the garden or forest as a place of revelation is one which is found in a number of recent Spanish films. In José Luis Borau's *The Poachers*, in Manuel Guttierrez Aragon's *In the Heart of the Forest* and in others, these areas are presented as the domain of fairy tales and legends, the place where mysterious magical rites are enacted. In speaking of the evocative power of the garden or woods Borau recently noted in a lecture: "The Spain of today is largely a dry and arid country worn out by centuries of erosion and war. But in ancient times, a Roman historian described Spain as a land with so many trees that a squirrel could travel from one end to the other merely by jumping from tree to tree." The garden or forest is a privileged place, a mythological space where the individual or the Spanish nation can find refuge from time and history. This is true for Antonio. Throughout the film the garden is shown in opposition to the house.[25] It is in the house that the father orchestrates the grotesque reenactments of Antonio's life and in the house that social rituals are performed. It is perhaps not by chance that Antonio's family is in the construction business, a point brought home by the photographs which his father assembles of the factories and buildings which they have constructed over the years. It is in terms of this dichotomy between the house and the garden that we should interpret the scene near the end of the film when Antonio meets the members of the board of his company. When they decide that he can no longer participate in the family business and cast him aside like a broken-down piece of machinery, his connection with the house is in some way severed. He returns to the garden for the film's final scenes, where in his own way, he will manifest the progress which he has made. There he rejects the fearful appropriation of his life by the people of the house, an appropriation not just of his past but of his future as well.

The fifth level of narration which Saura mentions is that of the protagonist's future. Throughout the film there is a movement from distant past, to recent past, to the moment of Antonio's accident, all juxtaposed with scenes from the present. When we arrive at the end of the film, we can anticipate

[23] Brasó, *Carlos Saura*, p. 288.

[24] Carlos Saura, *The Garden of Delights*, p. 55 (handwritten on a sheet labeled B).

[25] As Marsha Kinder has noted, the house is "a common dream environment for expressing one's life space." See "Bergman's Red Room," *Dreamworks*, Vol. 1, No. 1 (Spring, 1980), p. 63.

what his future will be like. Although his family seems about to give up on him, we know that he has begun to recuperate, completely on his own and in spite of their elaborate efforts. He is no longer in a wheelchair, is able to articulate some disjointed syllables, and has more memories of the past. Although he does not totally recover his past (he never does remember the number of the Swiss bank account), he is now in a position to resist the imposition of a future upon him.

This act of resistence takes place as he and his wife Luchy walk through the garden of Aranjuez. She reminds him of all of the suffering which he had caused her before the accident but promises to care for him, to devote herself completely to him, so that he may replace the children who no longer need her. At first Antonio does not seem to respond, but points to a boat on the lake. Once they are seated in the boat, in an awkward, violent and humorous way, Antonio articulates the words, *An American Tragedy*, the title of a well-known film adaptation of a novel by Theodore Dreiser made in the 1930's, in which a young man who wishes to marry a rich girl pushes his pregnant fiancee out of a boat and drowns her. As Antonio recalls this film which he might have seen, he makes frantic but futile attempts to push Luchy out of the boat. With this act, he manifests his desire to create his own story, to counter Luchy's version of the past and to keep her version of the future from becoming his reality. His inability to do so is brought painfully home by Luchy's laughter.

Nevertheless this violent reaction paves the way for the film's final sequence where, back in his own garden, Antonio has two visions. The first is a clear and vivid memory of his car accident, where he sees his own bloody body amidst the wreckage of battered autos on the lawn. He utters the words "Do what you want with my body but don't touch my head," words which are repeated by the other Antonio in the car. In this scene where there are two Antonios the fact that the invalid one perceives the other is a sign that he has established a link with his past, recapturing his own memory and bringing his biography up to date.

In the next scene which closes the movie, he sees all of the family members on the lawn moving silently around in wheelchairs, while he himself is at first walking through the woods and then seated among them. This is an ironic statement of what Saura has been showing us throughout the film: the man who has lost his memory is the healthy one.[26] Through fantasy and dream he has found his own individual truth and liberated himself from the social and political forces which have crippled his family and which had

[26] This scene is not found in Saura's shooting script. Indeed he seems to have had another ending in mind in which dogs were to eat up the people seated in the wheelchairs. See Brasó, *Carlos Saura*, pp. 284-88.

crippled him long before the accident. This scene offers a graphic illustration of a view expressed by Spanish novelist Juan Goytisolo shortly after the death of Franco: "A people who have lived nearly forty years in a state of irresponsibility are a people necessarily ill, whose convalescence will be prolonged in direct proportion to the duration of the illness."[27]

Implicit in the structure and themes of *The Garden of Delights*, is the notion of the family's illness as representative of the malady afflicting Spain after decades with Franco. They will not recuperate until like Antonio, they begin to reconstruct an authentic past, not on the basis of what they are told or shown, not on the basis of newsreel footage, public ceremonies or photographs, but by means of the workings of the inner psyche, through those hallucinations, dreams and memories which create an authentic reality, thereby releasing them from the hold of ideology, discourse, and representation.

Saura's interest in the recuperative powers of dreams, phantasms, and illusions, his joining of social forms and ceremonies with startling and often violent images, remind us of techniques which we have come to associate with another great Spanish director, Luis Buñuel. But while on one level these images are surrealistic, they also reflect certain characteristics of Spanish art and literature through the ages. Saura himself is very conscious of the ways in which his views "correspond more generally to our Spanish culture which one finds for example in the sixteenth and seventeenth centuries, in authors such as Gracian, Quevedo, Calderón, and of course, Cervantes. . . . This way of transfiguring reality through the imagination and (the tendency towards) dramatic representation are without doubt also due to the weight of the Inquisition upon the intellectual life of the period and the danger that existed in saying certain things, which necessitated indirect means of expression through stories, fables, symbolism and the presentation of the imaginary." [28] Faced with a similar impossibility of saying certain things, Saura rediscovered the solution of his predecessors. *The Garden of Delights* signifies a return not only to the past of the Spanish Civil War but also the reinstatement of a certain tradition of what we might call Spanish realism. On this point the filmmaker is explicit: "We Spaniards have been cut in great part from our roots. The Civil War was a catastrophe, the post-war period even worse. It completely halted the process of implanting Spanish culture in its past. And that past is not the glorious, idealized history which we were taught, but a

[27]Quoted by Roger Mortimore, "Reporting from Madrid," *Sight and Sound*, Vol. 49, No. 3 (Summer, 1980), p. 188.

[28]Guy Braucourt, "Entretien avec Carlos Saura," *Ecran 73*, No. 18 (Sept.-Oct., 1973), pp. 61-62.

fantastic, critical and realistic past that goes far beyond the narrow accepted meaning of the term realism. I think that there is a critical way of seeing reality, of showing the defects of a society, of a certain way of life and thought that is very Spanish."[29]

The realistic tradition with which Saura identifies is one in which dreams are intermeshed with reality, be it in the nightmares of a Goya or the more gentle dreams of Don Quijote. Both of these figures, in different ways, reflect a long-standing Hispanic preoccupation with the falseness of reality and the truth of dreams, a preoccupation which Saura translates to the screen. Like Segismundo in *Life is a Dream* who exclaims, "Yet I dreamed just now I was in a more lofty and flattering station," Antonio Cano wakes up one morning and finds that what he took for reality was "but a dream and dreams are only dreams." But in *The Garden of Delights* Saura goes one step further and suggests that the healthy mind dreaming certain dreams may use them in a constructive way: to help himself and his countrymen towards a more total perception of reality and of the problems of the day.

Much has changed in the decade since the release of *The Garden of Delights*. Following the death of Franco and the holding of free elections, film censorship was abolished and a number of documentary and feature films appeared which dealt with all aspects of the Civil War. At the same time, a host of foreign films which had formerly been prohibited flooded Spanish theatres, seriously cutting into the market for local films. Both of these trends have led to a change in direction for Spanish films over the past six years. Because of the new freedom of expression and the stiff competition of foreign movies, many Spanish filmmakers have abandoned the difficult symbolism and complex narrative structures which had characterized the films of the previous period. This is certainly true of Saura. Having exorcised the monsters from the garden of delights, he has moved towards simpler filmic forms, towards movies which are more autobiographical and less preoccupied with the past. Such films as *The Garden of Delights* correspond to a particular moment in Spanish life. They stand as documents in the history of consciousness of Spain, documents of a period which has been laid to rest. Now Saura, like his countrymen, is turning towards a future whose contours are only just beginning to emerge.

University of Southern California

---

[29] Enrique Brasó, "Post-scriptum sur *Ana y los lobos*," *Positif* No. 159 (mai, 1974), p. 25.

ONEIRIC VISIONS ON THE SCREEN
HOW BERGMAN CONVEYS NIGHTMARES IN
A CINEMATIC WAY

Vlada Petric

Bergman belongs to those filmmakers who believe that a script has to be the *inspiration* and *guideline* for the creation of a film, a "skeleton awaiting the flesh and sinew of images." This implies that true cinematic values originate in the very "flesh and sinew" of the film's structure. "A screenplay," Bergman continues, "can never express what the film intends to convey." In other words, no verbal description can do adequate justice to the cinematic vision shaped by the director's imagination and expressed through sight and sound. However, Bergman does not say that a cinematic event cannot be described in words; rather, he infers that the *experience* of such a description does not fully correspond to the emotional/sensorial experience of perceiving cinematic images on the screen. Therefore, it is important to keep the disparity between the *verbal* description and *visual* perception in mind while analyzing Bergman's films, particularly those parts which deal with psychopathic phenomena and dream processes. Moreover, Bergman's recognition of the unique impact of film on the viewer comes from a man who is a writer as well as a theater and television director. As such, he is a person most capable of drawing subtle but crucial distinctions between the various media of expression.

In his major films, Bergman deals with the psychic processes occurring in the human mind. He examines the unconscious mechanisms which relate intrinsically to our conscious activities, affecting them in the most puzzling manner. One of these mechanisms—anxiety—is revealed in the climactic sequences of Bergman's best films, providing a deeper insight into the characters and their relationships. It is possible, of course, to analyze the narrative content that contributes to an understanding of the physical activities and dramatic conflicts between the characters; there is no doubt that such an analysis would reveal the inner world of Bergman's protagonists and their complex psychologies. Without diminishing the importance of the thematic film analysis, this essay will concentrate on the *cinematic techniques* Bergman uses in presenting dream images, hallucinations, nightmares and paranoid visions in *The Hour of the Wolf* and *From the Life of the Marionettes*.

The Hour of the Wolf is a film about madness; it not only depicts the hallucinatory world in which the protagonist lives, but even more significantly, presents it as an outside world—reality—he has to cope with. According to Freud, hallucinations in dreams take place when the unconscious (repressed) wishes—filtered by the endopsychic censorship—can no longer find expression through action, but only through the hallucinatory imagery. Among the cinematic devices Bergman uses to convey hallucinations on the screen is, first of all, *light*. In most of the sequences conveying the mysterious atmosphere in which Johan Borg, the painter, finds himself after several paranoid crises, areas of brightness are presented on the screen in sharp contrast to those that are dark. The intensity of this contrast gradually increases as Borg's psychic trauma becomes more intense. Talking about the composition of the shot in his films, Bergman says: "Light has always fascinated me. All my visual experiences are bound up with light. My relationship with Sven (Nykvist) is based entirely on our experience of light—to decide what lighting will be in each scene" (from the statement made in Stig Bjorkman's film on Bergman). In the few theatrical productions of his I have seen, Bergman used Expressionistic lighting with chiaroscuro effects to emphasize the contrast between the dark environment and the bright illumination of the actors' faces. In his films as well, Bergman draws upon the style of lighting developed by famous German Expressionist stage designers, as well as film directors, of the 1920s. This is most evident in sequences which depict psychopathic states of mind, as in the climactic moments of *The Hour of the Wolf*, his most Expressionistic film. But it is equally important to point out that Sven Nykvist, as the cameraman, succeeded in transposing the old technique of lighting into a new style that fits modern shooting technology. How this was done?

The function of light is most dramatic in the climactic sequences of the film, such as the one which shows how Johan "kills" his wife Alma. After firing the pistol at her—although we do not see whether she is actually hit or not—the shots that follow are meant to represent projections of Johan's sick mind. In reaction to his conduct, Johan runs out of the house into the night: the black and white images of elongated shadows, filling the screen, stimulate a feeling of dread and delusion. Johan enters a mysterious castle where in one of the rooms he "sees" a man walking up the wall and moving upside down across the ceiling. The shot is photographed from Johan's point of view and marks the beginning of his nightmare: his perception of the outside world has been reversed.

With the understanding that a verbal description cannot be a substitute for the cinematic experience of a film, but in order to refresh the reader's memory of the narrative, I will give a detailed account of the shots to be analyzed. This description, manifestly, ought to be considered as a "supplementary documentation" that will facilitate the comparison between the sequence's cinematic structure and the literary description of the same event as presented in Bergman's script.

Johan's paranoia is enhanced by the pictorial transformation of his facial expression when Lindhorst makes up Johan's face, preparing him for his rendezvous with Veronica. Lindhorst then leads Johan through the long corridors of the vast castle (which is in an unspecified location). The shots are no longer stationary, but are executed by a moving camera; mise-en-scène is no longer frontal but perpendicular; the characters move toward the camera and often blur the image. Gradually, mise-en-scène transforms into mise-en-frame and mise-en-shot,[1] as the position of the camera sometimes intensifies the spatial perspective, and sometimes obliterates depth of field. In one shot in the corridor, Johan and Lindhorst approach the camera from the far background, and in the next, the camera, at a low angle, follows them down the hall. As the two men walk in front of the withdrawing camera in a medium shot, white pigeons fly in the far background. In the next shot the perspective is reversed: the camera is stationary and shoots through a dark doorway into the corridor focusing on Johan and Lindhorst approaching the camera from

---

[1] It is necessary to make a distinction between the two terms most confused by film theorists: *mise-en-scène* and *mise-en-shot*. The former term is borrowed from the theater and has been mechanically applied to cinema since the earliest days of film history/theory. Mise-en-scène is the arrangement of characters and objects on the stage, where movement is designed with a strictly frontal relationship to the audience; in most films, the camera becomes the spectator/audience and stage movements are directed towards a static or moving, relatively wide-angle lens. Many commercial entertainment movies are characterized by such a theatrical concept of mise-en-scène: the camera merely photographs what is arranged in front of it. Thus, the term mise-en-scène, when applied to cinematic imagery, basically has a negative connotation.

The moment a director decides to change the theatrical features of a photographed event, he begins to transpose mise-en-scène into something which meets the specific demands of cinema. When these changes reach the point at which mise-en-scène is sufficiently transformed (on the screen) into a specific filmic device, an entirely new phenomenon has occurred. Consequently, the perceived image can no longer be called mise-en-scène; rather, it is now *mise-en-shot*, or even more specifically *mise-en-frame* (i.e., the visual composition of each frame). Both devices depend on the relationship between the arrangement and movement of the photographed event and the framing or movement of the camera (which determines the film image). Hence, we must talk of mise-en-shot (instead of mise-en-scène) as the crucial element of the kinesthetic dynamism of a sequence, and we must talk of mise-en-frame as the basic unit of film structure.

the far background, while scores of pigeons, some blurred by proximity to the lens, fly in the close and middle foreground. These two visually dynamic shots are linked geographically, and function as a cinematic metaphor for the characters transgressing into a territory perceptually and sensorially different from that of common experience. Often the events are photographed through a doorway appearing as a dark frame in the foreground, which can be read as an "entrance" to the altered state of consciousness. The same connotation is enhanced by the fluttering pigeons, which create a dynamic semi-abstract figural movement in the foreground of this shot, particularly by their whiteness juxtaposed to the blackness of the background.

The images that follow are stationary: in a medium shot, the faces of Johan and Lindhorst are partially obscured by the pigeons flying around their heads. Unexpectedly, a medium shot of large mechanical wings waving behind Lindhorst is inserted. This creates an optical "shock"—almost like watching a flying creature from another world—appropriate to the horrified expression on Johan's face. The shock is meant to be drastic in the perceptual sense: it creates a visual tension on the screen that intensifies the mysterous atmosphere of the environment. The minimal duration of the shot with mechanical wings reduces its theatrical stylization; it functions as a subliminal "flash" which contributes to the eeriness of the sequence. These latter shots, especially those showing the perspective of the corridor, are more cinematic than those which occur earlier, in spite of the fact that the earlier shots depict more bizarre events (the man walking across the ceiling, vultures flying in close-up, monstrous faces). The reason for this is that the unreal atmosphere in the beginning of the sequence is executed by means borrowed from the theater (i.e., exaggerated mise-en-scène), while later the means of expression are unique to cinema (the camera movement and photographic dynamism of the shot composition). As such, they generate a greater sensory impact upon the viewer and serve as a preparation for the forthcoming events, marking the peak of Borg's nightmare.

Johan and Lindhorst's walk through the corridor lasts about one minute and is followed by a long shot of a dark hall with a brightly lit rectangular doorway centered in the middleground of the perspective. Through this doorway, a table on which a body rests draped in a white sheet is seen in the deep background. The dark doorway, like an image within an image, frames the white table placed against a white wall. On a pictorial level, the composition of this shot may suggest a symbolic gate leading into the world created by Johan's distorted mind: reality is gradually replaced by a subjective vision which, of course, contains all the elements of reality, but placed in different relationships. The atmosphere becomes more chilling and ambiguous. Although we cannot identify the person lying under the sheet on the table, we assume that it is Veronica (Pamina), since Lindhorst has already told

Johan that they were going to see her. Johan comes closer to the table while filmed by the camera slowly withdrawing in front of him, focusing on his face from a low angle in a medium shot, so that the dark ceiling is seen in the background. At the end of the shot, Johan has come to the foreground, thus reducing depth of field in the background, which oppressively dominated in the beginning of the shot. To a certain degree, this shot can be construed as expressing the subjective point of view of the person lying on the table. This intensifies the viewer's identification with the object Johan is approaching; indeed, it is even more intense because the viewer does not actually know who lies below the white sheet, i.e., he only suspects that it is Veronica.

The next two shots are photographed from a third person's point of view. In the medium shots, Johan is shown removing the white sheet to uncover the woman lying naked on the table. He caresses her body, passing his hand over her face, her eyes, nose, lips, ears, neck, left shoulder, arm, breast, stomach, hip, wrist, leg and foot. Photographed in close-up, this take functions as a micro mise-en-shot which underscores Johan's tactile sensations. In the following close-up, the movement of the heads of Johan and Veronica creates an exuberant play of light and darkness upon the screen. These two shots are related by the principle of "intervals" or cutting on movement. The movement of one shot (i.e., the camera gliding over the naked body from right to left) is juxtaposed to the movement within the succeeding shot (i.e., the motion of the two heads from left to right). The scale of both shots is in close-up, but whereas the former changes its composition because of the camera movement, the composition of the latter shot is changed by the movement of heads within the frame. The intense kinesthetic impact is enhanced not only by the graphic integration of the two different movements on the screen, but also by the very collision of the opposing movements which meet at the point where one image is connected (edited) with the other. This contrapuntal movement is interrupted by a distinctly histrionic shot of people standing, in strange positions, on the opposite side of the room, laughing as if they were monstrous witnesses to a nightmare. The shock is enforced by the "stillness" of the stationary shot which is inserted within a sequence of dynamic images. With demonic expressions, in prevailing darkness—since the only light comes from windows behind them—they face the camera, whose position is identified with that of Johan and, of course, the viewer. Histrionic in its formal arrangement, this shot is obviously intended to underscore the bizarreness of the situation, a sort of stylistic punctuation inserted into the sequence at the moment a new phase of Johan's psychic experience is about to occur. It is important to mention that in contrast to the shot with the people staring at the camera, the preceding shots are bathed in a nightmarish, chalk-white, consuming light which Bergman describes as being "intolerable and laden with anxiety and depression." This constant interaction of lighting makes it obvious that what appears on the screen is not reality, but rather an hallucination.

The next shot is a close-up of Johan: the make-up on his face begins to disintegrate, furthering the symbolism of his distorted fantasy and his own tragicomical position within it. As he retreats, the close-up becomes a medium shot of Veronica standing naked in the background. This shift of focus lasts only briefly: the image again changes as the camera moves forward blurring the image of Johan's face staring wide-eyed and open-mouthed, his make-up smeared. The push-and-pull effect of this shot gives a sense of the visual "respiration" of the film image, altering the composition of the shot and extending its focus from the foreground to the background; as such, it befits the "interior beat" of Johan's tensed psyche, paralleling the pressure exerted upon his brain, as if the camera had penetrated Johan's mind to record the distortions within. The next shot appears to be the most vivid manifestation of Johan's hallucination. Gazing fixedly "through" the camera with an expression of shock, Johan thus "summons" the next shot as the object of his vision. This last shot of the sequence, however, is brought to the screen not by a cut, but through a slow dissolve which reveals an overexposed image with restless black patterns floating across the white screen. The slow dissolve of one extremely figurative image (Johan's face) into another image which resembles an abstract painting reemphasizes transition from the real world into the unconscious. The flatness of the film image is gradually brought to an extreme: at first the floating patterns are reminiscent of black birds (associated with the white pigeons seen earlier), but as the photographic texture becomes less distorted, we recognize the image of dark water. Then, through the water, we see the floating body of the boy drowned by Johan earlier in the film. Consequently, we are fully persuaded that what we see is Johan's nightmare within an hallucination, since it is dubious whether Johan indeed drowned the boy or only fantasized that he did so.

The shot of the surface of the water is cinematic in its own way: it begins as an animated graphic abstraction (black patterns) and develops into a representational image of a narrative fact (the drowned boy). The psychological impact of this final shot in the sequence would have been weak, had it not been prepared for by the series of phantasmagorical shots described above. But the important point is that most of these shots are conceived and executed cinematically. The dynamism of the black-and-white contrast, together with a spatial exploration of the environment by the camera movement, parallels the distortion of the protagonist's mind, while stimulating in the viewer some of the neural sensations he himself could have experienced in similar psychic states. With all this in mind, one must conclude that the hallucinatory imagery and the depiction in *The Hour of the Wolf* is not intended merely to terrify the viewer, but to disclose the mental troubles of the character and intensify the viewer's involvement in Johan's frustrations.

In the synopsis-story which served as Bergman's only "script" during the shooting, Johan's hallucination is described in a way that is hardly reminiscent of the sequence in the film, yet the very spirit of the "mystery, dread and demons" is identical. Whereas the sequence as it exists in the film strongly emphasizes the character's movements in a mysterious environment (the castle), the literary description is focused on symbolic and surrealistic details (e.g., Lindhorst flies around the room "with his huge wings, black claws and a pair of bird legs") or on the histrionic appearance of the unidentified guests (who "look like insects with black bulging eyes and dark, gleaming limbs"). The segment of Bergman's prose which described this event reads as follows:

Mr. Lindhorst comes toward Johan with quick steps, his boyish, rather bloated face lit up by a cheerful smile.

LINDHORST: I knew that you would come at last. We know a trick or two, don't we? Let's see now if we're presentable. Veronica Vogler is an exacting woman, as you know. How pale you are, my dear fellow! You look a sight. Your lips are as blue as if you'd been eating blueberries. We must touch them up. A nice cupid's bow and a sensually swelling underlip are very titillating. Your eyes are bloodshot and swollen. Dab them with this. Now we'll draw a couple of lines in the corner of the eye. A shadow on the eyelid. No? Well, we mustn't overdo it. But a little fresher color in the face won't do any more. There! You look quite passable. You can borrow my dressing gown. It suits you. Or wait! Silk pajamas are the thing for trysts of this kind. Now for some scent. No? You prefer to smell of yourself. Of course. Each one has his own odor. But a little whiff of perfume all the same. I knew it! Now slippers. There you are. Take a look in the mirror. You are yourself and yet not yourself. The ideal conditions for a lovers' meeting. Here is her door.

Lindhorst claps him on the shoulder. As he raises his arm, huge wings sprout from his shoulders, and below his trouser legs powerful black claws and a pair of bird legs can be seen. Flapping his wings noisily, he rises from the floor, flies the room, and sails out through the open balcony door. Time and again he squawks like a pheasant.

Johan pounds on the door, but no one answers. He enters a fairly large room entirely without furniture. In the middle of the floor stand a couple of trestles. Over these lie some planks. On this primitive bier rests a body covered by a sheet.

He stands for a few moments at the door, bewildered. Then, driven by an irresistible desire, he goes over to the bier, lifts the sheet and exposes Veronica's face. Her very pale lips are slightly parted and an even row of white teeth glitter inside the soft opening of the mouth. The thick hair is combed in a simple coiffure, and in her small, well-shaped ears are a couple of thin gold rings. He draws the sheet from her body. Raising his hand, he touches her forehead, her cheeks, her neck, chin, and shoulders, her breasts, the curve of the hip, the tuft of hair covering the genitals, the long, thick thighs.

Suddenly she sits up, opening her legs. Laughing, she throws her arms around his neck and kisses him. She leans over him and he kisses her breasts. She takes his head between her hands and kisses his lips. Then he hears stifled giggles. He sees that the others have come into the room. In the dim light they look like big insects with black, bulging eyes and dark, gleaming limbs. They seem grave and expectant. The laughter, which can be heard all the time, comes from some invisible creatures somewhere up under the arched roof.

JOHAN: The limit has at last been· reached. The glass is shattered, but what do the splinters reflect? The void has finally burst the thin shell and meets—the void? In that case what a triumph for the void.

Alma and Johan's house. It is afternoon, as at the beginning of the story. Alma is sitting at the table, looking at the visitor. [2]

After reading this passage, one understands why Bergman insisted so much on the Expressionistic distribution of light and darkness in the composition of his shots. Light functions as an atmospheric component which underscores the overall feeling of "mystery, dread and demons," while mise-en-shot, montage, camera movement and the graphic composition (mise-en-frame) emphasize the inner meaning of the thematic flow. Following this tendency, Nykvist created mysterious atmosphere, surpassing the illustration concept of black-and-white pictorialism which can be traced in the silent Expressionistic films. In Johan's hallucination, light becomes an integral part of both thematic and formal structure of the sequence. As such, light contributes to the imagery which reflects the state of a deranged mind. Combined with the camera movement, light in *The Hour of the Wolf* becomes the major factor that stimulates the viewer's physiologicia mechanisms which intensify the experience of the film's narrative development. This is where Bergman's film substantially differs from conventional horror movies, and transcends the literal interpretation of the dramatic event.

Bergman insisted on the ambiguity of Johan's psychological relationship to Veronica and the drowned boy. Conversely, this ambiguity provided a ground for all sorts of interpretations, including the reading of Veronica as

[2] "The Hour of the Wolf," in *Four Stories by Ingmar Bergman*, trans. A. Blair (New York: Anchor Books. 1977).

a metaphor for Johan's suppressed artistic drive or the implication that Johan became creatively impotent because of his unfulfilled homosexual feelings. Whatever reading one considers more appropriate, it is not the interpretation that makes this sequence so powerful. Rather, it is the cinematic execution of the sequence which generates an hallucinatory feeling that goes *beyond any interpretive grasp of the photographed event*. Without such contrapuntal audio-visual interaction, the content of the sequence would remain literal and ineffective, or effective only in a thematic sense, without the kinesthetic impact *achieved by the specific filmic devices*.

In Bergman's other scripts as well, the most powerful cinematic moments related to the psychic states of his characters, are superficially described, or only vaguely mentioned. This tells us much about Bergman's cinematic imagination: although he is a man of theater and literature, he uses cinematic devices to convey his visions on the screen. Moreover, he is one of the few contemporary directors who realizes a striking similarity between the act of film viewing and the act of dreaming, trying to stimulate in the film audience some of the motor-sensory reactions they have while dreaming. Most of the cinematic devices singled out in the above analysis are realized during the actual shooting, presumably in the process of Bergman's viewing the event through the camera. This holds true for all genuine filmmakers: after reading the scripts of their films, no matter how meticulously written, one finds that they do not contain descriptions of the cinematic devices which are crucial for the cinematic impact of the most exciting sequences. The analyzed sequence in *The Hour of the Wolf* fully confirms this fact; this is how Bergman conveys nightmare imagery in a cinematic way.

It is elucidative that Bergman realized "all his films were dreams" just after (or probably during) the shooting of *The Hour of the Wolf*, which, as has been discussed earlier in this paper, successfully conveys the protagonist's hallucinatory experience *via* specific cinematic devices. One of these devices particularly strikes the viewer by a sudden intrusion of a dark or brightly lit object in the foreground. The film, shot in black-and-white, with many silhouettes, permitted Bergman and his camera Nykvist to achieve "the light as grey as ashes overloading a macabre environment" in which Johan experiences his unfulfilled sexual desires.

Bergman repeatedly emphasizes in his scripts that the dream sequences ought to have a "tangible" impact on the audience, and that they are supposed to be "mysterious in tension, yet real." As a matter of fact, Bergman's central problem in directing—and he admits it openly—is how to find the proper cinematic devices for the visions described in his scripts in a literary manner. Bergman does not wish to illustrate altered states of human consciousness by extravagant shots or optical tricks (which would easily lend themselves to Freudian or Jungian interpretation); rather, he seeks a correspondent auditory-visual structure capable of stimulating the viewer's sensory-motor centers as they are stimulated during dreaming. Properly devised, such a cinematic structure can intensify the perceptual impact of a dream content, making it more profound and captivating than if it were only photographically recorded as a strange, oneiric event. It is not a coincidence, therefore, that the dream sequences constitute the most cinematic portions of Bergman's films. One thinks of creating a "Dream Anthology" of Bergman's oneiric sequences, which would uncover a potent, though subliminal, connection among themselves and throw more light on Bergman's own psyche as well as on his work.

In his most recent film, *From the Life of the Marionettes*, there is an example of a dream sequence which marks a crucial point in the thematic development of the film. It reveals the motives and genesis of the protagonist's sexual frustration and his phobic obsession, resulting in his killing a prostitute (with whom he cannot make love), represented in his dream by his own wife. The film begins with the murder sequence (which, by the way, does not exist in the original script), while the rest of the film is a psychoanalytic exploration of the killer's (protagonist's) motives for committing the crime. Among a dozen or so sequences, the dream sequence best illuminates the act of murder and the state of mind in which the murder is committed. The cinematic execution and dramatic position of this sequence within the film's overall collage-like narrative structure, point to Bergman's particular concern for the visual aspect of dream imagery, and for the subconscious as a psychological axis around which unfolds the character's inner conflict.

Photographically the sequence is presented as a chalk-white over-exposed image, the camera moving over the bodies in close up, with an abrupt change of point of view. The action (involving the two lovers caressing each other) seems to occur in an indistinct space, "without the room's contours," yet the camera angles imply that the environment extends outside the screen frame. The "burning light" dominates the shots, thus separating the sequence visually from the rest of the film, as the first (i.e., murder) sequence, is set apart by being shot in color.

Directorial instructions in Bergman's original script (printed before the production began), clearly show his profound awareness of the difference between *cinematic experience* of a dream and its *verbal description*, however effective as literature the latter may be. This is particularly underscored in the writer's directions for the execution of the dream sequence. Bergman explicitly says that it is a "lucid dream" describing it as follows: "I dreamed I was asleep, I dreamed that I was dreaming . . . I am in a closed room with no windows or doors but also with no ceiling or walls, possibly confined in a sphere or an ellipse—I don't know exactly—I could never bring myself to examine the room's contours. The light was grey fluid, and undefined, rather like a winter's morning just before sunrise. . . . I knew at once that it was all a dream. I said to myself that this was a dream, much more real than other reality, it's true, but a dream all the same."

Bergman goes on with his description of a "horrible experience of a closed space," in which the dream event takes place, but he does not resolve the "dilemma" of how to express such a specific dream content cinematically. He reveals his quandary bluntly: "How the hell is this to be done? Where to put the camera, what does the background look like, is it a window, can the letter be seen, what sort of paper is it written on?" These questions arise from the dream description: "I write, I plead, I call, shout, bellow—can you hear me, or does something closer at hand occupy your thought, dear Mogens? If so, it would be only natural. Leave my letter. Put it aside or throw it away." Then Bergman goes on posing questions: "Does he (the protagonist) talk all the time? Is this a boring monologue or will there perhaps be cut-in shots of faces, bodies, twilight, or a stretch of water? It says in the text that he has eyes on his fingers. ("On every finger I had a little eye, which, with blinking delight, registered all this gleaming whitness and the floating itself.") Are we to order the enamel eyes from an optician and then stick them on the actor's fingertips? . . . I am jotting down words that are to represent pictures that I glimpse. There are no practical solutions—perhaps they will become apparent, perhaps not. I don't know. We can show burning skyscrapers or gorillas; it costs money and effort, but it can be done. But how are we to show a mental process?"

This final question is, in fact, the core of Bergman's directorial method; it is the essence of filmmaking which deals with inner visions and the human psyche. A close analysis of the dream sequence in *From the Life of the Marionettes* demonstrates Bergman's directorial approach to this problem in the process of shooting. The verbal soliloquy of six pages (in which Peter Egerman describes his nightmarish, lucid dream to his psychiatrist) is brilliantly transposed into a "sensual" and "tangible" (these are Bergman's terms) visual experience of a "strongly scented dream" (this is the first time that a Bergman script specifies "smell" as a component of cinematic perception).

As previously mentioned, the sequence is photographed in black-and-white technique, contrary to the instructions given in the script that it will be shot in color. The pulsating texture of the image suggests that the sequence was originally shot in color and then printed on black-and-white film stock, or that a particular development technique was used to achieve the "gleaming whiteness" which has a mesmerizing impact on the viewer. Throughout the sequence, the "grey, fluid and undefined light" dominates the shots, giving the illusion of an amorphous, fuzzy space, yet real and physical. This feeling is further enhanced by the meticulous camera movement, in close ups and medium shots over the two protagonists' bodies, which are contrasted to the extremely distant introductory overhead shot of the naked lovers asleep, representing a markedly stationary point of view, reminiscent of time-lapse photographs published to document the scientific research on the physiology of dreaming.

This is, by all means, one of Bergman's most cinematic dream sequences, and therefore more complex in its meaning than dream sequences in his other films. For example, one of the two oneiric sequences in *Face to Face* is also explicitly a "lucid dream," but lacking true cinematic intensity. After seeing herself lying dead in the coffin devoured by flames, Jenny exclaims, "If only I could wake up," confirming that she is aware of being asleep and dreaming. However, on the cinematic level, this sequence is executed theatrically in that it shows bizarre events (arranged in the form of a mise-en-scène) without sufficient auditory-visual components to intensify the eery mood and phobic tension of a dream caused by an overdose of sleeping pills.

Conflict between light and darkness is the visual substance of Bergman's dream imagery in general. He admits this by saying: "Light has always fascinated me. All my visual experiences are bound with light. My relationship with Sven Nykvist is based on our experience of light—to decide what lighting will be in each scene." In *From the Life of the Marionettes* it is, indeed, the light-dark contrast which transforms the literary narrative into a genuinely cinematic experience. That is probably why Bergman changed his initial decision to shoot all flash-back sequences in color, and ended up using it only in the brief introductory and closing sequences. The rest is a hypnotic combination of black, light and grey, or to use Bergman's own words, "the intolerable light laden with anxiety and depression."

The pristine, floating whiteness which saturates this sequence erases every material boundary ("contours") characteristic of a physical space. Immersed in such an "inexplicable light," human bodies are not perceived as levitating in the air (often done in the conventional dream sequences); rather, the whiteness—in its steadiness—functions as materialistic background against which the event takes place. The imagery is oneiric on its own phenomenological level, thus creating a real ("tangible") cinematic space, so powerfully visual that it is deprived of sound: the two lovers move their lips but the words are not heard. Yet, just like in our dreams, we *know* what is said although we do not hear people talking. Then a strange sound ("composed of only three or four tones") appears from nowhere to underscore the spatial (echoing) dimension of the whiteness. The motion of the two characters is gradually slowed down and segmented by time-lapse dissolves (which give the event a nightmarish look), while the camera moves in to a very close view of the protagonist's eye before fading into a complete white screen. This means that at the very end of this lucid dream, the whiteness of the shot's pictorial composition is identified with the physical whiteness of the movie screen. The viewer's perception is overloaded: whiteness within another whiteness. The illusion (dream), which a moment ago was affecting the viewer as reality, is destroyed and revealed as a rectangular white cloth. Here Bergman comes closest to the phenomenology of the motion picture projection, which is oneiric in its nature, mainly due to its stroboscopic effect. The identification-equation of the shot's whiteness with the whiteness of the screen is repeated four times in this sequence, which intensifies the light as the pivotal element of Bergman's directorial method. In addition, the shots—mostly in close-up—are connected by slow dissolves which "stretch" the cinematic time, just as the camera movement and lack of set "extend" the physical space of the unidentified ambient. The chalk-white photography is reiterated in the recollection sequence. At the moment when Peter describes his wife to the psychiatrist, Peter and Katarina's skin is perceived as transparent texture, while the background turns into a greyish formless backdrop.

On the interpretative level, the "lucid dream" sequence in *From the Life of the Marionettes* mirrors the philosophical connotation of the entire film. From the beginning, Peter feels low, alienated and claustrophobic, "entrapped" within his own depression, the source of which he cannot detect. In the kitchen sequence, after a sleepless night, he tells his wife, "All ways out are closed." She tries to help him, but with no result: their relationship rapidly deteriorates. The claustrophobic feeling is further enhanced by the fact that the entire film is shot in the interior, with ceilings hanging over the characters (only a few exterior shots of the night traffic and a garden entrance in twilight are inserted as transitions between the sequences). Near the end, in the brothel sequence, Peter tells the prostitute (whose name is the same as his wife's, Katerina): "All roads are closed." In order to get out he runs from one door to the other, while the prostitute calmly states: "Yes, every door is locked!" This mise-en-scène enhances physically the general mood of the narrative of the film which begins with the tragic finale: realizing that there is no exit for him Peter kills the prostitute, Katerina, and performs the sexual act with her dead body. As a result of this, his mind is completely demented: he breaks all contacts with the outside world and returns to an infantile phase of consciousness.

In the original script the narrative begins with the sequence entitled "A Conversation on a High Level," in which the psychiatrist (Mogens) reports to the Investigator how Peter Egerman phoned from the nightclub to tell him that he just "had murdered the girl [prostitute] and then had anal intercourse with her." Correspondingly the script ends with a similar sequence entitled "Concluding Conversation on a High Level," in which Mogens suggests to the Investigator that he place Peter "under strict observation" in order to examine "the patient's mental condition." Based on this type of narrative structure (i.e., story-telling framing), Bergman's original script was meant to describe the protagonist's tragedy through another person's (psychiatrist's) recollections of his patient's behavior, accompanied by the professional comments concerning his illness. Thus Peter's own recollections function as part (or a reflection) of the psychiatrist's opinion, including the lucid dream sequence which is adequately conceived in the script as Peter's letter to Mogens Jensen (though never sent to him). In the completed film, however, the first sequence shows Peter actually committing homocide, i.e. strangling the prostitute. As mentioned above, this first sequence is shot in color, but at the very instant Peter grasps for the girl's throat, the image "loses" its color and the flash back begins as black-and-white photography. Such a reemphasized visual transition may be read as a cinematic "penetration" into the protagonist's mind where the events from his past life take place; these series of recollections probably occur between the moment when Peter strangled the girl and the moment when his psychiatrist arrives at the nightclub. This narrative structure in the film justifies an often disjointed order of sequences, as if reflecting the fragile chain of associations in a deranged mind, and at the same time allowing them to be more than merely "objective." Consequently, and in contrast to the script, the final sequence of the film shows Peter being confined to the cell of a mental hospital, which further enhances the notion that the entire film is a projection of his own sick mind.

If Bergman's belief that all his films are dreams ought to be taken symbolically, it is indubitable that in the dream sequence he used his best creative imagination to find the appropriate cinematic expression. Obviously, it was not easy, and at one point in the script of *From the Life of the Marionettes*, he openly despairs, "Why do the dreams hide, why do they not let themselves be materialized by a machinery ideally suited to capture the most delicate movements in thought and feeling?" But in this film, Bergman proved that it is possible to achieve a cinematic vision which, in many ways, corresponds to the experience of dreaming. The words/concepts thus become moving pictures with perceptual ontological authenticity which has the tangibility of dream imagery.

Comparing Bergman's literary description of the dream content to its cinematic presentation, one would conclude that the script described the dream content as it exists in the sleeper's brain *before* being incorporated into the oneiric imagery triggered by the dream mechanism. In written form, the dream event is basically narrative in structure, without substantial visual features, despite the fact that it does stir concrete images in the reader's imagination. Such a narrative dream content is, then, visualized in the process of shooting, which can be compared to the "secondary revision" of a dream work. Cinematically, the "secondary revision" means giving proper "flesh and sinew" to the "subtle flux of the human psyche in its dreaming state." This also implies that the scripted dream content is transposed into cinematic imagery not merely by being photographed as it develops through mise-en-scène (dramatic situation), but that it is condensed, distorted, reorganized, displaced, abstracted and ontologically authenticated. Bergman's best oneiric sequences possess most of these features which make them climactic points within the film's narrative structure.

Bergman's decision to publish his scripts in initial form, without changing them according to the completed film, clearly proves that "all practical solutions" for the cinematic presentation of the described dreams become "apparent" *during the process of shooting.* That is the juncture at which Bergman's imagination begins to function in terms of the film medium. At that stage of creation, the literary devices used in the process of script-writing are replaced by cinematic ones, so that all metaphorical concepts and abstract ideas became palpable and credible despite their mysterious reverberations and elusive implications.

It may seem odd that Bergman even metaphorically considered the idea of putting "enamel eyes" on the actor's finger prints. In literary form this idea can be interpreted as a nightmarish metaphor revealing the protagonist's infantile imagination. It suggests the *naïveté* of the character's dreaming psyche, rather than the unsophisticated director's indication. In reality, however, the "enamel eyes" were not "ordered from the optician" for the shooting; instead the "camera's eye" was employed as a penetrative explorer of the mise-en-scène arranged in front of the camera. It is the camera's optical examination of the physical world that reveals the transcendental aspect of the dream experience in *From the Life of the Marionettes.* That is Bergman's unique way of showing mental processes; that is his cinematic treatment of psychopathic phenomena. The interpretation of Bergman's dream imagery and the subconscious can be more or less illuminating and useful, but only after one recognizes the rare cinematic values of Bergman's directorial method can the reading of his oneiric sequences be complete and rewarding. Only then will the viewer's experience of dreams in Bergman's films gain its full scope.

Harvard University

BERGMAN'S FILMS AS RECURRING NIGHTMARES:
FROM THE LIFE OF THE MARIONETTES TO THE DEVIL'S WANTON *

Marsha Kinder

From the Life of the Marionettes, made in Munich with a German cast, proves that Ingmar Bergman is capable of artistic growth when working outside his native Sweden. This latest masterpiece brings to full expression both narratively and visually and in the most intense, highly concentrated form, a murderous nightmare that runs throughout his canon. The emotional and aesthetic power of this stunning film is best appreciated when seen in the context of his entire body of work.

Recurring nightmares have four crucial functions in the films of Ingmar Bergman. First, they provide germinal images for the creation of specific films. Bergman claims the nightmare of humiliation that opens *Naked Night* and the haunting image of women in white drifting through red rooms that lie at the center of *Cries and Whispers* were based on his own dreams. When he adapts these images to his films, they are not necessarily limited to dream sequences, but provide the central thread out of which the entire film is spun.

Second, recurring nightmares control the structure of many key films. For example, the journeys of self-exploration in *Wild Strawberries* and *Face to Face* are controlled by a series of nightmares which help the rational doctors, Isak Borg and Jenny Isaksson, break through their constraining personae and confront their fear of death.

Third, the recurring nightmares unify Bergman's canon and illuminate his process of artistic growth. The repetition of images, faces, names, and situations enables his films to be seen as variations of the same recurring nightmare. They struggle with the same impulses, juggle the components into new configurations, but never escape the repetition compulsion. When he was

---

*Another version of this essay has appeared in *Film Quarterly* (Spring, 1981), pp. 26-37.

making his trilogy, Bergman took an important step toward dissolving the boundaries between nightmares and their surrounding reality.

> In the middle of the picture *Through a Glass Darkly* when Karin stands at the seaside and says three times, "Here comes the rain,": that's the exact feeling of dreams, and then everything turns over. You stop watching from the outside and become part of the madness inside.[1]

The nightmare becomes insanity when the dreamer no longer maintains the boundaries with waking reality. Earlier in *The Magician* (1958) this idea was verbalized by the scientist when he was terrorized by the surreal trickery of the mute illusionist. Trying to maintain control, he reasoned: I'm either dreaming or insane, since I can't be insane, then I must be dreaming so all I have to do is wait until I awaken. Once Bergman reaches *The Silence* (1963), the third work in the trilogy, his characters never awaken, for the entire film represents a nightmare from which there is no escape. Bergman became fully aware of this structural shift a few years later.

> Suddenly about a year ago while making *Hour of the Wolf*, I discovered that all my pictures were dreams. Of course I understood that some of my films were dreams, that part of them were dreams. . . . But that *all* my pictures were dreams was a new discovery to me.[2]

This realization made new relations possible among films. For example, black and white footage from *Shame* becomes a nightmare within *The Passion of Anna*, which itself is an anxiety dream in color, reworking the same dream thoughts. Although Bergman recently reported that he looks at a film for the last time three or four years after it's released, makes notes on what he likes and dislikes, and then pushes it out of his mind forever,[3] each new work seems to grow out of the previous ones and each leaves an indelible mark on his creative development. This complex interweaving extends from his latest film *From the Life of the Marionettes* all the way back to his cinematic debut in the forties.

Finally, the acting out of recurring nightmares is therapeutic both for Bergman and his audience. It's presented as an artistic and phenomenological alternative to psychoanalysis—like the Gestalt technique of dream

---

[1] Ingmar Bergman, as quoted in *Introduction to Ingmar Bergman*, a documentary produced for television by Lewis Freedman, 1967.

[2] Bergman, as above.

[3] Arnold Peyser, "'I am a voyeur': a Conversation with Ingmar Bergman," *L.A. Times*, Sunday, November 23, 1980, Part VI, p. 1.

reenactment. This is most clear in *Face to Face*, where the protagonist Jenny is a psychiatrist who experiences a psychotic break. In several ways this film is a continuation of *Through a Glass Darkly*. The titles of both films come from the same biblical quotation, revealing the focus on the two-way search for the self, from within and without:

> For now we see through a glass, darkly; but then face to face: now I know in part; but then shall I know even as also I am known.

In both films the journey into madness is triggered by the same germinal image—a woman staring at the patterned wallpaper. This image was based on an actual childhood experience that Bergman had when he (like Jenny) lived with his grandmother; he intended to include it much earlier in *The Devil's Wanton*, but omitted it because he could not make it work artistically or phenomenologically. In *Face to Face*, when Jenny visits her grandmother, ironically the old woman says: "I've put you in Karin's room. You won't be disturbed there."

Actually, Jenny condenses the mad wife Karin and the rational doctor/husband Martin from *Through a Glass Darkly*. Although she begins as a "mentally illiterate" psychiatrist who has never taken "extended reality seriously," Jenny continues Karin's descent into madness, providing us with an even closer look from the inside. Karin's brother Minus, who is unsure of his sexuality and whom she draws into incest and insanity, prefigures Tomas in *Face to Face*—the homosexual gynecologist whose mad sister doubles as Jenny's patient and Shadow. In contrast to Tomas, whose rescue of Jenny is based on his own experience of attempting suicide, Jenny's psychiatric colleague is of no help:

> Twenty years ago I realized the inconceivable brutality of our methods and the complete bankruptcy of psychoanalysis. I don't think we can really cure a single human being.

This doubt is echoed by the psychiatrist in *Marionettes*: "We're phenomenal at wiping out people's identities ... no self, no fear." Before attempting suicide in *Face to Face*, Jenny defines her own condition, not in analytic terms, but experientially:

> The dividing line between my outer behavior and my inner impoverishment has become more distinct.... We're gradually suffocated without knowing what is happening. At last there's only a puppet left.... Inside there is nothing but a great horror.

Although her nightmares are terrifying, at least they put her in touch with her actual feelings. When she awakens in the hospital, Tomas offers her an incantation for those who don't believe: "I wish that someone or something would affect me so that I can become real."

This is precisely the effect of Bergman's movies. Some might argue: but I'm not neurotic like Bergman and his sick marionettes! He counters with rational characters—the scientist in *The Magician*, the doctor/husband in *Through a Glass Darkly*, and Jenny in *Face to Face*—who demonstrate that those who cling to their personae are the ones in greatest danger of breakdown and victimization. In the Preface to the screenplay of *From the Life of the Marionettes*, Bergman says the central question is: "Why does a short-circuit reaction occur in a person who is in every way well adjusted and well established? *Face to Face* dealt with a similar theme."[4] All of his films imply there is no easy way out for anyone; that's why they are so threatening.

The most terrifying nightmare that recurs in Bergman's work is one where the dreamer commits murder; it always evokes the relationship between parent and child. In the rest of this essay, I want to trace this murderous nightmare through three key films in Bergman's canon: *The Devil's Wanton*, *The Hour of the Wolf*, and *From the Life of the Marionettes*. I have chosen *The Devil's Wanton*, also called *Prison*, and made in 1948/49, because it marked Bergman's debut as an auteur and contains the seeds of everything he was to develop in his later works.

The choice of *The Hour of the Wolf*, begun in 1966 and released in 1968, was made for several reasons. It marks the turning point when Bergman realized that all his films were dreams. Of all his films, it is closest to the horror genre, merging his personal nightmare with the cultural archetype. It's his first film to foreground the "Hour of the Wolf" motif, which reworks the werewolf and Little Red Riding Hood myths that imprinted Bergman as a child. He admits, "This cannibal motif, the hour of the wolf, goes back a long way."[5] Finally, it's a problematic work frequently attacked as being "insane" or out of control.[6] Yet it was made around the same time as *Persona*, one of his masterpieces. Originally he intended to make it the year before *Persona* when he wrote a script called *The Cannibals*. It's a work he

[4] Ingmar Bergman, "Introduction," *Four Screenplays of Ingmar Bergman*, trans. Lars Malmstrom and David Kushner (New York: Simon and Shuster, 1960), p. xiv.

[5] Bjorkman, Manns and Sima, *Bergman on Bergman*, trans. Paul Britten Austin (New York: Simon and Shuster, 1972), p. 215.

[6] See Linda Buntzen and Carla Craig, "Hour of the Wolf: the case of Ingmar Bergman," *Film Quarterly* Winter 1976-77, 23-34. John Simon also attacked the film on these grounds at the "Bergman and Dreams" conference held at Harvard University.

delayed, revised, and was never satisfied with; it clearly reveals his struggle to master this material.

The following patterns appear in all three films: (1) the hour of the wolf motif, (2) the use of a frame as a form of secondary revision, and (3) the three-stage revelation of the nightmare: the first stage, a bracketed theatrical insert, which displaces the nightmare by presenting it in a different mode or tone; the second stage, a verbal account of the dream; and the third stage, a visualization. By tracing these patterns through the three films, we will see how Bergman gains greater control over the materials, how he intensifies his use of condensation, how he shifts from coded surrealistic visuals to a richer phenomenological experience of the dream, how he moves his audience from an external observation and analysis of the events to a fuller participation inside the hallucination.

The Hour of the Wolf Motif

Bergman's early experience with the hour of the wolf is associated with his puppet theater and magic lantern. He says:

> The devil was an early acquaintance, and in the child's mind there was a need to personify him. This is where my magic lantern came in ... Red Riding Hood and the Wolf, and all the others. And the wolf was the Devil ... with a tail and a gaping red mouth ... a picture of wickedness and temptation on the flowered wall of the nursery.[7]

In Bergman's version of the fairy tale, the color red unites killer and victim as two faces of evil, which merge into the patterned wallpaper.

The werewolf myth is the story of the Shadow killer. Under the influence of the moon goddess, the good man is transformed into a wild animal, ready to devour his loved ones. Robert Louis Stevenson's version, *Dr. Jekyll and Mr. Hyde*, was also based on an actual nightmare. In all three films by Bergman, an essentially good man—the poet Tomas in *Devil's Wanton*, the artist Johan Borg in *Hour of the Wolf*, the businessman Peter Egerman in *Marionettes*—longs to murder his wife and commit suicide. The hour of the wolf is the time when the murderous impulses take over. Johan defines it most precisely:

---

[7]Ingmar Bergman, "Introduction," *Four Screenplays of Ingmar Bergman*, p. xiv.

> This hour is the worst. . . . The old folks call it the hour of the wolf.
> It's the hour when most people die. It's the hour when most children
> are born. Now is when nightmares come to us. And if we awake . . .
> we are afraid.

In Little Red Riding Hood, it is the grandmother who is transformed into
the wolfish killer, and her gaping red mouth is the primary object of terror.
These images are most explicit in *Face to Face*, where Jenny is dressed like
Little Red Riding Hood in her nightmares and confronts a demonic version of
her grandmother whose "face looked like a mad dog that was about to bite."
The color red is most intense in *Cries and Whispers*, which contains flash-
backs to the childhood memory of the magic lantern. These two myths are
reverse sides of the same cannibalistic fear—of devouring the mother, or being
devoured by her gaping red mouth. That's why Bergman's murderous nightmare always evokes the relationship between parent and child. These two
myths are also associated with two developmental stages, both crucial to the
child's emerging sexuality. The story of Red Riding Hood suggests the infantile oral stage where the .harmonious union with the loving mother is dis-
rupted by the development of ego boundaries, leading to a desperate power
struggle between the child's ravenous hunger and the mother's dominating
will. The werewolf myth is linked with adolescence, when the teenager
discovers strong sexual urges at the same time that the body undergoes
a physical transformation, including the growth of body hair.

In *The Devil's Wanton*, the werewolf and Red Riding Hood myths are
separated into two plots but united in the central nightmare. The werewolf
is the drunken poet Tomas, who talks about the hour of midnight 'when even
children sound cruel." He loses the boundaries between reality and hallucination, believing that he has actually murdered his wife; he brings a policeman
to search for her body in a closet (the very place where the grandmother is
hidden in Red Riding Hood), but discovers it was only a nightmare. In the
second plot the young prostitute Birgitta (with whom Tomas falls in love)
doubles as Red Riding Hood and the grandmother. Victimized by her cruel
older sister and her lover/pimp named Peter, she lets them take her child
and destroy it. At the beginning of her dream, Birgitta walks through a
forest of people (an image repeated in *Face to Face*) and is given a jewel
by her mother, who appears as a fairy godmother. Then the dream becomes
a nightmare as she experiences two violent transformations that reveal emotional truths which ultimately lead her to suicide. Tomas is transformed into
her sadistic customer Alf; she realizes that, like Peter, this lover is another
potential killer. She drowns a doll, which transforms into a fish—an image
that forces her to confront her own complicity in the infanticide. The nightmare reveals Birgitta to be both victim and killer.

In *Hour of the Wolf* all boundaries—between the two myths, between waking reality and dream, sanity and hallucination—completely dissolve. Just before Johan defines "the hour of the wolf," we see Alma and Johan walking through a forest with a full moon low in the sky; the hour affects even the placid Alma, who for the first time erupts into anger and threatens to leave Johan. Later, we watch close-ups of their faces illuminated by a match as Johan describes a painful memory of a childhood punishment, where he is locked in a closet, which supposedly contains a devilish little man who would bite off his toes. When he begged for release and admitted his guilt, he was beaten by his father and then forgiven by both parents and allowed to kiss their hands (like the gift of the jewel). A similar punishment is described in *Face to Face*, but there administered by a severe grandmother. This closet image can be traced back to the scene in *The Devil's Wanton* where Tomas takes the policeman (a substitute father) to search for the corpse of his wife (a substitute mother).

Following this narration, Johan describes to Alma another event, which he presents as a confession of an actual deed but which we interpret as a nightmare or hallucination, partly because of the style in which it is visualized. In the midst of this very dark movie, we suddenly see a sequence that is flooded in a harsh over-exposed light, which Bergman describes as "strong, unmoving sunlight that is always most frightening" and which dominates his "cruellest dreams."[8] In this nightmare Johan bashes in the head of a seductive child who tries to bite him and then submerges his body in water, like the drowning of the baby in Birgitta's nightmare. Johan's two narratives reveal that he, like Birgitta, is both killer and victim; he identifies both with the brutalized child and with the closeted demon—a pattern that exactly fits the sado-masochistic dynamic in the homosexual male, as delineated by Freud, and which is explicitly verbalized by the psychiatrist in *Marionettes*.

The transformation into the werewolf is most fully realized in a powerful hallucination, which absorbs and further compresses the previous narratives. It begins with Johan's shooting of his wife Alma, an act which totally bursts reality and transports him into his inner chamber of horrors, which is dominated by ominous birds, elongated shadows, and spatial disorientations. He meets the devouring woman (called Mother in the original story) who, in the midst of eating, makes him kiss her toes, reminding us of the closet demon and the forgiving mother; he watches the ominous grandmother peel off her face as if to expose a wolf, saying: "I must take my hat off, then I'll hear better"—a remark that echoes "the better to hear you with" from Red Riding Hood; he is costumed and made-up by the ominous puppeteer, who

[8]Ingmar Bergman, "Cries and Whispers," trans. Alan Blair, *New Yorker* (Oct. 12, 1972), p. 55.

functions here as a demonic director; finally, he reaches Veronica Vogler who lies on a slab like a corpse. When he runs his hand along her flesh, it's as if he is totally possessing it. Johan's erotic pleasure is interrupted when she awakens with hysterical laughter; when he turns to see the vampirish demons watching him from the ceiling, his own face is transformed by the smeared make-up and the surge of hatred into that of a leering wolf. Suddenly aware of his total descent into madness, he says: "I've reached the limit—the glass has been shattered." This moment is underscored musically by a blaring tone that sounds like the howl of a wolf and visually by a slow dissolve to water, and the boy's head bobbing up from the earlier nightmare, fusing the impulses of murder and lust. At the end of the film, we are not sure whether Johan has been totally devoured by his demons in the woods or whether he has committed suicide; we only know that he has disappeared from the island, leaving Alma wounded, impregnated, and imprinted by his madness.

From the Life of the Marionettes further compresses all of these elements into the opening color sequence, in which we see a man murder and sodomize a woman in an underground pornographic theater that is flooded in strong unmoving light, enclosed by red walls, and saturated in red brocade. The first image is a close-up of a woman's face. A man enters the frame, laying his head on her shoulder and saying softly, "I'm tired." She gently replies, "You must sleep now," and lovingly caresses his face with her hands. He erupts into fury, knocks her down, and in the struggle we see that she is bare-breasted, wearing only a choker necklace, red panties, red shoes and black stockings. She runs to hide in a closet, but he breaks in like a demon. Then she flees to a red theater, where he chokes her to death. During the actual killing we see only her legs going limp. As he lays her lifeless body on the red brocade and begins to rape her, the color drains out of the image.

Seen from the context of the rest of the film and the rest of Bergman's canon, we realize that every detail in the mise-en-scène contributes to the murder. The cruel light is as much to blame here as it was in Camus's *The Stranger*. The man's opening line, "I'm tired," has been used before both with his wife and mother. The victim's gestures of touching his face and suggesting that he sleep duplicate his wife's earlier attempts to console him during a sleepless hour of the wolf. This gesture and phrase are also typically used by a mother to quiet and control a demanding child before abandoning him to the solitude of his room. We gradually realize that the victim, a prostitute named Katerina, substitutes for the murderer's mother and wife, who is also called Katerina; she also condenses Alma and Veronica Vogler from *Hour of the Wolf* and Tomas's wife and the young mother/whore Birgitta from *The Devil's Wanton*. The murderer similarly condenses Birgitta's three lovers—the violent husband Tomas, the sadistic customer Alf, and her lover/pimp Peter—a trio whose unity was revealed in her nightmare.

In the Preface to the *Marionettes* screenplay, Bergman traces the names Peter and Katerina to the married couple—"two furious and disastrous persons"—who are minor characters in *Scenes From a Marriage*. Of all his works, *Scenes* is the most devoted to ordinary reality (though it contains a powerful nightmare sequence) and the most sympathetic to women and their growth.[9] Yet *Marionettes*, the most advanced into dreams, reveals the greatest hostility toward assertive women. Peter and Katerina are also the names of the participants in the beach orgy described by Alma in *Persona*. It is characteristic of Bergman to take minor characters from one work and transform them into protagonists of another film in a different mode; he follows the same pattern with the psychiatrist from *Persona* who becomes Jenny in *Face to Face*.

The rest of *Marionettes*, in black and white, is logically divided into eleven scenes, all dated and labeled, that occurred either before or after the catastrophe. This structure is similar to the numbered and labeled scenes in *The Rite*, an anagogic nightmare which also contains rape and murder. In *Marionettes* the labeled scenes range from Peter and the whore fifty minutes before the murder, to a psychiatrist's "definitive summary" of the event four weeks later. Both of these scenes immediately precede an epilogue, also in color, showing Peter in an insane asylum, where his behavior is described by a nurse to his visiting wife, whom he refuses to see (a sexual reversal of the situation in *Persona*). The labeled scenes function in relation to the opening sequence exactly the way the rest of Bergman's canon illuminates any specific film. Although the scenes are supposed to explain the catastrophe, they offer multiple perspectives that further complicate the reality. We watch Peter struggling in a deceptive marriage and dictating a deadening business memo; we witness his visits to his mother and psychiatrist, both of whom are interviewed by an investigator.

The investigator is seen only when he interviews Tim, who is one of the most illuminating characters in the film. The homosexual business partner of the wife Katerina, he is the one who introduced Peter to the murder victim. Like Tomas, the homosexual doctor in *Face to Face*, Tim is suffering from a recent rejection by a young lover and is a survivor of the same hidden forces that overwhelm the protagonist. He calls them "two incompatibles. The dream of nearness, tenderness, fellowship, self-forgetfulness—everything that's alive. And on the other side—violence, filthiness, horror, the threat of death. At times I think it is one and the same urge." Like Peter, he feels both hostility and affection for his partner Katerina. In two consecutive scenes, we watch him bare his inner emotional life, each time claiming that's only

[9] For a fuller discussion of these issues, see my review of *Scenes From a Marriage* in *Film Quarterly*, Winter 1974-75, pp. 48-53.

half the truth, as if the layers of masking and revelation are limitless. In one shot he sits before a mirror confronting his divided self, both images equally authentic. This composition reveals not only his narcissism, of which he is aware, and his function as the homosexual double for Peter, but also his acceptance of multiple reality. As he pulls at his face as if it were a rubber mask, he exposes the material base for the werewolf myth—the terrifying transformation that results from aging and that widens the gap between the view of the self from within and without: "When I shut my eyes I feel like a ten-year-old man and then when I open them, there stands a little old man, a childish old man." Like Tomas, his implicit incantation is, "Let me be real." Like Tomas, he is presented as an alternative to a psychiatrist who, as Bergman says in his Preface, "should be nearest to understanding . . . but is farthest away." Dr. Jensen tries to seduce Peter's wife and interprets the murder as the displacement of aggression toward a possessive mother committed by a latent homosexual. It's not that this interpretation is wrong, but merely that it's reductive and partial. Although Bergman acknowledges that the psychoanalytic framework describes the dynamics in his films, he seriously questions its powers of illumination.

Actually the most illuminating scenes are those that come closest to reenacting the opening sequence. They include two versions of the recurring fantasy of killing his wife, both addressed to the psychiatrist Jensen and both omitting the act of murder. In the first version, though Peter is verbally confessing his murderous obsession, the visualization remains beautiful and highly filtered. The germinal images are bright sunlight and silence. We see an overexposed image of Peter asleep in the foreground, while Katerina moves like a ghost in the background out of focus. The image dissolves to a screen through which he watches her combing her hair as he describes how he loves to watch her move. In both shots she is subdued and controlled. But then we see a huge close-up of her face staring directly into the camera, while Peter tells us she is looking in the bathroom mirror directly at him, knowing he has a razor in his hand ready to slit her throat, yet still smiling. He says, "I can feel the pulse in her throat." Both the image and the dialogue evoke the violent, loving encounter between actress and nurse in *Persona*, where they strike a similar loving pose in grey light and where Alma says while examining Elisabeth's face, "I can see the pulse in your neck, you've got a little scar there too." As in the earlier film, here the violence is checked. Dr. Jensen interrupts the fantasy by drawing the camera back to his office and describing the amount of blood that would be shed and that would stain the pristine whiteness of the vision. Like Peter's waking experience, the visualized fantasy remains alienated from his strongest drives.

In the second version, described in a letter that was never sent, the visualization is far more powerful and original. It begins with a white fade that dominates the visuals, though the screenplay reveals that the sequence was originally intended to be in color. As Vlada Petric has pointed out, Bergman shot it on color stock and had it printed in black and white, a process which enabled him to attain an extraordinary ethereal whiteness in this sequence. Bergman recently observed in an interview:

> Perhaps black and white is better, because color is never true. In black and white, you create the color yourself. Fantasy is created with black and white.[10]

First we see a huge close-up of part of Peter's face as he describes the experience. When he tells us it was no ordinary dream, "I dreamed I was asleep," we see a very realistic overhead shot of Peter and Katerina sleeping in their bed; it looks like one of the time-lapse photos of recent studies of body positions during sleep. Later when Peter says, "I dreamed I was dreaming," transforming the mode into a lucid dream, we see a similar overhead shot, but this time they are naked and set against a white shimmering surface that has no boundaries. He describes it as a closed space, perhaps a sphere, which creates the sensation of floating. The size of their bodies and the selection of details keep changing, always linked by dissolves and white fades. As he runs his hand along her body, an image that is reminiscent of the necrophiliac eroticism between Johan and Veronica in *Hour of the Wolf*, Peter says: "I felt a direct connection between my brain and . . . fingertips, on every finger I had an eye." When we cut back to the close-up of the narrating Peter, he totally accepts the dream and its contradictions: "A thought floated like a ribbon through my mouth. If you are death, then welcome my death. If you are life, then welcome my life." This acceptance allows him to reach the next stage of lucidity, for now he dreams that he awakens out of deep sleep, perhaps heading for a "night terror". He knows it is still a dream and that the only danger is to be afraid, or to scream. He tries to waken Katerina but can't reach her; he finds her "soft and indifferent in an exciting way." When she does awaken and smile at him, he feels an insane rage—as if he has lost control of the fantasy. As in *Hour of the Wolf*, they move their lips but we don't hear their words; violence erupts in slow motion in the white glare. As he looks at her, the camera moves into a tight shot of his eyes before fading to white. Then there is a moment of tenderness where they embrace, striking the pose of the pieta that Bergman used earlier in *Cries and Whispers*. When the image returns to a close-up of Peter as narrator, there is another abrupt shift. He says, "Then it happened all at once, Katerina was dead." We see a brief flash of her lying on the floor with blood spilled from her slit throat

[10]Peyser, p. vi.

and Peter standing behind her, almost fading into the whiteness. Then the image turns quickly to the safer reality of Peter awakening in his bedroom while Katerina sleeps on, as he asks the psychiatrist in a voice-over: "Am I in fact alive or was the dream ... my one brief moment of life—of conquered and experienced reality?" In this nightmare he moves closer to a fusion of word and image, of inner feeling and outward action, of the contradictory realities described by Tim.

Peter takes the next step toward violence in the following sequence where he attempts suicide after an argument with Katerina. In his first visit to Dr. Jensen, Peter had described his violent marital quarrels in theatrical terms: "It's all like a play with the lines rehearsed ... though the lack of an audience is fatal." In the suicide scene he stages a dress rehearsal for the murder, even arranging for a male friend to be present as audience. In an upside-down facial close-up (a recurring shot in *Persona*), Katerina describes the sexual origin of their fight: Peter tried to sodomize her but failed, she laughed, he became furious and tried to choke her. Making his exit from the scene, Peter proclaims with deliberate melodrama: "What a handsome couple you two would make," and then adds unexpectedly, "when Christ was on the cross, he said, Woman behold thy son! Son, behold thy mother." One suspects Peter learned his theatrics at his mother's knee.

In scene after scene we constantly return to the image of mother and child. In the grainy flashback to Peter's visit to his mother, their embrace is captured in a freeze frame. Although she tells the investigator that Peter had a happy childhood, she actually reminds us of the motherhood story from *Persona*. A famous actress like Elisabeth Vogler, she gave up her career for her husband and children; yet, as her daughter-in-law observes, she is still terribly self-centered and remains "a decaying monument to her husband's god-damned tyranny." The mother looks like an older version of Katerina, with whom she aggressively competes for control over Peter.

The final step toward murder occurs when Peter enters the pornographic theater fifty minutes before the catastrophe. The sequence opens with a startling assault on our senses—a writhing nude body doing bumps and grinds to sensual punk rock. We recognize images from the previous nightmares—the glaring lights, the familiar gestures and phrases, the disturbing smells and Peter's fear. On one of the walls we see an unexpected picture of a mother and baby. We share Peter's feeling of entrapment for we know all the repetitions are leading inevitably to murder. The narrative structure reaffirms Peter's refrain: "All roads are closed." What we see dramatized so powerfully is that Peter and the whore play exactly the same power games he has played with all females; he wants to direct a passive woman and becomes impotent as soon as she shows signs of life. Although Dr. Jensen says that with the prostitute "suddenly everything was possible," the repetitions imply precisely the opposite. Although this scene is the prelude to the murder, the actual killing is not repeated. Bergman forces us to experience the repetition compulsion from the inside. We have a strong urge to see the opening climax again, realizing that when we first experienced it we didn't understand what was happening. It almost becomes an erotic frustration. The murder remains an elusive nightmare partially remembered and beyond our reach. As the wife Katerina says of their former reality, "What has been can never return . . . it's gone like a dream."

THE FRAME

In most of his films Bergman uses a dramatic frame, as if to control the extended reality or as a form of secondary revision. Yet in the earlier films it doesn't always work.

In *The Devil's Wanton* the frame defines madness as a source of artistic inspiration: a professor, just released from an asylum, goes to a director with an idea for a movie—a vision of hell on earth controlled by an anarchistic Devil, showing that "life is a cruel but seductive path between birth and death." At the end of the film, the director decides *not* to make such a movie because the questions it raises are too dangerous: what is the meaning of life? why not suicide? Of course, these are precisely the questions raised by all of Bergman's films, including the two inner stories of Tomas and Birgitta. The frame defines them as two examples of hell on earth and also links them structurally. When Tomas hears of the movie idea, he immediately thinks of Birgitta, whom he has interviewed for an article on prostitution. But in the flashback to the interview, she hides her inner life. Ironically, fictional melodrama proves far more revealing of emotional truth than naturalistic documentary.

In *Hour of the Wolf*, Bergman cut out most of the original frame:

> The *Hour of the Wolf* is extremely personal. So personal I even made a prelude and a postlude of it, playfully 'boxing it in.' Nothing is left of this but the dialogue which accompanies the titles. In this prologue and epilogue I was guilty of a self-deception. It was better not to play at any aesthetic games to hold this film at a distance. So I took these two bits away in two stages.[11]

Despite this omission, the interview of the wife Alma remains as another frame. As in the interview with Birgitta, the truthfulness of documentary

---

[11] *Bergman on Bergman*, p. 212.

cinema is subverted, for Alma reveals very little and is cut off in mid-sentence while questioning the interviewer. What is most revealing is her face, which is captured in one long take and carefully studied in the final close-up. Bergman is still dissatisfied with the remaining frame.

> The difficulty with the picture is that I couldn't make up my mind who it was about. Had I made it from her point of view it would have been very interesting. But no, I made it the wrong way. After it was finished, I tried to turn it over to her; we even reshot some scenes, but it was too late. To see a man who is already mad become crazier is boring. What would have been interesting would have been to see an absolutely sane woman go crazy because she loves the madman she married. She enters his world of unreality, and that infects her. Suddenly, she finds that she is lost. I understood this only when the picture was finished.[12]

In *Marionettes*, Bergman resolves these problems by turning the frame inside out. Only the prologue and epilogue are in the present tense and in full color. Only they enable Peter to escape his marriage, in which he is trapped as a lifeless puppet acting out a charade and which dominates the black-and-white sequences of the interior. Only in the underground theater and the asylum is he able to act out fully his infantile desires and become fully alive, but, like the earlier nightmare, the prologue is only a *"brief* moment of . . . conquered and experienced reality." This idea is expressed visually when the color drains out of the image as soon as the victim is dead, softening the boundary between the prologue and the black and white sequences to follow.

The epilogue of Peter under observation in the asylum also merges with the previous sequence where Dr. Jensen presents his analytical interpretation of the events—a pairing that is bound to suggest the ending of *Psycho*. As we watch a huge close-up of Peter's face, moving to a tight shot of his eye with the color fading in, we are reminded of a similar shot in the nightmare; we hear Jensen saying in voice-over, "Only someone you kill can you possess . . . only someone who kills himself possesses himself entirely." Though incarcerated and alone, Peter has finally gained full possession of his experience. In his barren room, he stands at the window, duplicating a shot from Johan's final hallucination in *Hour of the Wolf*. His only diversions are a chessboard, reminiscent of the death game in *Seventh Seal*, a teddy bear that evokes both the circus bear who is shot as a substitute for suicide and murder in *Naked Night*, and the stuffed bear that hangs inside the automobile which Anna was

---

[12]Charles Thomas Samuels, "Ingmar Bergman: An Interview" in *Ingmar Bergman: Essays in Criticism*, ed. by Stuart M. Kaminsky (New York: Oxford University Press, 1975), pp. 131-32.

driving when she killed her husband and child in *The Passion of Anna*. In *Marionettes*, the final image is of the yellow teddy bear, a silent puppet that Peter is at last free to dominate in peace.

It is fascinating that the screenplay of *Marionettes* contains no prologue or epilogue: the narrative begins and ends with the psychiatrist, the asylum scene is placed in the center as a poetic interlude, and the murder scene is omitted entirely. While Freud identified secondary revision as a process that operated both within the dreamwork itself (particularly through displacement) and in the subsequent dream report, in both instances it was a censorship mechanism whose primary function was disguise. In *The Devil's Wanton* and *The Hour of the Wolf* the frame functions in this way, as a means of holding the terrifying dream thoughts at a distance, or to use Bergman's phrase, of playfully "boxing them in." But in *Marionettes* the frame does precisely the opposite—it exposes rather than disguises the aggression and sexuality in the latent dream thoughts. This form of creative adaptation is as revealing as Freud's own technique of free association to specific images. In Bergman's creative process, this kind of revelation is always carried much further in the visual adaptation to film than in the verbal adaptation to the screenplay.

THREE-STAGE PATTERN OF REVELATION

The recurring pattern of the three-stage revelation of the nightmare can be seen either as over-determination or as another instance of secondary revision. In all three films there is a bracketed theatrical insert, which presents the nightmare in a different mode; a verbal narration of the dream; and finally a visualization. While they seem always to be three versions of the same story, they exhibit varying degrees of displacement and disguise.

In *The Devil's Wanton* all three versions are placed in the center of the film as consecutive scenes, each moving deeper into non-ordinary reality and decreasing the amount of displacement. The insert is a farcical film, which Tom shows Birgitta and which actually is Bergman's remake of footage he bought as a child for his first projector. It appears again in the opening montage and jarring interruption within *Persona*. This little farce contains the deep structure and many germinal images for the grim stories of Tomas and Birgitta and for Bergman's entire canon. A sleeper/dreamer starts a fire in his bed, an event that brings forth Death and the Devil, who have been hiding in his room. Running from both of them, he goes to the closet where he discovers a killer with a long knife, who functions as a Shadow or closet demon. A policeman enters, seeking the guilty one, but chases both dreamer and killer who pass the knife back and forth. Amidst the chaos a spider is dangled over the bed—an image that prefigures the terrifying vision of a predatory God in *Through a Glass Darkly*. Still fleeing Death and the Devil, the dreamer/Ego, the killer/Id and the policeman/Super-Ego somersault out of three adjacent windows.

Immediately following this interlude, Birgitta narrates a recurring dream to Tomas, which she describes as beautiful and in which her mother gives her a jewel. When we see another version of this dream in the next sequence, it transforms into a nightmare, alerting us to the latent horror in the previous two scenes. Like dreams, Bergman's films teach us to trust visuals over words as more accurate signs of emotional truth. Yet in this early work the visualization of the nightmare is dominated by the same kind of theatrical surreal trickery that was used by the mute illusionist in *The Magician*.

In *Hour of the Wolf* the three-stage revelation contributes significantly to Alma's increasing participation in Johan's madness. In some ways, this film is another version of *Through a Glass Darkly*; it continues to probe madness on the island of Faro, but reverses the roles of the spouses. In the earlier work, we never actually see the mad wife's visions, and this helps to keep both the sane husband and Bergman's audience somewhat removed from the insanity. In *Persona* Bergman reworked the situation; this time the hallucinations are visualized, yet they are the mutual creation of both the "mad" artist Elisabeth Vogler and the "sane" nurse, also named Alma. As in *Hour of the Wolf*, at the end of the film the artist disappears from the island while the camera observes the surviving woman who has absorbed the other's deepest fears—a process that parallels Bergman's imprinting of his audience. Only in *Hour of the Wolf* does one character's visions actually infect another; the verbal and visual accounts of the disturbed artist enable Alma, as well as Bergman's audience, to participate fully in the madness, while the theatrical insert offers a means of escape.

Before the titles, we are informed that this film is based on Alma's verbal account and Johan's diary. Before she sees the first demon, Alma listens to Johan's verbal descriptions and sees his sketches of the cannibals. The demon leads her to take the next step—the reading of Johan's diary, which enables her to visualize three hallucinatory encounters as conventional flashbacks: in the first, the Baron invites the couple to the castle: the second encounter with the teacher introduces Johan's violence; the third meeting is with Veronica Vogler, who is used (like Mozart's "Pamina") as a demonic incantation that lures not only Johan through lust, but also Alma through jealousy. Once Alma accompanies Johan to the dinner party at the castle, she is a full participant in the madness.

This party is the context for the theatrical insert—a puppet show performance of a scene from *The Magic Flute*, which provides an alternate deep structure for Bergman's canon, one in which the forces of Love, Reason and

Order triumph over the demonic forces of passion and anarchy. Mozart's celebration of the triumph of harmony makes us all the more painfully aware of Johan's disintegration into madness.[13] Bergman says: "If you distract the audience temporarily from the course of events and then push them into it again, you don't reduce their sensibility and awareness, you heighten it."[14] As in his filmed version of this opera, here he focuses on the faces of the audience; Mozart's music seems to soothe even the demons, except for the puppeteer. Like a dream-within-a-dream structure, the insert represents an attempt to escape from the most threatening aspect of the nightmare into another reality. Its illusionary nature is underlined when the puppet stage is transformed into a live opera; these conflicting realities are linked by a close-up of Alma's face, as if this is her last chance to avoid being overwhelmed by Johan's vision. The opera provides a glimpse of the world outside Johan's madness. Hence the insert functions, not as the inner dream, but as the outer frame. Bergman claims: "It's good for people to be woken up a moment, then drawn back into the drama."[15]

When Johan confesses the murder of the child, both Alma and we in the audience are even more deeply infected by his insane vision—for his murderous images are visually imprinted in our minds. Though he claims it actually occurred, the visual style forces us to interpret the sequence as a nightmare, and the harsh discordant music makes us contrast it with Mozart's harmony from the insert. Again the words seem least reliable, yet they are essential as a triggering mechanism that releases the visual memory and authenticates its reality. In *Marionettes*, this point is made explicit, when Peter tells the psychiatrist: "So long as I don't utter a word, my anxiety is like a dream." Once he commits murder, there is no longer a need for verbalization. The same is true of Johan in *Hour of the Wolf*; once he shoots his wife, he dispenses with words and moves totally inside the hallucinatory experience—a shift that is signalled not only by surrealistic codes of ominous birds, peeled faces and dislocated eyes, but also by Bergman's cinematic distortion of space and light.

In *Marionettes*, we are presented with two very brief inserts—a fashion show in slow motion and a highly erotic nude dance. Both events have a logical place in the narrative, but their manner of stylistic presentation emphasizes their disruptive nature. Both intrude into the preceding sequence, coming before the label that introduces the scene to which they belong. Both

[13] For a fuller discussion of Bergman's use of *The Magic Flute*, see Houston and Kinder, *Self and Cinema, A Transformalist Perspective* (Pleasantville, New York: Redgrave Publishing, 1980), chapter 1.

[14] *Bergman on Bergman*, p. 222.

[15] *Bergman on Bergman*, p. 222.

performances reveal women as dehumanized puppets being manipulated by artists, merchants and consumers to communicate sexual fantasies, but they offer a stark constrast. While the fashion show displays the Persona, featuring costumes that express social codes, the nude dance directly exposes and addresses the Id. The comparison raises the question of whether the bracketed insert reveals or disguises the impulses behind the narrative. Of course, this same question is relevant to the theatrical inserts in the two earlier films. Yet in *Marionettes*, it also applies to the opening sequence, which can be seen as another theatrical insert, bracketed by being in color and by being labeled as prologue. On the one hand, this is the only film in which the dreamer fully acts out the impulse to murder in waking life, yet the victim is still a surrogate for the wife and mother. Like the fashion models, nude dancer, and even the stuffed teddy bear and chess pieces in the asylum, she is merely an icon being manipulated by the dreamer. As his fantasies take over his experience, Peter finds he prefers a silent partner—one who is sleeping, or preferably dead.

When Peter's mother tells us that he and his younger sister played with dolls and had a puppet theater, she immediately evokes Bergman's own childhood experience as a precocious puppeteer. This parallel emphasizes that the opening of *Marionettes* is the most highly compressed model for all of Bergman's films—one he almost omitted. All of his works feature his marionettes acting out his violent nightmares in theatrical settings, allowing him to project his dual identification with the ravenous wolf and the ravished child.

University of Southern California

FRANZ KAFKA:
OUTSIDER IN HIS OWN WORLD

Arnold Heidsieck

Those wishing to understand Kafka's hermetic and troubling stories must pay a great deal of attention to his socio-political environment, the dynamics of his parents' family and his inner biography.

During Kafka's lifetime an intense cultural and political struggle existed between the four million Czechs and the 2.5 million Germans in Bohemia; caught in the middle, a hundred thousand Bohemian Jews had to decide where their loyalties fell.[1] Most of them felt close to the German culture because, since the late 18th century, the Austrian empire had steadily moved to give them equal rights. Ninety percent of all Jewish children in Prague and Bohemia attended German-speaking schools. Since the Jewish middle class participated in the struggle for cultural and political emancipation, and since it produced many candidates for the German liberal and social democratic parties of Bohemia as well as many of the journalists writing in the liberal papers of German-speaking Prague and Vienna, most Czechs considered Jews either as Germans or as supporters of German supremacy in Bohemia.

Throughout the second half of the 19th century the nationalist movements of the Czechs and the Germans in Bohemia became more and more infused with economic, political and racial antisemitism. An exception to this development was German-speaking Prague itself, where nationalism and its concomitant antisemitism could not uproot the traditional upper-class liberalism which remained free of both nationalism and antisemitism. Whereas the German nationalists in the rest of Bohemia used their antisemitism mainly as a non-violent weapon in the political and economic struggle against the Czech majority (they occasionally referred to a "Czech-Jewish conspiracy"), Prague and other Bohemian cities witnessed many antisemitic and

---

[1] For this and the following paragraph see the two historical essays by Peter Hilsch (on Bohemia) and Christoph Stölzl (on Prague), in the new comprehensive *Kafka-Handbuch* (2 vols., ed. Hartmut Binder [Stuttgart: A. Kroener, 1979]), I, pp. 3-100.

anti-German progrom-like riots on the part of the Czech lower middle classes
and the so-called "Young Czechs," Bohemian patriots who were fighting for
a Czech nation state. Due to these riots roughly ten percent of the Bohemian
Jews left their homeland between 1900 and 1914.

Kafka, although not a political Zionist, felt a very strong cultural identification with Jewish nationalism in his later years.[2] He was a subscriber, avid
reader of and occasional contributor to the Prague-based Zionist paper
Selbstwehr (*Self-Protection*); in 1914 he donated money for Palestine; he
became proficient in the writing of Hebrew and, after the Balfour Declaration
of October 1917, he talked about plans of settling in Palestine as a book-
binder. The experience of the rampant antisemitism in the Hapsburg empire
and its successor states after 1918 heightened Kafka's deep-seated feeling of
worthlessness; it made his self-doubting understanding of himself as a Ger-
man-Jewish writer even more difficult, and it twisted his problem-ridden
relationship with his father even further. I quote from a letter written in
1921, after the establishment of the Czechoslovakian republic:

> I've spent all afternoon in the streets, wallowing in the Jew-baiting.
> 'Prašivé plemeno'—'filthy rabble' I heard someone call the Jews the
> other day. Isn't it the natural thing to leave the place where one is
> hated so much? (For this, Zionism or national feeling is not needed.)
> The heroism which consists of staying on in spite of it all is that of
> cockroaches which also can't be exterminated from the bathroom.
> Just now I looked out of the window: Mounted police, *gendarmerie*
> ready for a bayonet charge, a screaming crowd dispersing, and up
> here in the window the loathsome disgrace of living all the time
> under protection. (*M*, p. 213)[3]

Kafka's consciousness as a Jew played a strong part in his relationship
with his father. At the age of 36, Kafka wrote a long letter to him in which
he relates his father's ruthlessness toward him to his, the elder Kafka's,

---

[2] See Binder, in *Kafka-Handbuch*, I, pp. 436, 503-7, 570-78.

[3] Kafka's works are abbreviated as follows:

D   *The Diaries of Franz Kafka*, 2 vols. (New York: Schocken, 1948/49).

DF   Franz Kafka, *Dearest Father: Stories and Other Writings* (New York:
Schocken, 1954).

F   Franz Kafka, *Letters to Felice* (New York: Schocken, 1973).

L   Franz Kafka, *Letters to Friends, Family, and Editors* (New York: Schocken,
1977).

M   Franz Kafka, *Letters to Milena* (New York: Schocken, 1953).

STO   Franz Kafka, *The Complete Stories* (New York: Schocken, 1971).

T   Franz Kafka, *The Trial* (New York: Random House, 1969; Vintage Books
Edition).

exaggerated ambitions as a businessman, to his vulgar materialism, social Darwinism, and his total cultural assimilation into the bourgeoisie of western Austria. He also accuses his father of abuse and of "dispossessing" him:

> It was enough that I should take a little interest in the person—which in any case did not happen often, as a result of my nature—for you, without any consideration for my feelings or respect for my judgment, to butt in with abuse, defamation, and denigration. Innocent, childlike people, such as, for instance, the Yiddish actor Löwy, had to pay for that. Without knowing him you compared him in a dreadful way that I have now forgotten, to vermin and, as was so often the case with people I was fond of, you were automatically ready with the proverb of the dog and its fleas. (*DF*, pp. 146-47)

> You reinforced abusiveness with threats, and this applied to me too. How terrible for me was, for instance, that 'I'll tear you apart like a fish,' although I knew of course, that nothing worse was to follow (admittedly, as a little child I didn't know that), but it was almost exactly in accord with my notions of your power and I saw you as being capable of doing this too. (*DF*, p. 152)

> But since there was nothing at all I was certain of, since I needed to be provided at every instant with a new confirmation of my existence, since nothing was in my very own, undoubted, sole possession, determined unequivocally only by me—in sober truth a disinherited son—naturally even the thing nearest at hand, my own body, became insecure. (*DF*, p. 178)

The most damaging element of Hermann Kafka's power over his son was his ambivalence in sexual, moral, and religious matters—an ambivalence which Kafka experienced as an unbreakable double bind.[4] His father set very high social standards as far as his son's later marriage plans were concerned but sent him, at age fifteen, to a brothel to be sexually enlightened. He wanted his son to be strong, decisive and successful, but termed all his attempts to break away from home "ingratitude, extravagance, disobedience, treachery, madness" (*DF*, p. 159). He forced him to observe the conventions of orthodoxy but obviously lacked faith himself and was revolted by all signs of his son's Jewish nationalism.

More than the menacing social and family environment, it was also a far more deep-seated psychological problem which stifled Kafka's efforts to secure self-confidence, a place in the world, trust and constancy in his

---

[4]See Stölzl's essay on Kafka's "Letter to His Father," in *Kafka-Handbuch*, II, pp. 519-39.

relations to other people, and trust in the most ordinary conventions of his life. In a letter of 1920 Kafka compared himself to someone who

> each time before taking a walk, had not only to wash and comb [his hair] and so on—this alone is indeed tiresome enough—but he also (since, each time, he lacks the necessary for the walk) has to sew his clothes as well, make his shoes, manufacture his hat, whittle his walking stick, and so on. Of course he's not able to do all this very well, perhaps they hold together for the length of a few streets, but when he reaches the Graben, for instance, they suddenly all fall apart and he stands there naked among rags and tatters. And now the torture of running back to the Altstadter Ring! (M, p. 219)

Kafka's anxiety was based in his deep-seated distrust of his own ability and strength, in his belief that nothing in his daily life offered even a modest support. It seems that at each moment of his waking life—and even in his dreams—his ego had together itself up from a zero state. It had to create the most ordinary social conventions anew, and still it failed—to the point of grotesque humiliation. From numerous passages in his diaries and letters it becomes clear that he was relentlessly critical of himself (with the exception of himself as a writer), ashamed of his body, plagued by masochistic guilt feelings, indecisive, passive, depressive and despairing. In a late diary entry (1922), Kafka complains:

> I have not shown the faintest firmness of resolve in the conduct of my life. It was as if I, like everyone else, had been given a point from which to prolong the radius of a circle, and had then, like everyone else, to describe my perfect circle round this point. Instead, I was forever starting my radius only constantly to be forced at once to break it off. (Examples: piano, violin, languages, Germanics, anti-Zionism, Zionism, Hebrew, gardening, carpentering, writing, marriage attempts, an apartment of my own.) The center of my imaginary circle bristles with the beginnings of radii, there is no room left for a new attempt; no room means old age and weak nerves, and never to make another attempt means the end. If I sometimes prolonged the radius a little farther than usual, in the case of my law studies, say, or engagements, everything was made worse rather than better just because of this little extra distance. (D, ii, 209)[5]

---

[5] This self-portrait is, of course, overly negative, especially as regards Kafka's high professional competence as "Konzipist," (official writer/editor of all external communications) for his employer, the public "Workers' Accident Insurance Agency for the Kingdom of Bohemia." See Binder, in *Kafka-Handbuch*, I, pp. 356, 447, 530.

Kafka despaired of experiencing happiness in life, and he feared for his sanity. He also dreaded the loss of love from his women friends, upon whom he was extremely dependent; the delay of an answer to his enormous daily correspondence with Felice Bauer and Milena Jesenská could bring about violent, sometimes suicidal, self doubt. He had an enormously difficult time with relationships, even within his own family; he lived in extremely close proximity with them for almost all his life, yet sometimes spoke to no one for months. He broke off three engagements in despair and later seemed to be unable to have his meals in the company of others. It has been suggested that Kafka suffered from a disturbance of his primary narcissism and of his ego identity, that he never formed the basic trust necessary for sustained object-relationships.[6] A diary entry of 1911 reads: "a sad but calm astonishment at my lack of feeling often grips me. I am divided from all things by a hollow space and I don't even push myself to the limits of it" (*D*, I, 180). A diary entry of 1922 states: "Hesitation before birth. If there is a transmigration of souls then I am not yet on the bottom rung. My life is a hesitation before birth" (*D*, II, 210). In a letter to a friend, Kafka said in 1921: "nowadays I cannot endure the eyes of people (not out of misanthropy, but merely the eyes of people, their presence, their sitting there and looking across at me, all that is too much for me)" (*L*, pp. 305-6). And in four earlier letters to his fiancée Felice Bauer he wrote:

> if, when discussing the most trivial things with someone, he turned his head only slightly to one side, I at once felt rebuffed, and could see no way of drawing the other's face back toward me and thus holding on to it. Once I did succeed in almost wholly convincing Max [Brod], usually quite impervious to these states, that things with me were steadily deteriorating, and that no one, no matter how much he loved me, however close he sat beside me, looking into my eyes to reassure me, even putting his arms around me (more out of desperation than love), could possibly save me. I would have to be left to my own devices, which I actually preferred, and for the rest be tolerated for as long as humanly possible. (*F*, pp. 175-76)

> I cannot live with people; I absolutely hate all my relatives, not because they are my relatives, not because they are wicked, not because I don't think well of them (which by no means diminishes my "terrible timidity," as you suggest), but simply because they are people with whom I live in close proximity. It is just that I cannot abide communal life (*F*, p. 287)

---

[6]See Hartmut Böhme, "Mother Milena: On Kafka's Narcissism," in *The Kafka Debate*, ed. Angel Flores (New York: Gordian Press, 1977), pp. 80-99.

> I have always had this fear of people, not actually of the people
> themselves, but of their intrusion upon my weak nature; for even the
> most intimate friend to set foot in my room fills me with terror.
> (*F*, p. 279)

> As a boy I was alone a lot, but it was more from force of circum-
> stance, rarely from choice. Now, however, I rush toward being alone
> as rivers rush toward the sea. (*F*, p. 510)

These last words are strange indeed, considering the fact that they conclude a
letter to his fiancée. Loneliness, the feeling of being "divided from all things
by a hollow space," appears to have been Kafka's defense mechanism against
the intrusion of others upon his "weak nature." Thus he chose the "border-
land between loneliness and fellowship" (*D*, II, 198), or mere loneliness, as
his preferred state. Although he perceived loneliness as the most terrible
deficiency of his life, he saw it at the same time as the precondition of his
writing. Two years before his death in 1924 he wrote to his friend Max Brod
from one of the sanatoria he visited because of his incurable tuberculosis: "I
cannot talk to the people here, and if I did so, it would only be a heightening
of loneliness. And I have a nodding acquaintance with the terrors of loneliness, not so much of lonely loneliness as of loneliness among people . . . But
what is it about loneliness? Fundamentally, loneliness is my sole aim, my
greatest temptation, my opportunity, and assuming it can be said that I have
'arranged' my life, it was always with the view that loneliness can comfortably fit into it" (*L*, p. 359).

Torn between his daily obligations and his obsession to separate himself
from everything in order to write, Kafka felt himself to be in a world of his
own: "All is imaginary—family, office, friends, the street, all imaginary, far
away or close at hand, the woman; the truth that lies closest, however, is
only this, that you are beating your head against the wall of a windowless
and doorless cell" (*D*, II, 197). "What will be my fate as a writer is very
simple. My talent for portraying my dreamlike inner life has thrust all other
matters into the background; my life has dwindled dreadfully, nor will it
cease to dwindle" (*D*, II, 77). In two letters to Felice, Kafka imagines the
degree to which his life might be permitted to dwindle: "What I need for
my writing is seclusion, not 'like a hermit,' that would not be enough, but
like the dead. Writing in this sense, is a sleep deeper than that of death, and
just as one would not and cannot tear the dead from their graves, so I must
not and cannot be torn from my desk at night" (*F*, p. 279).

> I have often thought that the best mode of life for me would be to
> sit in the innermost room of a spacious locked cellar with my writing
> things and a lamp. Food would be brought and always put down far

away from my room, outside the cellar's outermost door. The walk to my food, in my dressing gown, through the vaulted cellars, would be my only exercise. I would then return to my table, eat slowly and with deliberation, then start writing again at once. (*F*, p. 156)

In another letter to Brod in 1922 he wrote:

on what frail ground or rather although nonexistent ground I live, over a darkness from which the dark power emerges when it wills and, heedless of my stammering, destroys my life. Writing sustains me, but is it not more accurate to say that it sustains this kind of life? By this I don't mean, of course, that my life is better when I don't write. Rather it is much worse then and wholly unbearable and has to end in madness. But that, granted, only follows from the postulate that I am a writer, which is actually true even when I am not writing, and a nonwriting writer is a monster inviting madness. But what about being a writer itself? Writing is a sweet and wonderful reward, but for what? In the night it became clear to me, as clear as a child's lesson book, that it is the reward for serving the devil. This descent to the dark powers, this unshackling of spirits bound by nature, these dubious embraces and whatever else may take place in the nether parts which the higher parts no longer know, when one writes one's stories in the sunshine. Perhaps there are other forms of writing, but I know only this kind; at night, when fear keeps me from sleeping, I know only this kind. (*L*, pp. 333-34)

A week later, in another letter to Brod, he summed up the purpose of his writing: "I am away from home and must always write home, even if any home of mine has long since floated away into eternity. All this writing is nothing but Robinson Crusoe's flag hoisted at the highest point of the island" (*L*, p. 340). Kafka the writer saw himself as a Crusoe in a distant, almost inaccessible place, sending out private communications dealing with his innermost conflicts and anxieties which he nevertheless wished would contain something universal to be shared with others.

Of "The Judgment," the first of his own stories that he liked without reservation, Kafka wrote: "Only *in this way* can writing be done, only with such coherence, with such a complete opening out of the body and soul" (*D*, I, 276). Kafka here employs the traditional device of a double, the hero's unmarried and unsuccessful childhood friend in far away Russia, to show that Georg Bendemann's denigration of his friend is the struggle within himself, between his wish to succeed in life, marriage, and profession, and his wish to remain a bachelor.[7] To remain a bachelor, of course, means to fail as far as the communal norms of his family and tradition are concerned. The father unmasks his son's decision to get married and to take over the family business all by himself as phony and parasitical, a mere disguise of his basic inability to become an independent member of society. The son accepts his father's reasoning and willingly carries out the father's death sentence himself. The story reflects Kafka's life-long struggle to break away from his family and to start a family of his own, but also Hermann Kafka's belief, which he by no means hid from his son, that Kafka was unable to make it in the rough-and-tumble outside world.

Kafka somehow believed that this unconventional, nightmarish story was sufficiently transparent to be recommended to his fiancée's father as a true portrayal of his, Kafka's, situation. Since the story is narrated entirely from the perspective of Georg Bendemann who gradually recognizes his inability to stand up to his father and to preserve his self-worth, the reader would be expected to experience the breakdown, self-condemnation, and suicide of the hero as the gradual intrusion of the nightmarish into the every-day bourgeois family life. But there is an indication that the father's death-sentence against his son, in the struggle between the generations, has been a foregone conclusion: "So now you know what else there was in the world besides yourself, till now you've known only about yourself! An innocent child, yes, that you were, truly, but still more truly have you been a devilish human being! —And therefore take note: I sentence you now to death by drowning!" (*STO*, p. 87). The father's slight grammatical-logical deviance, this "still more truly," reveals the injustice of his judgment. Without knowing it the son is placed under the paternal double bind: is he the loyal child, innocent of any design on the father's social role, or the father's natural but "devilish" successor?

The *Metamorphosis*, one of Kafka's most grotesque stories, continues and, at the same time, modifies the working-through of this basic conflict, the choice between success or failure, guilt-ridden self-preservation or "innocent" self-denial. At the time he wrote this story Kafka had tied up all his resources in a new venture, a family-owned asbestos factory. He faced the possibility of having to take over the business himself, thus becoming forever tied to the hated lifestyle and demanding daily duties of his father. Furthermore, Felice Bauer seemed to have broken off their relationship, and Kafka dreaded the possibility of being absorbed by a torturing job while remaining a bachelor. These prospects threw him into suicidal despair (*D*, I, 248; *L*, p. 88). In the story Kafka projects this dreaded possibility on to a fictional

---

[7]See Walter Sokel, "Perspectives and Truth in *The Judgment*," in *The Problem of 'The Judgment,'* ed. Angel Flores (New York: Gordian Press, 1977), pp. 193-237.

plane.[8] The elder Samsa has gone bankrupt; the son Gregor takes on the role of the family's sole bread-winner. His life becomes totally empty and monotonous. Because of the father's heavy indebtedness to Gregor's employer, there is not the slightest hope for change.

The story begins with the fact of his metamorphosis: upon awakening "one morning from uneasy dreams he found himself transformed in his bed into a gigantic insect. He was lying on his hard, as it were armor-plated, back and when he lifted his head a little he could see his domelike brown belly ... Oh God, he thought, what an exhausting job I've picked on! Traveling about day in, day out ... The devil take it all! He felt a slight itching up on his belly; ... identified the itching place which was surrounded by many small white spots the nature of which he could not understand" (*STO*, pp. 89-90). This microscopic realism is unsettling because minute details take on a magnified and threatening significance; they seem fixated, independent of a personal narrator's perceptions and judgments or of the laws of the physical world. Several years later, Kafka spoke of the "microscopical eyes" (*M*, p. 65) and confusion one develops in reaction to an emotional threat. The story's nightmarish fantasy in all its precise detail, with Gregor's serious, rationalizing attempts to keep his "cool reflection, the coolest possible" (*STO*, p. 93) and the rest of the family-life fully intact and unchanging, clearly has its origin in Kafka's experience of the separation of his inner self from the threatening circumstances of his external life.

In his letters, Kafka often imagines himself as an animal, in ways that seem to abbreviate metaphors into statements of fact, suggesting masochistic self-punishment and isolation from all surrounding humanity: "My body is afraid ... [it] would prefer slowly to creep up the wall" (*M*, p. 143). The paradox of this metaphor and of the story itself is that the anxiety of human existence cannot be affected even by the most thorough-going metamorphosis. Gregor's grotesque humiliation is heightened, because in his new state he fears, now more than ever, that the chief clerk may ruin him by giving an unfavorable report of the incident to the head of the firm: "at Gregor's very first words the chief clerk had already backed away and only stared at him with parted lips over one twitching shoulder ... the suddenness with which he took his last step out of the living room would have made one believe he had burned his foot.... Gregor perceived that the chief clerk must on no account be allowed to go away in this frame of mind" (*STO*, pp. 101-2). Kafka's "realism of detail" captures the behaviorial expressions of the antagonists, their moods and ambivalent intentions—not necessarily from under the predominant narrative perspective (in this case from Gregor's point of view), but as spontaneous reactions to the story's momentary happenings. This

---

[8] See Heinz Hillman, "Schaffensprozeβ," in *Kafka-Handbuch*, II, pp. 24-25, 30-31.

realism achieves a sophisticated overlap between the minutely portrayed real and the surreal or incomprehensible, between the more and more self-reflexive, insightful perspective of the narrator-hero and his anxious conjurations of guilt, "shame" (*STO*, p. 112), hopelessness and death.

Kafka's portrayal of the court system in *The Trial* is a working out of his dilemma on the wider social plane. The paradox of this court system is that it has the appearance of a self-contained, hierarchically structured order, but at the same time presents itself as a thorough-going disturbance of the everyday conventions and norms of bourgeois society. At the same time this novel was written, at the beginning of World War I, the Austrian military administration had extraordinary dictatorial prerogatives; for instance, it suspended the freedom of assembly. But the court system in *The Trial* is certainly more vicious, more arbitrary and dictatorial than this. The trial proceedings which are kept secret from the accused and always lead to a conviction (so that, in K.'s opinion, a "single executioner could do all that is needed"); the ever-vengeful officials who are "confined day and night to the workings of their judicial system;" the goddess of justice who is depicted as the "goddess of the Hunt in full cry"—all point to the secret but relentless aggressiveness or perversion of the social system which Josef K. is faced with. In some of the scenes, such as the flogging of Franz and Willem, Block's humiliation and near transformation into a dog, and Josef K.'s butcher's knife-execution ("like a dog"—*T*, p. 286) at the hands of his two "companions," this aggressiveness becomes extremely grotesque and sadistic.

Kafka himself once associated the hero's humiliation and destruction with his own masochistic guilt feelings over his break-up with Felice Bauer (*D*, II, 65); he believed that he deliberately deceived her for years through his intense letter-writing. But more importantly, Kafka's hopeless double bind situation vis-à-vis his father informs the workings of the court system as sketched by the lawyer Huld, the painter Titorelli and the priest. This double bind is especially well illustrated by the legend "Before the Law" and its numerous conflicting interpretations. To the priest, interpretation is basically futile: "The right perception of any matter and a misunderstanding of the same matter do not wholly exclude each other" (*T*, p. 271). "The scriptures are unalterable and the comments often enough merely express the commentators' despair" (*T*, pp. 272-73). It "is not necessary to accept everything as true, one must only accept it as necessary," to which K. answers: "A melancholy conclusion ... It turns lying into a universal principle" (*T*, p. 276). This chapter and the following, dealing with K.'s execution in the loneliness of a deserted quarry on the outskirts of the city, point to K.'s hopeless isolation from human understanding and from his fellow-men. But of course, this isolation was the main thrust of the novel from its beginning. K. strives for a thoroughly rational comprehension of his situation, yet again and again he is "deflected from this perspective into a helpless absorption in the specific details of any given situation in which he finds himself, studying the relations of others the way the man from the country studies the fleas in the doorkeeper's collar. The Inspector's charge, in the first chapter, that Joseph K. is insensitive to the nuances of his situation, indicates that the Court appears to encourage this attitude also."[9] With the overemphasis on detail, the linear progression of the narrative produces successive "revelations," very much like those in a detective novel; yet these revelations often prove shortsighted, to be contradicted later, and for the most part they are more disorienting than explanatory. The narrative fractures into detailed fixated moments; it starts and stops, and begins anew—whether in fictional reality or in the thought of the protagonists (through the device of "narrated speech") one does not always know. Joseph K.'s perception of the proceedings against him becomes more and more confused and dissociated,[10] obsessed with the hope for help from people—Leni, the priest, any "human figure" (*T*, p. 286)—who prove incidental to his trial and execution.

In *The Castle* as well as in many of Kafkas's later stories the position of social outsider or outcast becomes even more pronounced. Kafka often uses animal-metaphors to relate a sense of isolation and anxiety. He sees himself as an "animal condemned to silence and separation" (*F*, p. 233), as "some kind of beast at the farthest pole from man" (*D*, II, 98). In "A Report to an Academy" an ape, or rather a former ape, undertakes to justify, through the learned capability of speech, his integration into the human race, its professional and rational aspects, while remaining sexually and morally free from its norms. The report of the ape demonstrates the necessity of assimilation to the social rituals of civilization while implicity denying their legitimaticy. Whereas the ape still lives in the human world, in "The Burrow" a giant mole (or a badger) has built a labyrinthic system of pathways through the earth, absolutely self-contained and secure with the exception of the entrance, and it controls the system with obsessive vigilance. The burrow is the ultimate metaphor for Kafka's desire to retreat into a completely private inner world inaccessible to others, and at the same time a metaphor for the impossibility of such desire. The animal must leave the security of his home in order to protect it.

[9] James Rolleston, "Introduction," in *Twentieth Century Interpretations of 'The Trial,'* ed. Rolleston (Englewood Cliffs, N.J.: Prentice Hall, 1976), p. 7.
[10] See Karlheinz Fingerhut, "Die Phase des Durchbruchs," in *Kafka-Handbuch*, II, pp. 287-93.

The burrow has probably protected me in more ways than I thought
or dared think while I was inside it. This fancy used to have such a
hold over me that sometimes I have been seized by the childish
desire never to return to the burrow again, but to settle down
somewhere close to the entrance, to pass my life watching the
entrance, and gloat perpetually upon the reflection—and in that
find my happiness—how steadfast a protection my burrow would
be if I were inside it. Well, one is soon roughly awakened from
childish dreams. What does this protection which I am looking
at here from the outside amount to after all? Dare I estimate the
danger which I run inside the burrow from observations which I
make when outside? Can my enemies, to begin with, have any
proper awareness of me if I am not in my burrow? A certain awareness of me they certainly have, but not full awareness. And is not
that full awareness the real definition of a state of danger? So the
experiments I attempt here are only half-experiments or even less,
calculated merely to reassure my fears and by giving me false reassur-
ance to lay me open to great perils. No, I do not watch over my own
sleep, as I imagined; rather it is I who sleep, while the destroyer
watches. (*STO*, p. 335)

These obsessive ruminations characterize Kafka's reductionist style, the
smashing up of an emotional trauma into ever more tentative and narrow
propositions. In *The Castle*, Kafka's last novel, a wandering stranger makes
numerous but equally frustrating efforts to be admitted to the close-knit
society of a village and the inaccessible castle overlooking it. His desperate
isolation from the important people of this small territory becomes ever
more dominant. Through constant shifts of the narrative's perspective, his
attempts at communication make everything he seems previously to have
ascertained ever more vague and uncertain—to the point of the dissolution
of his sense of time, space, and emotional orientation.[11] The more he learns
about the administrative procedures of the castle and engages in speculations and interpretations of his observations, the more he tries to obtain
some recognition as a member of this community, the more starkly he
emerges as the totally isolated outsider. Whereas in the earlier stories—
"The Judgment," "The Metamorphosis," and *The Trial*—the ordinary perspective of the protagonists turns into total, nightmarish isolation, the heroes
of the later stories are divorced from the human world to begin with, either
as animals ("Report to an Academy" or "The Burrow") or as *The Castle*'s

---

[11] See Winfrid Kudszus, "Changing Perspectives in *The Trial* and *The Castle*," in
The Kafka Debate, p. 386.

K., an outsider seeking admittance in vain. The author's distancing reflexiveness, ego weakness and emotional uncertainty and his work's shifting thematic and narrative perspectives mesh in the position of the outsider.[12]

University of Southern California

[12] Rolleston has used the term *outsider* as a central "intellectual pattern" (p. 115) in his interpretation of *The Castle* (*Kafka's Narrative Theater*, Pennsylvania State U. Press 1974, pp. 112-29). I am applying it, in a much broader sense, to Kafka's entire work and life. —I would like to thank Wilhelmina Hotchkiss for editorial assistance.

DREAMS, AGGRESSION, AND INDIVIDUALITY

Joseph M. Natterson, M.D.

Important interrelationships exist among dreaming, aggression, sexuality, individuality, and creativity. A dream and pertinent clinical data from a psychoanalytic case will be presented. This will be followed by a discussion which demonstrates the above connections.

The dream is as follows:

> My mother, Jimmy's mother, and I are in a hollow, near a trestle. It is a glade with rich soil, which I know very well. The women are digging up Boston ferns which grow there. I am running about frantically through the bushes and tall grass, hoping I can find Jimmy, to warn him that his mother is going to kill him. Suddenly a black snake appears; it is very menacing. Mother, Jimmy's mother, and I flee. I am terrified, and I awaken.

Sam is a middle aged man, a fine and successful writer. When Sam was four years old, his closest friend was Jimmy. Sam's siblings were as yet unborn. He and Jimmy were like alter egos. Sam's mother and Jimmy's mother were closest friends, as were Sam's father and Jimmy's father. One day Jimmy's mother was hunting squirrels with a shotgun, while Jimmy played nearby. She "accidentally" shot Jimmy's head off—having mistaken him for a squirrel. Sam still remembers Jimmy's mother staggering down the road, carrying Jimmy's headless body—his blood and brains smeared over her hands and face and clothing, moaning, "I've killed my baby." Although it was officially an accident, Sam knows that she killed her son because she and her husband had conceived him three years before their marriage. She could not bear this living reminder of her shame and sin. Relatives, friends, and authorities in this rural Baptist stronghold all concurred: it was a terrible accident, but somehow God's will had been served.

To this day Sam cannot discuss Jimmy's death without sobbing—he grieves, he wishes to repair the damage, he feels he should have died instead of Jimmy, and he shudders with relief that his life was spared instead of Jimmy's. Understandably, serious problems exist in his relationship with women. When he masturbates, the seminal ejaculate on his hands appears as blood, Jimmy's blood on his hands.

To paraphrase Sam, this was the single most awful and awesome experience of his life. His world view; his relations with his parents and siblings, and his wife and children; sexuality and aggression; his present and his future; work, religion, and art—all have been enormously influenced by this event. Instead of tracing the relationships to these many existential issues, the rest of this paper will dwell on the creative linkage.

Sam's entire artistic career has been devoted to a happy, romanticized reconstruction of the past. In his writing, the helpless horror of his personal past is replaced by a hopeful enthusiasm accompanied by plausible happy endings. Since Sam is unafraid of ruthless self study, he states categorically that Jimmy's murder, and its experiential consequences, propelled him into writing. Even more particularly, the event impelled him to focus on the loving aspects of family intimacy, in order to repair, to undo the damage.

In the psychoanalytic situation, Sam's anguish has been sizeably diminished, and just in the past week, he boldly stated he no longer *needs* the nightmare. The statement is indicative, although premature. Sam also notes that he is beginning to write about "tougher" people and themes. He feels more able to treat life as it really is, in its harshness and its tragedy.

Now departing from Sam, it seems possible that the creative effect of this trauma could have produced literature, sculpture, or other art of tortured rather than relieving quality. This would have depended on a multitude of antecedent and subsequent experiences in the artist's life.

The crucial issue in all this is the role of aggression in creativity.

The person with the soul of an artist, but without the talent or training, does nevertheless have a creative opportunity, namely, the achievement of individuality. The accomplishment has much in common with artistic creativity. Dreaming is a significant concomitant—causal and/or reflective and indicative. Charles Rycroft has advised that analysts utilize Freud's theory as a quarry rather than as an edifice. Thus with some dreams, one may usefully employ Freud's dictum that the analytic focus be on latent dream content, but in other situations, more heuristic possibility may exist in the manifest dream. Optimal blurring of the distinction between manifest and latent dream should exist. Dreams constitute the most intimate and powerful expression of the psychic life of the individual. With greater or lesser clarity, dreams reveal the psychic structures which establish a person's individualty, or the possibility of its attainment. These pain-saturated themes run through the dreams of every patient.

Aggression and sexuality are the ancient and powerful twins. Freud saw them as the cosmic opponents, locked in eternal embrace. A person's encounter with aggression may, if successful, establish a new quality of individuality and a more stable platform for the freer utilization of sexuality, the immediate instrument and source of creativity. The aggression of any person is crucially derived from the traumata, the pain and suffering of that person. And, therefore, the agonies of the human experience establish both the patterns and the motive force for the person's uniqueness. The relationship between aggression and individuality is by no means new. Among the important contributions to this subject are: Freud's *Civilization and Its Discontents*;[1] Marcuse's *Eros and Civilization*;[2] Rogow's *The Dying of the Light*;[3] and now Lasch's *The Culture of Narcissism*.[4]

Aggression and sexuality, as portrayed in manifest dreams, typically share a common fate in the early and middle phases of an analysis; however, they diverge *notably* and *very significantly* in the late phase of an analysis. Here is a summary description: Early in analysis both sexuality and aggression tend to be furtive, disguised, and allusive. The superego effect is predominant. As the analysis progresses into the middle phase, the sexuality and aggression are still convergent: they have become much freer and more exuberant—and are expressed in the manifest dream without guilt. However, an instructive divergence becomes evident in the final stage of the analysis: the sexuality remains free and unrestrained, but the aggression now possesses civility. It has become subdued, tamed, non-violent. To be graphic: the anxious, hurt dreamer of the initial stage changes into the ax murdering dreamer of the middle stage who becomes the unapologetically indignant dreamer of the final stage. The savagery of the middle phase has vanished.

The double helix of aggression and sexuality circles in marvelous ways around the dream axis. Each person's dream theme has its own portrait of aggression. As the dreams are recalled, reported, thought about and interpreted, transformation of the aggression occurs, and there is a corresponding augmentation of the person's individuality, wisdom, and maturity.

The psychological development of the individual does not occur according to some rigid and happy timetable, disturbed only by the empathic lapses of inadequate parents. Kohut's ideas, which are the rage in psychoanalysis, are, I am afraid, despite their clinical pertinence and appealing simplicity, based on just such a non-conflictual, non-dialectical premise. Empathy is invaluable in parents and in psychotherapists, but I doubt its sufficiency

---

[1] Freud, Sigmund. *Civilization and Its Discontents*. Standard Edition, (1930), Vol. 21, pp. 64-145.
[2] Marcuse, Herbert. *Eros and Civilization* (Boston: Beacon Press, 1955).
[3] Rogow, Arnold. *The Dying of the Light* (New York: Putnam, 1975).
[4] Lasch, Christopher. *The Culture of Narcissism* (New York: Norton, 1978).

for the generation of rich and varied personalities. Aggression is the prime existential commonality of our time: politically, economically, psychosocially, interpersonally, and intrapsychically. Each of us must wrestle with the devil, and sometimes be seriously injured in the process. A person who has not confronted aggression externally might grow into adulthood as symmetrical and unblemished as a baby's behind—and be just as interesting. Without the crookedness, the asymmetries, the scars—humans succumb to homogeneity and a terrible conformity.

Nightmares can be viewed in several ways regarding their relevance to individuality and therefore to creativity. First, and obviously, the traditional ascription of function to a dream such as Sam's is that it represents a reworking of a severe trauma which threatened ego function, and it remains necessary to repeat the incident in the dream to help maintain optimal ego function. Conversely, as is also well known, a nightmare can be one part of a larger pattern of psychological events which constitute a fragmentation of the ego and a loss of self cohesion. Fortunately, this is not a present danger for Sam. It might also be postulated that the dream, through its symbols, sharpens Sam's appreciation of his artistic tasks of reparation and restoration through a new artistic creation. This is especially evident in Sam's work in which he rescues the innocence of the past, just as in his nightmare he attempts to save the innocence of Jimmy. John Mack's book, *Nightmares and Human Conflict*,[5] gives numerous examples of severe life problems, the creative representation of these problems in "bad dreams," and then the use of these remembered dreams in the author's current writing. Another important creative function of a nightmare may be to raise the level of creative anxiety. Perhaps it would be more accurate to think of the anxiety as existing in unconscious, potential form. Through the nightmare the anxiety is brought into conscious access, and thus is transformed into creative anxiety. This function is essentially non-symbolic and non-cognitive, although it cannot be completely separated from the thematic aspects of the dream. Sam is exceptionally attuned to the tragic dimensions of the human experience, and his dreams are significant components of the dramas by which he attempts to illuminate and resolve.

In every analysis hundreds of dreams are worked with. Many of these are nightmares. In my experience such dreams tend to be more analytically valuable than less anxiety laden dreams. A vintage nightmare may be of special importance. My earliest remembered dream, from around six years, was a nightmare. I was unable to analyze it until I reached my forties, and then I put it to good use.

[5] Mack, John. *Nightmares and Human Conflict* (Boston: Little, Brown and Company, 1970).

One final clinical point: The aggression, which is the invariably essential component of a nightmare, may not always be immediately evident. Here is an example of this type of disturbing dream. A man dreamed that as he observed his wife's face, it aged and became his mother's. He watched transfixed and horrified and then awakened. He has good reason to detest his mother. Recently, he discovered a serious betrayal by his wife. The pain generated by his wife's betrayal pushed the dreamer reluctantly into his therapeutic and creative misrecognition: picturing his wife as his mother, and thus becoming aware of the tremendous levels of aggression within the marriage.

The student of dreams may not begin his study with nightmares, but in due time he will discover that such dreams are rich with psychological and existential meaning. It is quite impressive that so many nodal dreams in analysis have a terrifying component. The analysis of these dreams may have creative consequences of great significance.

University of California, Los Angeles

NIGHTMARES*

Claude T. H. Friedmann, M.D.

INTRODUCTION

A journey into the "nightmare" is both a journey into the occult and a short sojourn through the history of psychiatry. It is, in addition, a trip into modern neurological science. Perhaps no other area of study focuses so acutely on our past and future, as regards mysterious and frightening mental disturbances. It serves as a reminder that it is only in the last few decades that emotional illness has emerged from the medieval shrouds of sorcery and spirits into the more rational concepts of the unconscious and dopamine. It further serves as a sobering lesson to those of us who have lost sight of our supernatural and irrational collective past; a fitting reminder that our scientific advances are but a few steps away from the ghosts, devils, religiosity, and parapsychology which permeate the various subcultures and strata of our diverse society.

The interconnection of past to present, occult to scientific, is particularly well illustrated in the vocabulary we will use in this chapter. To begin with, let's take the word "nightmare" itself. This noun is derived from both the French "couchmar" and the German "nachtmar."[1] A "mar" is a "devil." If you are French, you talk about the "pressing devil" which is couched upon your chest; if German, about the "night devil." At any rate, when we say the word "nightmare," we may mean many things, but we imply that a devil has come upon us while asleep.

Another term is "pavor nocturnus." "Pavor" is Latin for "terror." We speak then of nocturnal terror. Some authors have used it as a synonym for "nightmare," while others reserve it for deep sleep (Stages 3-4) phenomena

*Also published in *The Dream in Clinical Practice*, ed. J. Natterson (New York: Jason Aronson, 1981).
[1] Broughton, "Sleep disorders: Disorders of Arousal?" *Science*, 159 (1968), pp. 1070-78.

only, preferring to call the "bad dream" that occurs during Rapid-Eye-Movement sleep a "nightmare." To add to the confusion, and really jazz up the parapsychological end of things, we have the peculiar terms "incubus attack" and "succubus attack." An incubus is a spirit or demon who "lies upon" sleeping women for the purpose of sexual intercourse. A succubus "lies under" sleeping men for the same purpose. Some nightmares, most especially Stage 3 or 4 night terrors, are sometimes termed incubus attacks.[2] In addition, night terrors are related to enuresis, somnambulism, and sleep talking.[3] To round things out, nightmares are often a symptom within a constellation of severe diurnal psychopathology.

Broughton,[4] Fisher[5] and others have begun to bring both the light of science and the order of classification to this murky semantics. Before summarizing their findings, however, let me say a bit more about the symptoms. It is probably no coincidence that medieval concepts, demons, devils, and "pavor" have found their way into the vocabulary of nocturnal sleep disturbances. One can hardly imagine a more terrifying event in the life of a "normal" human being than the nightmare. Fast asleep, all ego defenses down, there suddenly emerges into one's consciousness an irrational, hallucinated, emotional episode, often so frightening as to awaken the sleeper, who parenthetically, may well find himself in a cold sweat, his hands trembling and his breath short and labored. The nighttime equivalent, as Freud[6] put it, of the anxiety attack. True angst. Jones[7] wrote of a triad: (1) dread, (2) weight on the chest, (3) paralysis. Both he, Freud, and others of their school spoke of the Oedipal and psychosexual conflicts which they considered the root cause of such difficulties. Yet some[8] today see Freud and Jones as probably dealing with REM sleep "bad dreams," and not with true night terrors. Or, at least, as not clearly differentiating between them. As terrifying as the REM nightmare is (and, I suspect, we've all had them), the true "night terror" is even more frightening.

Keith[9] reviews the salient differential points which separate the REM

---

[2] Broughton, "The incubus attack," in *Sleep and Dreaming*, ed. E. Hartmann, (Boston: Little Brown and Co., 1970) pp. 188-92.

[3] See note 1 above.

[4] Ibid.

[5] Fisher, "A psychophysiological study of nightmares and night terrors: II. Mental content and recall of stage 4 night terrors," *Journal of Nervous and Mental Diseases*, (1974), 158:174-188.

[6] Freud, "On the grounds for detaching a particular syndrome from neurasthenia under the description 'anxiety neuroses'," *Standard Edition*, (1895) vol. 3, pp. 87-117.

[7] Jones, "On the nightmare," *American Journal of Insanity*, 66 (1910), 383-417.

[8] See note 5 above.

[9] Keith, "Night terrors: A review of psychology, neurophysiology, and therapy," *Journal of the American Academy of Child Psychiatry*, 14 (1975), 477-489.

"nightmare" or "bad dream" from the Stages 3-4 "night terror." In so doing, he points us further along the trail blazed by the analysts: out of the Middle Ages and into the age of science. He also gets us into a position to understand Fisher and Broughton. That will get us into position for trying to understand our case study. A night terror, pavor nocturnus, possesses, according to Keith, the following features: It usually occurs during Stage 4 (deep) sleep, with arousal to an awake, alpha, pattern in the EEG; there is pronounced autonomic activity during the attack (fast pulse, perspiration, rapid breathing); there is also pronounced physical activity (thrashing, somnambulism); verbalizations almost always signal the onset, and there is often loud screaming; content of the dream, if recalled, is terrifying, violent, aggressive, and of a singular nature as to the thought or emotion; the patient is confused, disoriented, and amnesic if awakened.

In contrast, the "bad dream" or "common nightmare," called by Keith the "anxiety dream," occurs during REM (Rapid Eye Movement) sleep, with only minor autonomic changes, decreased muscle tone, little physical movement, only occasional verbalizations, little screaming, and elaborate, vivid, mental content. If awakened from a REM anxiety dream, the dreamer is easily calmed and quickly lucid. The memory for content is much greater in the REM "nightmare" than the night terror.

Broughton[10] has demonstrated that the night terror of adults and children, as well as somnambulism and nocturnal enuresis, all involve a specific neurophysiological mechanism, namely, a sudden change in the mental state from that of deep sleep (slow-wave EEG pattern) to an arousal pattern (alpha-wave EEG). Thus, although the person is physically asleep, the brain is in a "dissociated" state of arousal. This "arousal" state is normal to all of us, and occurs at regular cycles throughout the night in each and every one of us. It is in parallel with this state, interestingly enough, that virtually all night terrors occur. Why some people have night terrors, enuresis, or sleep-walking during these periods of arousal, is a question we will address, albeit gingerly, later on in this chapter. For the moment, though, we will pause. We have just briefly traced the "nightmare" through its metaphysical, analytic and scientific history, and paved the way for the study of a most unusual case. Although most problems with nightmares occur in children, the adult is far from immune. Our patient, an adult, suffered from nightmares for twenty years. As we unfold her tale, we should try to answer the following questions: (1) Did she suffer from "anxiety dreams" or "pavor nocturnus?" (2) What is her psychiatric diagnosis? (3) What dynamics could explain her problems? (4) Are we dealing with a neurophysiologic difficulty, a psychogenic illness, or a combination of both? (5) Was her treatment optimal?

Without, then, further ado, the case of Miss T.

[10] See note 1 above.

THE PATIENT

HISTORY

When one combines intelligence, energy, and perfectionistic traits with a degree in psychology, suicide attempts, self-mutilation, and theatricity, one has the ingredients for a most complicated and fascinating therapeutic encounter. If, in addition, one adds a history of terrifying, but unrecollected dreams since a rape at age eleven, one has the ingredients for a chapter in this book. If that's not enough, there's one more thing: the patient is a crack shot, and threats of violence are never very far away.... In case you need any more excitement.

When I first met Miss T., she was sitting tensely in a chair in my office. Her legs were crossed and she was hunched forward. She stared at me with small, dark, angry eyes. Then she began to cry. She was thin. I thought at times that I was speaking to a small child. A ten year old? Yet she was thirty-one. She pleaded for my help, then kicked me in the shins. Then she cried again and apologized. Her history, given in obsessional detail, was thus wrapped in a shroud of overt, demonstrative emotion. Schizophrenia? Hysteria? Obsessive-compulsive disorder? I had, at that moment, no idea whatsoever.

What she recounted went, more or less, like this: she'd been "falling apart" for two years, out of work for one, and in "very bad shape" for eight weeks. Her symptoms included nervousness, insomnia, weight loss, decreased appetite, and "nightmares." In addition, she occasionally hallucinated voices. Sometimes she impulsively and uncontrollably broke objects in her room, bones in her body, or bruised her extremities. She had abused placidyl on and off for two years, but had stopped a month before we met. She was afraid she might kill herself—she'd tried a year ago. She was even more concerned about killing someone else—most particularly the uncle with whom she lived. Guns and she were by no means strangers.

There was little doubt that she required hospitalization, and she was admitted to the Inpatient Service at the UCLA Neuropsychiatric Institute, where I helped care for her for two months. Over time, as we talked, the rest of her story unfolded. We also became friends. I didn't get kicked again. But sex, guns, and violence—especially violence against men—were constant topics.

The patient was the only daughter of a rather soft-spoken, homespun, "unliberated" mother, and a hard-nosed, chauvinistic, rustic father. Indeed, "rustic" is a good term with which to describe the entire family: almost like a page out of your favorite Western. Daughters in this family were not of much value: Miss T. was to have been, like her older and younger siblings, a son. Her father never forgave her for it. She hated him in turn, and he was to become the focus of many of our talks. Her mother never came up, until we began to have family sessions. Miss T. tried very hard to be a son: she was a tomboy, got a master's degree, learned to shoot arms, wore her hair short, talked tough, and never backed away from a fight. But when we talked, and she turned inside out, I saw a very frightened little girl.

When she was about eleven, she babysat regularly for a family next door to her home. The child's father, "Larry," came in one night and raped her. He threatened to kill her younger brother, Tom, if she told anyone. Until she told me, she had lived with this hellish memory and agonizing fear, without sharing them with a soul. For twenty years the trauma was, literally, locked up inside her. It became, as it were, her personal "devil." Her "nachtmar." For from that day forward the nightmares, hallucinations, and physical destruction began.

With varying frequency, over the subsequent twenty years, she has experienced the following: she awakens suddenly in extreme confusion and terror, often screaming, often crying for help. Then she may get intensely angry, get out of bed, and break something in her room. Once in a while the object of her rage becomes herself, and she has banged her arms and legs against the wall, kicked herself, hit herself with a hammer, and once even broke her own knee. She told me that her uncle, with whom she's lived since age eighteen, is roused by her screams. If he is able to awaken her quickly enough, the destrucive behavior is aborted. Usually this is done by holding her down on the bed until she is fully awake. Her uncle has informed her that she will often scream his name aloud, or the name "Larry." She, however, never remembers a single thing. In fact, she has never recalled a single dream in her entire life—as far back as she can remember. Whatever it is that rouses and terrifies her is completely unknown to her. Ghost? Devil? Suppressed unconscious drives? Incubus? I was fascinated, but baffled.

I was even more baffled when she told me that, despite her constant "nightmares," repetitive self mutilation, and a very lethal suicide attempt, she had never had any psychiatric care, even though she herself was a psychologist! And, what's more, her family thought she was a very normal girl! Or, at least, that's what they told her. I began to harbor the desire to meet this extraordinary family. I was not to be disappointed—colorful, to say the least, they were.

But before we go into that, let's complete the history. First off, this lady had strengths: Despite her handicaps, she obtained both an M.S. and an M.A. in psychology and counseling. She actually worked for a couple of years as a school counselor until, in April of 1970, she "over-identified" with a junior high student who, like her, had a hostile father, problems with boys, and was called "ugly" and "no good" by her peers. Our patient became extremely anxious and actually fainted upon hearing the pupil's woes. She abruptly quit her job, and, after a respite, became a teacher. She didn't like teaching, so quickly left that for a job in a bank which she held for about twelve months. About a year and a half before admission (half-way through the bank job), she fell in love with "George." Six months later they became engaged. Her family organized a large engagement party for them, but George never showed up. Six days later she loaded her shotgun, called him up and asked him over to her house. He arrived to find her comatose from twelve placidyl, the loaded gun at her side. She never saw him again, and, as she put it, "everything has gone downhill since then." "Then" was thirteen months before admission—thirty days later she quit her bank job. She hadn't worked since.

About three months before I met her she began to hear voices. This was not a new phenomenon for her—she'd suffered from such things on and off since the rape. Always terrified by the voices, she nonetheless knew that they were a figment of her own imagination. They always consisted of men arguing: her uncle, father, brothers, Larry, George, and Andy.

Oh, yes, Andy. Andy was the man who finally got Miss T. into treatment. He was a very effeminate, quiet, shy young man—a fitting contrast to this outwardly masculine woman. They had met at a skeet shoot, and he'd been impressed when she hit forty-nine out of fifty targets (a fact which, I must admit, I also found impressive. My supervisor, who'd recently been shot at by one of his own patients, virtually panicked!). As Andy pressed his suit, she became nervous and hostile. He thought an encounter group might help them. When Miss T. physically assaulted the group leader, Andy suggested UCLA. Two weeks later she was at my door. Andy never deserted her, but she eventually was to outgrow him. Yet she would forever be in his debt.

Let's sketch in the rest of her past so we can get to the story of her hospitalization. For it is in that story that the true excitement of her case unfolds—and the puzzling facts of her nightmares are revealed. Miss T. was born and raised in the Los Angeles area. At age eighteen she and her father had a severe disagreement. He felt college was wasted on females. She wanted to go. So she left home and moved a block away to the home of her bachelor Uncle Clyde, her father's brother. There she stayed until her hospitalization. Her two brothers eventually married, but, of course, she did not. She loved and idolized her younger brother, but loathed the older one. She had never used alcohol, but, as stated above, had abused placidyl. Physically, she always had been in good health, and had never required medications.

So, on November 19, 1973, we began to unravel the intriguing mystery of Miss T.: her terrifying, repetitive dreams, her poor sexual identity, her self-destructive impulses, auditory hallucinations, and suicidal thoughts. Although we never totally clarified the diagnosis, or, for that matter, the nature of her nightmares, we effected a very fine therapeutic result. What will follow is a description of her hospital course, with a special emphasis on her nightmares.

HOSPITAL COURSE

We can follow her hospital course using three threads: her nightmares and hallucinations, her family sessions, and her medications. All three intertwine, and the result is an intriguing pattern, a pattern which comes into increasing focus over time, but not without accruing a deeper texture of mystery.

We began systematically observing Miss T.'s nightmares shortly after her admission. She had at least one of them every night until the 21st of December. We would be apprised of her "devil" by loud shrieks of panic, then come upon her thrashing wildly in her bed, her legs and arms rattling the side rails as she banged against them. Her fists were usually clenched, her face frozen in fear, and her eyes open. On December 6 she screamed, "Don't hit her." On December 7, she sobbed "It is gone, it is gone!" On December 10, after a leave from the ward, during which Andy and she tried having intercourse, her night outcry was: "Larry says he'll kill them all!" The next night she yelled, "I'll kill him!" On December 14 she screamed "Dr. Friedmann promised *he* wouldn't be here." After being awakened by the nurses, she couldn't recall who "he" was. After each nightmare, which would last from two to five minutes, she would either fall back to sleep, or, if the nurses were alarmed by the violence of her thrashing, be awakened by them. She could never remember the dream, and often was reported confused and disoriented during the first minute or two after waking up.

Her "nachtmar" would begin fifteen to twenty-five minutes after falling asleep, last, as I said, two to five minutes, and always be accompanied by loud screaming, talking, and much sweating and physical activity. Yet, her pulse was never recorded as greater than ninety beats per minute. When she awoke, she was unable, for a brief period, to recognize the people around her, and she often talked incoherently. About five minutes later she would fall back to sleep, exhausted, and only occasionally be bothered by a second terror in a given night. On December 17 she awakened screaming "Larry is trying to kill Dr. Friedmann." On December 20, she yelled "Clyde, don't." On December 21 I had one of the most extraordinary experiences of my life: and Miss T., after that, never had another nightmare.

I was "on call" and had pre-arranged for a videotape machine to be placed in the patient's room. She had consented to have a nightmare recorded. The nurses were instructed to phone me when it began and to turn on the machine. At about 1:00 A.M. I came rushing in and observed Miss T. to be thrashing about and screaming, "Clyde, Clyde!" She then sat bolt upright in bed and opened her eyes. "Larry's gonna kill you!" But she wasn't talking to me. She looked right past me into space. I decided, on a hunch, to talk to her. "Miss T.," I said, "it's Dr. F. Can you hear me?" "Who?" She whimpered. "Dr. F. You're having a dream. Tell me about it." "They're all here. Larry's gonna kill Clyde. He told me not to tell. Now he's gonna kill my brother, and you, and everyone." "Where is Larry?" "Right here in the room. Can't you see him?" "No." "He's right here." "It's only a dream. No one is here but me."

We went on like that for a good twenty minutes. Then she laid down and went to sleep. The next day we viewed the tape together. "Who's that woman?" she exclaimed. "That's not me!!"

As I said, she never had a nightmare again. In fact, she began to have, for the first time in her life, pleasant and recalled dreams! Several people viewed the tape with me. None of us was ever certain she was awake during it, or in an altered state of consciousness.

Let's go back, briefly, to December 10. That was the day Andy and she attempted sexual intercourse. She had taken off all of her clothes and laid back on his bed. But when he disrobed she literally froze in panic and couldn't move. After several attempts to mollify her, Andy had given up, dressed, and left the room. From that moment on, her auditory hallucinations became loud and constant. They consisted of the same personages who appeared during her recorded nightmare: Larry, George, Andy, Clyde, her father, and her brothers, arguing and yelling at each other, at her, and at me. Larry would often threaten to kill her, me, or us all. Subsequent to the videotaped dream, her voices reached a crescendo. It almost seemed as though her unconscious night terrors had become conscious, daytime hallucinations. We increased her Navane to 35 mg. daily on December 22, and within a week the hallucinations were gone.

Miss T. had been given Navane since December 14, in an attempt to quiet her auditory hallucinations and to diminsh her daytime anxiety. In addition, she'd been taking Valium since November 21. The Valium was taken 10 mg. at bedtime from that date until her discharge. The Navane was increased steadily from 5 mg. b.i.d. on December 14 to 35 mg. q.d. on the 22nd. So, when she was discharged on January 18, her regimen was 35 mg. daily of Navane and 10 mg. at bedtime of Valium.

Meanwhile, we'd been conducting the usual individual and group therapies customary to inpatient milieus, and, in addition, family therapy. Without going into all the details, we can sketch a few outstanding moments. On December 3, during the second family session, she informed her parents and uncle that she'd been raped at age eleven. Her father wept openly and hugged her, her uncle declared he'd "get Larry," and the mother almost collapsed. This was truly a non-communicative family: silent mother, angry father, and loving uncle. Only Miss T. seemed capable of talking about her feelings, at first. But after the "secret" was divulged, they all opened up. By the eighth session we were all "friends," although there was still much ambivalence in the father as to whether psychiatry had anything of value to offer. Her trust in me and the ward seemed to transcend her family's pathology, and they slowly overcame their last doubts when Uncle Clyde reported three consecutive nights without a nightmare, during a weekend pass. By the time Miss T. left the ward, they were all "eternally grateful."

The one sad note was for Andy. Miss T. "broke up" with him on December 26. She felt all he wanted of her was "a sick patient to help," and "now that I'm healthier, he doesn't seem as excited by me anymore." Miss T. was truly growing up. She was discharged on January 18, 1974 to the Day Treatment Service of our hospital, where she remained for three months before being transferred to weekly outpatient group therapy with a private therapist. She required ever decreasing dosages of Navane, got a job and a boyfriend, and seemed to be making profound strides in other areas when I last heard from her, about nine months after she had left the ward.

DISCUSSION

With the exception of the autonomic phenomena, our patient clearly displays the signs and symptoms of pavor nocturnus. The timing (first third of the night), length of episode (two to five minutes), onset with a scream, violent content, sleep talking, severe terror, lack of recall, thrashing, somnambulism, and disorientation on waking are all classical features of the stage 4 night terror. Yet the nursing staff never recorded tachycardia or hyperpnea, which are usual features of this type of nightmare. One must, I think, assume that the nurses came upon our patient too late in the process of the attack, after the pulse rate and breathing had returnedstosnormal. After all, our ward was not a sleep lab, and staff didn't come to her until after she began to scream. We tried several times to record a sleep EEG, but Miss T. never was able to fall asleep with the electrodes in place: she was too anxious to do so, and a recording was never made.

Some of the staff speculated that Miss T. suffered from the anxiety dream type of nightmare, and others felt that her nightmares were really a theatrical feature of an hysterical personality, somehow "put on," or at least part of her hysterical neurosis. The former speculation is quickly ruled out by a second look at Keith's[11] summary (see "Introduction"). The latter is a bit harder to dismiss. Miss T. was a very histrionic, neurotic woman, with severe sexual conflicts, amnesic episodes, a great need for love and attention, labile

---

[11] See note 9 above.

affect, and auditory hallucinations. But to assume her severe terrors of twenty years duration to be a "put on" might be a bit far-fetched, especially since she fits so nicely into a classical entity. And remember, night terrors don't usually exist in isolation. As with so many others, Miss T.'s night terrors were not an isolated mental phenomenon in an otherwise normal personality. Flenenbaum[12] states that the incidence of night terrors in children is roughly 3-4%; the incidence in adults is less. Keith[15] notes that adult patients like Miss T. who have frequent night terrors are generally neurotic and anxious during the day. Put another way: most adult patients who suffer from night terrors also have daytime psychopathology. Most hysterics, borderlines, schizophrenics, etc., do not, in contrast, suffer from night terrors. She may have been severely neurotic or even psychotic, if you wish, but she also was afflicted with night terrors.

As to her overall psychiatric diagnosis, her chart reads like a summary of the DSM II. Two observers called her "schizophrenic," two others "hysterical neurosis, dissociative type," another "obsessive-compulsive neurosis," and still another "anxiety neurosis with depression." An argument could easily be made for all of these, and many an hour was spent around the table debating the merits of each classification. We tried to resolve the question with some psychological tests: the Wechsler Adult Intelligence Scale, Rorschach, and Draw-A-Person Test were given. But Miss T. became acutely anxious during the testing and literally threw the materials at the psychologist while storming out of the assessment lab. Although she finally was able to return and finish them, the results were certainly contaminated. In any event, her full scale IQ came to 115, verbal IQ to 123, and performance IQ 102. The "readout" was: "Anxious, intellectualizing, paranoid, hallucinatory, poor sexual identity." Beyond that, nobody's neck was stuck out.

I suspect that by today's light and the retrospectoscope she would be called "borderline." Her poor self-identity, constant anger, transient psychotic-like symptoms, suicidal and homicidal ideation, labile affect, difficulty with relationships and separations, etc., etc., clearly fall within the concept of "borderline" as summarized by Grinker, et al.[14] At the time, we treated her as an hysterical neurotic with obsessional traits, steering clear of any psychotic diagnosis, and thus, at least giving her the benefit of the therapist's

---

[12] Flenenbaum, "Pavor Nocturnus: A complication of single daily tricyclic or neuroleptic dosage," *American Journal of Psychiatry* 133 (1976), pp. 570-72.

[13] See note 9 above.

[14] Grinker, Werble, and Drye, *The Borderline Syndrome: A Behavioral Study of Ego Functions* (New York: Basic Books, Inc., 1968).

positive expectation for change and recovery, an important factor in any healing process.[15]

Since the purpose of this chapter is a discussion of the nightmare, let's leave the issue of diagnosis and dive into the muddy waters of theory and therapy. Although I suspect all the mud will not settle as we proceed, some of the water, at least, may become potable. Melitta Sperling[16] has suggested that the night terror can be split into two types: Type I, with hypermotility, psychotic-like behavior during the attack, and retrograde amnesia, and Type II, the post-traumic night terror. In Type II the nightmare is a repetition of the trauma, and she speculates that the waking up from the nightmare is a way of mastering the trauma. Type I she sees as merging with such states as petit mal, fugue, and frank psychosis in children. The onset is early and insidious, the parents often overtly sexually seductive to the child, and the prognosis often poor. Our patient would seem to be a Sperling Type II, but she also has some Type I characteristics (psychotic-like states, fugue states). Perhaps, then, the distinction between Type I and II pavor nocturnus is somewhat of an artifact—or, at least, worthy of rethinking.

What is, frankly, the most fun for me at this point—and perhaps the most enjoyable aspect of psychiatry as a whole—is the chance to continue along the paths of the various theoretical speculations regarding night terrors. What makes the job baffling is the fact that each of the three major theoretical frameworks, the parapsychological, the analytic, and the neurobiological, can explain some or all of Miss T.'s afflication. But, before we do that, let's dismiss a few old wives' tales. Large adenoids or tonsils resulting in anoxia due to partial apnea, heavy meals and indigestion, and the telling of ghost stories are a sample of these, according to Stern.[17]

An incubus, as you recall, is a male demon who has intercourse with sleeping women. If I were a believer in the occult, I could easily convince myself that Miss T. was being raped nightly by such a ghost or spirit. The contents of some of her outcries, the belief that Larry was with her and ready to attack all other men, would be "data" I could use to support my point. Since I am a physician and scientist, my inclination is to dismiss these speculations with the same swiftness as the "wives' tales" outlined above. But, then, I am a rather firm disciple of the "Age of Reason."

[15] Friedmann, Procci, and Fenn, "The role of expectation in treatment for psychotic patients," *American Journal of Psychotherapy*, 34, (1978), pp. 188-196; Frank, *Persuasion and Healing: A Comparative Study of Psychotherapy* (Baltimore: Johns Hopkins University Press, 1973).

[16] Sperling, "Pavor Nocturnus," *Journal of the American Psychoanalytic Association* 6 (1958), pp. 79-94.

[17] Stern, "Night terrors: Etiology and therapy," *New Yorker Medical Journal* 101 (1915), pp. 951-52.

The Freudian and neo-Freudian notions of trauma, repetition of trauma in the hope of mastery,[18] Oedipal conflicts and repressed sexual impulses;[19] Jones's[20] notion of intense psychosexual conflict; Klein's[21] notion of the child's aggression against the Oedipal mother, all have a ring of truth to them as well: in Miss T. we find a woman raised to be a man, a woman who hungered for her father's love and esteem and learned to despise herself and her mother, a woman who was raped at eleven and whose incestuous impulses must have been roused by that event, a woman who lived with her own uncle as a combination "wife" (she did all his housework) and "child" (he controlled her at night and "fathered" her), and a woman who was never able to achieve physical or emotional intimacy with men. Her "nachtmar" and daytime hallucinations recapitulated the intense conflicts: Larry was both her attacker and lover, her "men" constantly fought over her, her "voices" toyed with death for herself, her father, her brother, and her doctor. Clearly the trauma of her rape, placed within the context of her family and her Oedipal conflicts, could easily pave the road to her subsequent psychopathology.

But, according to Keith,[22] Fisher,[23] and Broughton[24] there is still another necessary element before the crucible can give rise to night terrors. That element is what they term the "Disorder of Arousal." Briefly put, there occur during each sleep cycle periods of arousal from deep (Stages 3-4) sleep to an alpha (awake) EEG pattern. For most of us, these brief periods are without problem. Some people, however, do not fare so well: they have enuresis, somnambulism, or night terrors during these periods of arousal. Broughton[25] has found that those individuals who do have these disorders are generally "hyperactive" physiologically during the entire night, and the arousal period merely pushes them "over the edge" clinically. That is, enuretic children have an increased number and depth of bladder contractions during sleep as opposed to normals; people with night terrors have increased cardio-respiratory rates throughout the night. The night terror, then, could be the "cart," not the "horse:" the feeling of terror could come out of a "void" occurring in a person with an abnormality of the neurological and/or cardio-respiratory system. When the pulse and respiration pushed to a super-rapid

---

[18] See note 16 above.

[19] Freud, "The interpretation of dreams," *Standard Edition*, 4 and 5, (London: Hogarth Press, 1900).

[20] See note 7 above.

[21] Klein, *The Psychoanalysis of Children* (London: Hogarth Press, 1932), pp. 59-60.

[22] See note 9 above.

[23] See note 5 above.

[24] See note 1 above.

[25] Ibid.

rate during the alpha arousal periods, a subjective feeling of terror might occur. The nightmare itself, the mental content, could be the "cart," i.e., it would be "filled in" later as an attempt to explain the phenomena to the victim's conscious or unconscious mind. That is, rather than having sexual conflict, etc., as the root cause of the nightmare, the neurophysiology could trigger the terror, which in turn, as an afterthought, gives rise to mental content.

As a rule, I try to steer clear of chicken-egg arguments until all the evidence is in. To date, so far as I can tell, the jury is still out. Did Miss T.'s night terrors stem from her conflicts and trauma, her terror being the result of her repressed past intruding into the unguarded ego of deep sleep? Or did the physiological correlates of an abnormal arousal state during Stage 4 sleep give rise to the physical equivalent of terror, a feeling so close to that felt during her rape at age eleven that, in her mind, the two became eventually coupled? I don't know.

Finally, why on earth did she get better? Was it the videotape? The family therapy? The ward milieu? Group therapy? Individual therapy? Medications? Or, as Fred Silvers and I[26] postulated in a paper about the multi-modal treatment of an obsessive-compulsive inpatient, a synergistic combination of all of these? Fisher et al[27] have demonstrated that diazepam in doses from 5-20 mg. per day reduces Stages 3-4 sleep, as well as the incidence of night terrors. They note, however, that the nightmares may go away without the Stages 3-4 reduction, and, vice versa, the nightmares may remain even if the stages are completely obliterated. Miss T. had been on 10 mg. q.h.s. of Valium for about thirty days when her nightmares ended. Was it cause-and-effect? Or a synergy? We felt at the time that the videotape replay of her night terror was the key, but maybe not. On the other hand, her night terrors did not decrease slowly over time, but dropped out suddenly, and we did not push the Valium to the hilt. Which is to say, we don't know for sure.

In addition, there were many dramatic moments during her family therapy, such as the one when she admitted her rape to her parents. She also learned to relate to peers better, to me as a therapist, and to men in general.

I guess, to sum it all up, she and we were just plain lucky. Or were we? If we look at it another way, since ghosts, conflicts, and synapses all seem theoretically reasonable causes of night terrors, by hitting at all three areas

---

[26] Friedmann and Silvers, "A multimodality approach to the treatment of obsessive-compulsive disorder," *American Journal of Psychotherapy* 31 (1977), pp. 456-65.
[27] Fisher, Kahn, Edwards, and Davis, "A psychophysiological study of nightmares and night terrors: The suppression of Stage 4 night terrors with diazepam," *Archives of General Psychiatry* 28 (1974), pp. 252-59.

(via videotape "exorcisms," analytic-like therapies, and medications), plus throwing in a few nonspecific and adjunctive therapeutic modalities, we both hedged our bets and attacked at all possible levels. Eclecticism may be, after all, a viable answer to the mystifying and fascinating phenomenon known as the night terror.

University of California, Irvine

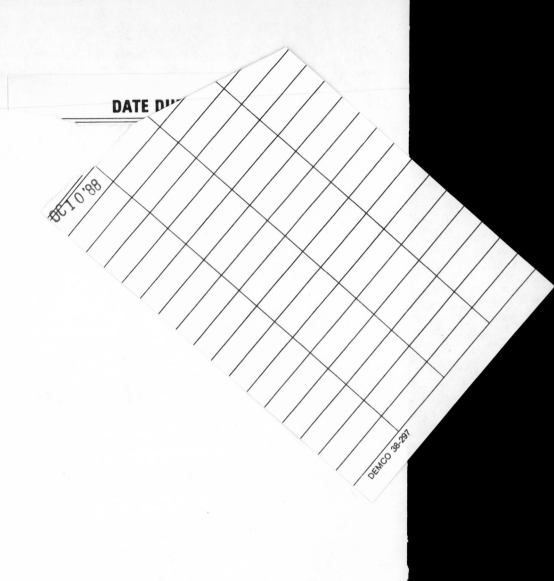